PRAISE FOR *DELIVERING THE DIGITAL RESTAURANT*

"It's time for every restaurant to evolve beyond their four walls. Sandland and Orsbourn explain why consumers are demanding improved off-premise convenience and how technology is enabling new ways to interact with food. As an owner, executive, investor, or general manager, this is a must-read."

GREG CREED, Former CEO, Yum! Brands

"The next frontier for restaurants is to expand hospitality through technology. This book reads as a how-to guide for restaurateurs looking to apply technology to benefit the consumer, not just tech for the sake of tech."

DANNY MEYER, CEO, Union Square Hospitality Group; Founder, Shake Shack

"Any aspiring or current leader in the food industry will love *Delivering the Digital Restaurant*. It will help you build your unique vision for how a restaurant wins in the years ahead."

KAT COLE, Former President, Focus Brands

"*Delivering the Digital Restaurant* illuminates the impact of evolving consumer behavior and expectations on the restaurant industry and how entrepreneurs are leveraging technology to reimagine the restaurant of the future."

EURIE KIM, Managing Director and Investor, Forerunner Ventures

"What an informative and cutting-edge read. The industry has never had a book like this: the business of restaurants. If you're in the restaurant industry, it could be the most important book you ever buy."

BETSY AND MATT BORLAND, Founders and Owners of East End Tap and Table in Lexington, Kentucky

www.amplifypublishing.com

Delivering the Digital Restaurant: Your Roadmap to the Future of Food

Second printing. This Amplify Publishing edition printed in 2022.

Cover design by Westwords Consulting

For more information, please contact:
Amplify Publishing, an imprint of Mascot Books
620 Herndon Parkway, Suite 320
Herndon, VA 20170
info@amplifypublishing.com

Library of Congress Control Number: 2021910020

CPSIA Code: PRBANG1121B

ISBN-13: 978-1-64543-948-6

Printed in the United States

To Melissa Lora, who introduced me to the business of restaurants.

and

To my wonderful husband, Scott, who made writing this book and so many things possible.

—*Meredith*

To Betty and Mike, whose imaginative stories and encouragement to try any dish once led me to a life full of exploration, curiosity, and love of all things food.

and

To my darling Elicia and the moments we cherish in the world's most amazing restaurants and those we share in the comfort of our home.

—*Carl*

DELIVERING
THE DIGITAL RESTAURANT
YOUR ROADMAP TO THE FUTURE OF FOOD

MEREDITH SANDLAND | CARL ORSBOURN

an imprint of Mascot Books

CONTENTS

FOREWORD

This book was written for a guy like me. And I suspect you will find it as helpful as I did.

I've been in the restaurant industry for thirty-six years. I run three very successful restaurants in Southern California. During my tenure, Café Japengo was awarded the California Restaurant Association Gold Medallion Award for "Best Sushi" eight years in a row. Today, James' Place is a specialty Asian fusion concept offering a casual fine dining menu nestled in the heart of La Jolla Playhouse grounds. My team takes great pride in delighting our guests every time they join us.

It's only recently that I realized how much is changing for my guests and the impact these changes have on my restaurant. My son, Anthony, who works with me, represents the next generation of restaurant operators. I hope he carries on the traditions that we've started, but there's so much to add that will take him and this industry onward to even more incredible things. Already when he talks about how he and his friends live, I can see that he will evolve our restaurants to meet the needs of the next generation. This book will surely help him on that journey.

Any restaurant owner today will tell you there is a bewildering array of new technology available to improve the restaurant experience. At a conference, a fellow restaurant owner shared their "tech stack," and I was shocked to realize first, that so much different software is now required to run a restaurant. And second, that if I were to honestly look at my own tech stack, it would have just as many different elements involved. Now, in addition to being a chef, a human resource professional, an accountant, and a purchasing agent, restaurateurs are becoming technologists. Every sales call I receive offering me some new piece of software has just become noise. What happens as a result is that I just carry on doing what I know best—providing excellent service to my dine-in customers and doing what I can to support those who prefer delivery or takeout.

There's no doubt that through the COVID-19 pandemic, delivery and takeout food kept my business afloat. I'm sure I'm not alone. But at what cost? With the impact to restaurants from COVID-19 pandemic lessening, I'm growing tired of paying high fees, handling drivers from who knows where, taking my food to my faceless guests five miles away. In many ways, I just wish things would return to how they use to be.

I've known Carl for over fifteen years, and together with Meredith, he's helped paint an accurate picture of how restaurant professionals like me can see the opportunities in this new world for food. Their wise words, jargonless clear explanations of what's going on, and concrete examples provide, as they say, a roadmap for every restaurateur. As a result, their book has helped me recognize the steps I need to take to move forward and embrace the change as something to consider positively.

This is not a how-to book, but it is a wakeup call. *Delivering the Digital Restaurant* will help you diagnose where to improve your digital offering. The book highlights the exciting progress early pioneers have made. While by now, many restaurant operators have found some way to operate their business online, generate a social media page, and use a tablet or two, this book will be the kick that we all need to take things up a level or two. I hope you find it as valuable and insightful as I did.

James Holder
You can learn more about James and his
restaurant James' Place at jamesplacesd.com

INTRODUCTION

In normal times, running a restaurant is one of the most rewarding—and challenging—business endeavors out there. The pride of service, atmosphere, recipes, and hospitality inspire many people to open a restaurant of their own. Maybe you are one of those people who took the leap and opened your own local version of hospitality. There are probably also people you know who have the scars to prove that a restaurant is no easy undertaking. Consumers are finicky, competition is heavy, and running a restaurant requires responses to a hundred different demands each day. These challenges have always been true, but the role of a restaurateur has never been as hard as it is today.

The accumulation of millions of people making small changes in their daily lives lead to seismic shifts in our economy. These shifts are most apparent in sectors where they have progressed the furthest, like department stores making way for online shopping. These shifts are less apparent where they are just starting, like restaurants. It has taken a global pandemic and twenty years since digitization began for the restaurant industry to face the same existential threat as many retailers did back at the turn of the twenty-first century.

The revolution that began in retail with the birth of mainstream e-commerce has arrived on the doorstep of the restaurant industry. Over time, the outcomes will be all the amazing things that have already transformed retail and consumer products: one-to-one marketing, micro-niche products, digitally-native brands, the subscription economy, the gig economy, massive logistics networks, bankrupt storied brands. In the short term, the disruption created by this innovation will create opportunities and perils for every operating restaurant.

At the time of writing this book, the restaurant industry is facing the most significant challenge in its history. The more than six hundred thousand restaurants the United States boasted at the start of 2020 were decimated by one hundred thousand casualties in just six months, with many more expected to follow.[1] The industry laid off three million workers and lost a quarter of a trillion dollars in revenue in 2020. The COVID-19 pandemic hit the restaurant industry particularly hard, but in truth, the restaurant industry was primed for disruption long before COVID-19 became part of our everyday vernacular. Restaurant profit margins, already squeezed thin by a hugely competitive environment and increasing minimum wage, now have the promise of off-premise growth and the challenge of third-party fees to deal with. Much as the 2008 recession sped the disruption of retail, the COVID-19 pandemic has accelerated the digital disruption of restaurants.

We are going from an era in which people go to food to an era in which food goes to people.

When we each left our corporate jobs running large chains behind us, we did so believing that the future of food was changing in front of our eyes. We each wanted to be a part of the change. We joined Kitchen United, one of the country's leading ghost kitchen providers, and established the operating model to scale the concept across the country. Along the way, we witnessed the challenges many restaurateurs were facing as they worked to adopt new approaches to win in a digital landscape.

And there is so much more change yet to come. As we have seen in retail, there are likely to be many business casualties brought down by their reluctance to change or their blindness to how both sociological shifts and technological advancements are transforming the restaurant business model and the desires of the everyday consumer.

Those who understand the elements, process, and direction of this disruption will be better positioned to survive and thrive by embracing the innovation that consumers are demanding. Those who resist will surely be left behind. The purpose of this book is to make it easy for restaurant owners, landlords, investors, and patrons to understand what's happening, why it's happening, how we all can navigate the changes we're facing—and together, shape the future of food.

—Meredith and Carl

Chapter 1

WE EAT AS A NUCLEAR FAMILY NO MORE

"Late again," Jessica Gray chided herself as she turned out of the office parking lot toward home. Her 5:00 p.m. meeting had run over; it was 6:35 p.m., and her day had not ended. Now she faced the long commute to her home in the suburbs of Columbus, Ohio, and it was her turn to make dinner when she got there. She had promised her husband, Andrew, and their nine-year-old son, Jackson, that she would cook. Considering how long it would take her to get home, figure out what to prepare, and actually make it, that home-cooked meal was looking increasingly unlikely.

You probably know a family like the Grays. Maybe you are like the Grays. After all, they're a typical American Millennial family. Jessica and Andrew married twelve years ago, when they were in their late twenties. Jackson was born a few years later. Six months into her new role as VP of Digital Advertising for an advertising agency, Jessica works long hours. But the job comes with a full benefits package, and she provides the primary regular income for the family. Even though they are a dual-income household, Andrew's work as a Realtor combined with Jessica's job doesn't generate enough to upgrade from their townhouse rental to buying their own home. It isn't so much that they don't earn enough to cover a monthly mortgage payment—it's that their student debts have held them back from saving up enough for a down payment.

"Call Andrew," Jessica says, using voice command in her car. When her husband answers, she tells him, "I'm going to order delivery."

"Sure," Andrew agrees immediately, even as he mentally calculates the hit to their monthly food budget. Seems they've been ordering takeout a lot more often since Jessica got her promotion. Sure, she was earning more now, but the costs stacked up pretty fast. To be fair, Andrew would be the first to agree that he was not the best of cooks. "Functional" was the most complimentary word to use for the meals he prepared. Sometimes they weren't even that—Andrew found it hard to figure out what to cook that their gluten-free son could eat. The one or two recipes his grandmother taught him seemed to require much more planning and time than he ever seemed to have.

At the next set of red traffic lights, Jessica opens an app on her phone, finds a restaurant she has been meaning to try out, ticks a few boxes next to options she knows will work for her family, clicks through to checkout, and presses her fingerprint against the phone sensor to authorize payment. The meal will be on her doorstep in thirty-five to forty-five minutes. Her GPS tells her she will be home in thirty minutes. "Perfect," she whispers in relief and returns to the podcast she was listening to on her commute that morning.

For the Grays, time is the one commodity they always seem to lack. That's true of many—if not most—families in twenty-first-century America, no matter where they sit on the income spectrum. It's true because, like it or not, families are not what they used to be. And maybe the typical family never was what we imagined it to be anyway.

The romanticized ideal of the nuclear family—mom, dad, and two kids in a home of their own—belongs to past generations. Family looks different now, and the nuclear family model is losing ground.

Ask almost any American—married with children, empty nester, or twentysomething—if they feel stretched, and they would agree: there isn't enough time in a day. Part of the squeeze is real: more Americans are working more hours, children are more "programmed," and lots of us have side hustles—even our kids. Another part of the squeeze is perceived, but no less palpable for that. We live in an "always on" technology-enabled world, and it is hard to protect any time as our own. The phone is constantly buzzing with a notification of some kind—call, text, email, message, an app requiring attention. Combine the real with the perceived, and you end up with a time-starved society.

No wonder convenience reigns supreme in many parts of the consumer economy: think smartphone check deposits, dry cleaning pickup services, or electronic signatures replacing notary visits. In food, too, convenience has become paramount. With the increase in demands on our time, something had to give, and that "something" is the time we used to spend shopping for food, preparing meals, eating together, and cleaning up.

You could say that the transformation of family life in the United States all boils down to time. Or timing, to be more precise. Young adults today are slower to marry than their parents and grandparents. Just 22 percent of Millennials (born after 1980) are currently married. Back when Gen Xers were the same age that Millennials are now, three in ten were married. For Baby Boomers, four in ten were married at that age, and for the Silent Generation (ages sixty-five and older) more than half were married.[1]

As a consequence, for the first time in American history, "singles now outnumber married adults," according to the *Christian Science Monitor*. "In 1950, married couples represented 78 percent of households in the United States. In 2011, the US Census Bureau reported that the percentage had dropped to 48 percent."[2] Marriage and cohabiting are no longer life events that we can necessarily take for granted. In 2018, there were 35.7 million single-person households, representing 28 percent of all households in the US. Back in 1960, by contrast, only 13 percent of all households were single-person arrangements.

Fertility is following a similar downward curve, with babies arriving later or not at all.[3] The National Center for Health Statistics reported, "The general fertility rate declined to 58.3 births per 1,000 women aged 15–44 in 2019, another record low for the United States."[4] At the same time, mothers starting families are doing so later than at any point in history. A recent article in *USA Today* studying the CDC data found that the only age group for whom birth rates are increasing is women over forty-four years of age.[5]

Old is the new young. As a society we are having fewer children, later, but we are also living longer than ever before. According to the CDC's findings, life expectancy rates increase more than two months every year. A baby born in 2018 could expect to live 78.7 years (averaged out for male and female life spans).[6] This means that, even for those who grew up in a traditional two-parent household and subsequently have a nuclear family of their own, the portion of their life lived in this arrangement is declining.

In a recent article for *Quartz*, social psychologist Bella DePaulo noted, "In 1970, more than 40 percent of households were comprised of nuclear families; today, that figure is not even 20 percent."[7] As the author of *How We Live Now: Redefining Home and Family in the 21st Century*, DePaulo spent years traveling the US, scouring government reports, reviewing scholarly writing, and interviewing people about their home lives. She found that the nuclear ideal is not only on the wane—it was only ever a fleeting phase in the history of civilization.

Commentator and columnist David Brooks agrees. Writing in *The Atlantic*, he observed:

> When we have debates about how to strengthen the family, we are thinking of the two-parent nuclear family, with one or two kids, probably living in some detached family home on some suburban street. We take it as the norm, even though this wasn't the way most humans lived during the tens of

thousands of years before 1950, and it isn't the way most humans have lived during the fifty-five years since 1965.[8]

So what is going on?

We are living longer and living in very different circumstances than those of our parents. As the "mom and dad and two children" model fades away, many of us are living with parents, friends, or alone rather than with a spouse and children. The American Community Survey has shown that following the Great Recession of 2007–2009, the rate of young adults living with parents or roommates increased to higher levels than any previous generation. But it would be wrong to see this as a new phenomenon. "The ways that many present-day Americans are pushing back on modern living arrangements closely resemble what came centuries, even millennia, before in other parts of the world," writes Ilana E. Strauss for *The Atlantic*. "Family members, relatives, neighbors, and strangers are coming together to live in groups that work for them—a bit like medieval Europe."[9]

Here, however, the comparison with medieval households ends. Today's Millennials are blessed with education and cursed with debt in a way other generations could never imagine. "American tuition fees have increased faster than wages, with the average annual cost for attending a public four-year university at just over $19,000 (2015–2016)," Kevin Dickinson observed in *Big Think* in 2019.[10] "At $1.5 trillion, today's student debt has surpassed loans for cars and credit cards, stymieing those who hold it from putting that money toward asset accumulation."

People hold far more debt far earlier in life than would have been the case even fifty years ago. As a result, many Millennials cannot afford to buy homes or even start families as their parents did at the same age. Looking at that fact in the most optimistic light, it does at least reduce the pressure for young professionals to save for the purchase of a house. Homeownership may simply seem an impossibility. With interest rates close to an all-time low, saving for the future is not necessarily at the front of a young person's mind. There are so many temptations and distractions in the here and now that seem much more appealing too. Our ancestors and even our parents could never have dreamed of the abundance of choice we now enjoy in retail channels, travel experiences, and leisure activities offered through the Groupons of this world. Even if they had, providing for a young family's needs and a roof over their heads would have prevented our predecessors from clicking "buy now" (or its historical equivalent).

With the incentive to save so low, Millennials and Gen Z are the opposite of "house poor." These young people are what we call "renting rich." While their overall income and wealth lag behind that of prior generations, their disposable income is higher. No mortgage payment, no car lease, no insurance, and no maintenance on assets they do not own opens up a significant portion of their take-home pay to spend on "experiences."

Which brings us to food.

Chief among these experiences is eating at restaurants. Forty-nine percent of Millennials spend more on restaurant meals each month than they save for retirement. In 2013, Millennials spent 10 percent more each year on restaurants than Boomers did—in spite of their lower incomes and debt-saddled negative wealth. A Millennial today spends $1,000 less per year on groceries than someone in their age cohort did just ten years ago.[11] Where is that $1,000 going? Well, a good portion of it is now redirected toward restaurants, delivered food, and ingredient or meal-kit subscriptions.

When one of us (Meredith—not a Millennial) started seeing delivery affect the business she was working in, the appeal of delivery wasn't obvious to her. What was the draw for a Millennial market that was meant to be so in love with experiences? Luckily, she had a Millennial on hand to ask: her husband, Scott.

"If you guys love experiences so much, why do you want to sit at home bingeing on Netflix while you eat something that was brought to your door?"

"You're misdefining the word *experience*," he explained. "An experience isn't just about going somewhere. It's how I'm choosing to live at a particular moment. If the choice I have made is to run around in the backyard with my kid or play an online video game with my friend who lives two hundred miles away, I don't want to be interrupted from that experience to go get—or even worse, make—something to eat."

Point taken. Scott's words made her reflect on how different their lives were from those of previous generations in her family. Meredith's grandmother was a stay-at-home mom who cooked every meal for her husband and children. She would never dream of going to a restaurant on a weeknight. For her, eating out was reserved for a special occasion. Meredith's mother worked as a teacher, yet she was still expected to serve up a home-cooked meal every night. When Meredith was growing up, her family tended to eat out more often than her grandparents, but it was definitely not the norm.

Now she is married with a child of her own. Scott and Meredith both work, and they tend to eat out or get food delivered most weeknights. When they do cook, it's more of a special weekend event so they can plan for it and set aside some time.

Theirs is a familiar story that exemplifies the trends we're talking about in this chapter. In the last few years, the number of restaurants has expanded in line with the rise of women entering the paid workforce. Only two generations ago, women such as Meredith's grandmother were largely restricted to the homemaker role, supporting male breadwinners and their families as their full-time job. "Homemaking" is no longer a presumed role for women but one choice among many careers both parents can consider—if they are lucky enough to afford it. According to the Pew Research Center, in 1960, 50 percent of children under 18 lived in a home with both parents where the father worked and the mother stayed at home. In 2014, that number had dropped to 14 percent.[12]

"Women outnumbered men in the US paid workforce, with their new majority buoyed by fast job growth in health care and education over the past year, as well as the tight labor market," wrote Rachel Siegel for *The Washington Post* in 2020. Furthermore, she says, "Of the 145,000 jobs picked up in December throughout the economy, women won most of them—139,000, according to Labor Department data."[13]

In their move from the informal to the formal economy, women are also fast displacing men on the income front. According to a 2017 *Daily Beast* article, "A new study says that young, single, and childless women under

30—who live in cities—make more money than their male counterparts."[14] Though Equal Pay Today reports American women earn eighty cents to every dollar earned by their male peers today, they are catching up fast. Already, the National Bureau of Economic Research reports female college graduates outnumber males. And according to the American Enterprise Institute, "Women earned the majority of doctoral degrees in 2017 for the 9th straight year and outnumber men in grad school 137 to 100."

It's not surprising, then, that women are playing a bigger role in household budget allocation. Men, meanwhile, have taken on more household chores—though not so much that there isn't a gap. A US Bureau of Labor Statistics study in 2015 found that women engage in about an hour more a day on household activities than men do.[15] As women increasingly work outside the home, the shortfall is covered by outsourcing to cleaning services, gardening services, and home maintenance services, as well as delivery services and restaurants. Even with outside help, according to OECD Gender Data, the gender gap in leisure time still sits more significantly in American men's favor relative to other countries.[16]

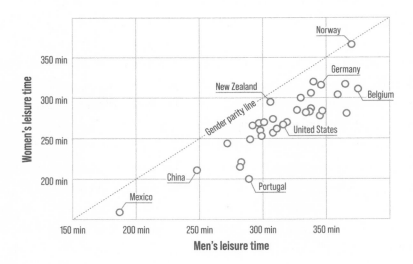

1.1 Gender Gap in Leisure Time[17]

There's really no time to handle the shortfall any other way. The Gray family, whom we met at the start of this chapter, are by no means an exception. Instead, their story is reasonably representative of an overworked and overscheduled country. According to the Institute for Women's Policy Research, women on average worked just under forty hours per week while men worked just over forty, but a staggering one in five women and one in three men worked well above forty hours per week.[18]

At the same time, in between sports, enrichment activities, and work obligations, most Americans now spend most of their time consuming media as opposed to other leisure activities like spending quality time with their family or friends.[19] Longer work commutes compound this problem further and prevent parents from having the bandwidth to cook. As Christopher Ingraham explains for *The Washington Post*: "The average American commute grew to just over 27 minutes one way in 2018, a record high, according to data released in September by the US Census Bureau."[20] As a result, Americans spend only sixty-six minutes a day eating food—some thirty-seven minutes less than China or sixty-seven minutes less than the French.

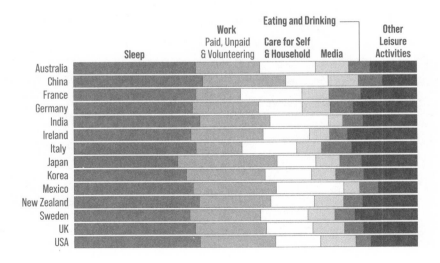

1.2 How Do People Spend Their Time?[21]

The uptick in women working, the housework that still needs to get done, and busier schedules for everyone (toddlers and teens as well as parents) has led to fewer in-home meals prepared from scratch. As we've seen in this chapter, the nuclear family sitting around the dinner table most nights of the week has become the exception rather than the norm. The reality for most families is this: we are time and asset poor, live in unconventional settings, and depend on both parents working inside and outside the home. In place of the home-cooked meal, we are turning to dining out and, increasingly, delivery services.

Restaurants who understand their customers are responding to this new reality. Convenience alone isn't enough: families also expect more choice, higher quality, speed, and value for money. For all of that, they are willing to pay.

The rise of e-commerce has brought us a phenomenon called "I Want What I Want When I Want It," or IWWIWWIWI for short. Millennials are creating an on-demand economy—same-day delivery, anyone? IWWIWWIWI is a mantra for retail shoppers growing ever-more accustomed to instant gratification. It also represents a demand for a seemingly endless array of choices in other areas of life too. Food is no exception. We want what we want to eat, and we want it on our plates now.

As we're about to see, fulfilling that desire isn't as simple as putting food on a plate (or in a box). In this new world of eating, food has become much more than a means to service a twang of hunger. Now, food reflects your identity, your values, and your consciousness of the direct effect of food upon your health.

Chapter 2

OUR TASTES ARE CHANGING

ndrew Gray's stomach grumbled as he looked at his watch. He had just got the text from his wife that tonight they were to eat from Kwixo. He hadn't heard of them before, but Mediterranean food had been a favorite of his and Jessica's ever since their honeymoon cruise around that part of the world.

Theirs was not the easiest family to feed. Only a few years earlier, the Grays had watched a documentary on Netflix about how the food industry was conspiring to make Americans eat more meat than is good for our health. Later that weekend, they met with Andrew's elder sister, who had recently turned to veganism because of her growing concerns about the environmental effect of the meat industry. Andrew adored his sister and, with the documentary fresh in his mind, half-jokingly agreed to support her efforts. His diet shift wasn't as difficult as he first expected it to be. Before he knew it, he had fully accommodated the switch to veganism, felt great, and never looked back. Having access to several local restaurants with vegan options, plus the niche products available on a growing number of grocery store shelves and online, helped him eat the foods he felt were right for him.

Unfortunately for Jackson, Andrew and Jessica's nine-year-old son, dietary restriction was not a preference, but a matter of life or death. His peanut allergy was identified by the pediatric allergist they were referred to after Jackson experienced anaphylactic shock. His intolerances to gluten and dairy were less proven. Jessica was fascinated with a new nutrigenomics client she was supporting at work, so she started researching possible causes to Jackson's behavioral challenges online and began adjusting his diet in ways that seemed to help.

What Jackson ate had to be carefully monitored. This wasn't uncommon, though: many of Jackson's classmates also had some kind of dietary restriction. Most of the kids in Jackson's school had access to far more knowledge about food and its impact on their well-being than their parents had had during their childhoods. And many parents were now learning right along with them.

Armed with a staggering amount of information at their fingertips and driven by a passion to share experiences, today's consumer hungers for greater variety and choice in their food. It's also perhaps no surprise that many of us have a wider culinary perspective than ever before. The rate of legal immigration in the United States has more than doubled since 1970. Since the introduction of the 1965 Immigration and Nationality Act, immigrants have come from an ever-widening array of regions across the world. According to the Pew Research Center, 1960s-era immigration to the United States was 67 percent European. In 2013, 52 percent came from Latin America and the Caribbean, 27 percent from Asia, 4 percent from Africa, and just 13 percent from Europe.[1] Such an increase in total immigration, as well as the increased diversity within the immigrant population, has brought with it diverse eating patterns on a scale large enough to penetrate the entire US food industry and create a cultural food awakening in all US consumers—not just the recent arrivals.

You see it in the schoolyard: 22 percent of Gen Zers have at least one immigrant parent, compared to 14 percent of Millennials, making Gen

Z the most diverse generation in American history.[2] These children of immigrants are as likely to open lunchboxes filled with lamb koftas as the peanut butter and jelly sandwiches we grew up with. Exposed to different food types at an early age, children's culinary curiosity is awakened, and their food horizons expand.

Each successive wave of immigrants contributes to American cuisine. Padma Lakshmi's television series *Taste the Nation* demonstrates that American food *is* ethnic food, as she explores how each migration has brought something new to what we consider American: flavors, forms, and cooking methods. The show takes Lakshmi all over the US, talking to indigenous and immigrant populations about their food and culture. Speaking on the podcast *Ask Me Another*, Lakshmi says that American food is "a microcosm of all the world's foods and . . . an ever-evolving organism . . . It is shaped by waves and waves of different generations of people that have come here from all over the world."[3]

The restaurant Jack's Wife Freda is a perfect example. Dean Jankelowitz and wife Maya operate the New York City boutique restaurant, named after Dean's South African grandparents. When Dean arrived in the US in 2003 in pursuit of the American dream, he met fellow immigrant Maya, who had arrived from her homeland in Israel. In 2012 they opened their first restaurant, its menu filled with an eclectic mix of South African and Israeli favorites brought together from their families' generations-old recipe books. The restaurant has a colorful and vibrant Instagram feed (#jackswifefreda), while Dean and Maya's younger son, Benjamin, has his own hashtag (#benniethegangster)—and probably the best lunchbox in town.[4]

In the nation's transition from grilled cheese to empanadas, television has been far more than an observer on the scene—it has urged us to greater taste adventures. Years before e-commerce sites like Amazon conditioned consumers to expect access to any product imaginable, a culinary revolution was erupting in America led by celebrity chefs. Writing for *Time* in 2010, Lisa Abend explained how this vocation birthed legends more akin to rock stars than cooks through TV shows like *Barefoot Contessa, Throwdown!*

with Bobby Flay, and *Hell's Kitchen*: "These days, the Emerils, Marios, and Gordons of the world scarcely need the qualifier *chef*—they are celebrities, plain and simple. But between the television shows, the food festivals, the Vegas outposts, the spaghetti-sauce labels bearing their names, and the fans rabidly tracking everything from new dishes to failed love affairs . . . it's easy to overlook the impact that fame has had on the once disparaged profession of cooking."[5]

In the early 2000s, munchie-seeking stoners, workaholic C-suite execs, and soccer moms found common ground in salivating over epicurean dishes beamed directly to their TVs. Channels like Food Network took off, introducing the public to exotic delicacies like shrimp pad thai, Kogi BBQ, and vegetable pakoras. Inspired by such influences, the designation "foodie" exploded, and "food porn" selfies the world over caught fire. Posting a shot of a lobster roll or foie gras to Instagram could bring social cachet and respect, a badge of honor in a society rushing headlong toward gastro diversity.

The exoticism spread to grocery stores like Trader Joe's and Whole Foods, who profited from offering items such as kombucha and kimchi, once only found in ethnic food stores. Alan Jackson, the visionary behind the California restaurant chain Lemonade, comments on the rise of such food multiculturalism and experimentation: "Today, people are interested in powerful flavors and the American palate is more willing to try new things."[6] Celebrity chef and owner of Chica restaurant, Lorena Garcia, agrees: "People are much more open to trying new flavors. The American staples are always going to be the American staples, but you see a fusion of the cultures."[7]

Around the same time consumers were expanding their culinary horizons, a host of awareness-raising books and documentaries shined a light on nutrition, clean eating, and the possible unintended consequences of Americans' long-term love affair with red meat, dairy, sugar, and processed foods. In 2001, investigative journalist Eric Schlosser's *Fast Food Nation* opened many eyes to the dangers of fast food, the obesity epidemic, and the problems of industrial food preparation. More recently, documentaries exploring the dark side of food have included *Super Size Me*; *Food, Inc.*; *Forks Over Knives*; and *Fat, Sick & Nearly Dead*.

Food preferences once considered fringe became mainstream. Consumers began demanding food products that met organic standards with clear labeling for accountability. By 2019, organic food sales accounted for 5.7 percent of total food sales and were growing at nearly three times the rate of overall food sales.[8] Awareness of unsustainable industrial farming practices increased. Restaurants earned back trust—or built it—by offering free-range or grass-fed meat to demonstrate their commitment to animal welfare. The largest food purveyors in America, McDonald's and Walmart, both announced they would migrate to cage-free eggs. Nutrition solutions to what had formerly been considered purely medical matters are now common, often spearheaded by online gurus. The phrase "food as medicine" turns up nearly a million results on Google.

Considering the SAD (dietician lingo for the Standard American Diet) state of typical eating patterns in the US, can we really believe that Americans are starting to change their behavior after watching some TV shows and browsing a few healthy eating websites? American scores on the USDA "Healthy Eating Index" are dismal (59 out of 100 at the most recent reading), but they have improved three points in eight years; it is perhaps the start of an upward trend.[9]

The rise of plant-based eating is one trend that may have contributed to the improvement in our health. A 2018 consumer study by NPD Group found that "14 percent of US consumers, which translates to over forty-three million consumers, regularly use plant-based alternatives such as almond milk, tofu, and veggie burgers, and 86 percent of these consumers do not consider themselves vegan or vegetarian." The trend is rolling into restaurants as well as home kitchens. David Portalatin, a restaurant industry expert with NPD, said in 2019, "When we look at shipments from broadline food-service distributors into commercial restaurants, plant-based alternative sales are up 30 percent year-over-year, proving that veggie burgers are not just showing up on restaurant menus, consumers are ordering them."[10]

Leading the way among chains entering into this sea change are companies like Chipotle, which offers Lifestyle Bowls to promote healthier well-being with "real ingredients adhering to a particular diet regime," including vegan, keto, Whole30, and paleo. Most major chains have created vegetarian menus or launched meatless burgers, like Beyond Meat or the Impossible Burger.

Individual chefs and restaurant owners are also seeing a new mindfulness about food and experiencing it themselves. Restaurateur Lorena Garcia has embraced new dietary choices—much to her own astonishment, it seems: "Me, Lorena Garcia, stopped eating red meat two years ago! Even though I love red meat medium-rare. I am mindful of what I am putting in my body." Her choices are both personal and commercial: "In my restaurants we have to have a vegan menu. It is something that wouldn't happen before. Now it is upfront in the conversation about the food."

The high-growth chain Sweetgreen has made a mission of bringing healthier food to America. "We build healthier communities by connecting people to real food," says Cofounder and CEO Jon Neman.[11] He points to the current state of affairs: Americans spend the least amount per capita on food and the most on health care. He says, "Nobody made healthy food cool, and that's what we're doing. It should be a lot easier to eat healthy, nutritious, sustainable food." The only restaurant "unicorn" (start-up worth more than $1 billion) has just over one hundred restaurants and a higher valuation than Dine Brands, which has thirty-five hundred restaurants.[12] Sweetgreen was the #6 restaurant on Evercore's 2020 survey of brands loved by young adults and teens. The restaurants that beat out Sweetgreen—like Chipotle and Starbucks—each have thousands of restaurants.[13]

There's no better demonstration of the attraction of eating for health than restaurant brand True Food Kitchen. Founded by Dr. Andrew Weil—a physician and doctor of integrative medicine—and backed by Oprah, True Food Kitchen is one of the few full-service restaurant concepts that is currently growing. CEO Christine Barone explains it this way: "Our core is Dr. Weil and his life's mission to teach people that eating actually greatly impacts your health over your lifetime. But eating healthy doesn't mean it isn't delicious." Offering food that people don't enjoy eating would be counterproductive, she reasons. "If we limit our audience, we limit our mission." And consumers are responding. "We have guests who ask, 'Could you just set me up for a delivery at 7:00 p.m. every single night?'" says Barone of the restaurant's fanatical patrons.[14]

Dr. Weil wrote in his 2012 book *True Food*, "One of the most remarkable changes in American food culture in the past fifty years has been the mainstreaming of once-fringe food philosophies. When I was a kid in the 1950s, vegetarians (including my Aunt Rebecca) were kooks . . . In the intervening years, three intersecting trends—emerging affluence, a growing emphasis on individuality, and an explosion in nutrition science—fostered explosive growth of these diets."[15] In other words, the fifties are over. We no longer have to conform. Human beings are not all the same, and it's appropriate that we should be able to tailor our restaurant experience to fit our unique physiologies, ethics, or tastes.

Which brings us to another revolution in our food expectations: made-for-you options and entire menus catering to you as an individual.

Americans now enjoy a remarkable freedom in what we eat, when, and where. More than that, each of us eats differently from our friends, family, and coworkers. And restaurants are responding. The first step toward personalization in restaurants came with the Subway-style interactive assembly line that has since been adopted by sandwich shops, burrito shops, and pizza shops from Bend to Boston. Based on the idea of "mass customization" first popularized by furniture chains like Room & Board, these businesses were able to offer a product that felt entirely custom by restricting choices (and therefore time and costs) on a few key dimensions. The interactive process also co-opted the customer into "self-checking" the accuracy of their order and the desirability of their own choices.

Starbucks went a step further by applying mass customization principles not only to their menus, but to their restaurant design. Now you could enjoy your extra hot, tall, vanilla skim half-caf latte in a coffee shop that had its own character—and the company could achieve this "localization" without ordering fifteen thousand different sets of furniture. They just assembled different ambience "ingredients" in a customized way at each location.

Historically, pizza has been outside of this trend, but then in 2012, Blaze Pizza came along and made pizza personal. "It was a celebration of individuality," says Elise Wetzel, Cofounder (with her husband Rick) and consumer clairvoyant. "It wasn't just personalization of pizza, it was the entire experience—valuing self-expression and making your own art."[16]

Blaze Pizza uses a "cocreated" assembly line format that lets guests choose one of the menu's signature pizzas or create one of their own. Most people go custom. "Our sales are 80 percent custom-made pizzas, even though we offer 'signature' recipes that are the Blaze take on classics," says the Wetzels' long-time business partner, Bill Phelps. "The customer wants to go down the line and make up their own. It's the experience and fun of cooking."

The proof of the pizza is in the numbers: Blaze became the fastest concept to reach two hundred restaurants in history (just four years from creation to two hundred locations). Blaze nailed many aspects of a strong concept to achieve this quick success, but the primary brand tenet was personalization. Elise describes the initial flash of insight. "We were at a Chipotle—because fast casual pizza didn't exist at that time [2011]—and I thought, 'Why can't everyone have their own pizza?'"

"Our kids are now [in their twenties], but we lived through many years of ordering the same two pizzas every Friday night," Rick adds. "One would eat pepperoni with no sauce. The other, cheese and sauce only. So, we were kind of left with these two pizzas over and over again." It's a story that rings true for many families. "This is a category that has always been a shared format," Rick says. "And now we wanted to take it to an individual format. Let everyone do their own thing."

To design the Blaze menu, Rick and Elise enlisted chef Brad Kent, owner of the nationally acclaimed Olio restaurant and pizzeria, whose pizzas Zagat called "one of ten pies in the country worth traveling for." The dough was the first thing to get right, and next came outstanding ingredients. "We wanted to serve something that would be available at a great pizza restaurant and simply make that product, with those ingredients, accessible: at a location nearby, with a price point that's affordable, at a speed that works with your life," Elise explains. "Having those ingredients was very important to us. And I think it's aligned with this whole personalization trend. People are actively seeking out foods that are representative of their lifestyle right now."

Blaze's commitment to great ingredients that matched individual lifestyles did not end there. Soon they launched gluten-free dough. Gluten is part of what makes pizza crust so good, giving it a crispy, yet at the same time, chewy quality. To offer a crust with no gluten that met their standards was a tough haul. Once again, though, Rick and Elise had a personal motivation for making it happen. Rick says, "We've got some very good friends who have a son who is gluten-sensitive, and so we made a commitment that we were going to launch a gluten-free dough as well."

Personalization will continue to be a "key tentpole" of the brand as it innovates into the future, and technology will only fuel Blaze's—and other brands'—ability to do so. Indeed, the Blaze founders see the demand for personalization as being driven by technology. "Look at this thing," Rick says, holding up his cellphone. "It's—what? Ten, twelve years old? And it has changed our expectations of everything. My apps are completely different from your apps. The weather report I see is for my specific location." Elise expands the point: "Technology has enabled concepts across the board to customize. And when we start to give guests a taste of customization, they want more and more. Now we are being served ads that are custom-created just for us. If I'm a vegan, you shouldn't be serving me an ad for a pepperoni pizza. You know, that's the ultimate personalization."

The Internet's capacity for creating a customized experience has started to affect nearly every consumer vertical. Particularly in consumer goods, we can use the Internet to order custom shoes, custom shampoo, custom fragrance, and custom candy. Niches that would have once been impossibly small suddenly become economically viable—and it's happening in food too. If a consumer loves walnut butter, they may not find it on the shelf in their local grocery store. After all, it's a niche product that doesn't maintain high enough sales to be carried in every mainline grocery store. But it can be bought on Amazon. And while you're there, you can order smoked salmon directly from the Alaskan fisheries that catch it and cook it. Want to go one step further to give your baby the best of everything? You can order internationally produced organic formula through a website that curates the best formulas from each country into one digital storefront.

Once consumers change behavior in one area of their life, they expect to be able to repeat that pattern in other areas. It's the IWWIWWIWI factor (I Want What I Want When I Want It). When we are used to choosing anything we want via the Internet, we will not put up with selecting from the limited range that a large brand has decided we should be offered.

Clever restaurateurs will leverage that desire. A vegan restaurant might struggle to draw foot traffic on a certain street in a certain town, but if that restaurant can expand its market using delivery and digital ordering, then there are vegans aplenty to support the location.

When Taco Bell was repositioning their brand in 2012, the management team had a realization: what they were undertaking reflected a society-wide shift in attitudes. Then-CEO Greg Creed described it as a shift from "Food as Fuel" to "Food as Experience."[17]

Food as Fuel made sense to the Gen Xers, who just needed as much energy for as little money as possible. The Fuel era produced giant muffins, burritos the size of an adult's arm, and restaurant chains like The Cheesecake Factory and Claim Jumper, which are known for their portion sizes. Then Instagram, created in 2010, helped to make the *experience* of eating so much more important than the *function*. How did the food look? What was the restaurant like where you ate it? Who were you with? Would eating there help you get additional follows and likes?

What, where, and how we eat has shifted yet again. Now, we care not just about the experience, but we use our food preferences to define and share our identity. Food is a message bearer that expresses our personalities, values, and choices. Here's a sampling of the food identities we hear and see all around us:

- Health ("I'm gluten-free")
- Economic ("Farm to table")
- Diet ("I'm keto")
- Environmental ("I'm vegan")
- Trendy ("I always eat at the newest chef-driven concepts")
- Diversity ("American food is a collection of ethnic foods")
- Hospitality ("I'm always baking something for my grandkids")
- Political ("I only eat American beef")

One of the admirable qualities of the Internet is that it makes it so easy for us to be individuals together—in other words, to find a like-minded community. Sure, it's also easy for the Internet to become an echo chamber of facts selected or invented to reinforce a belief the audience already holds. But on the positive side, the most particular niche can now attract a following. Products that were once impossible to produce at reasonable cost can now find a large enough market to make sense. People with viewpoints or lifestyles that were once considered outlandish in their small town can now find an online community that shares their values.

People take pride in sharing their food philosophy and personalizing their order. Ordering online expands our restaurant options and personalizes our choices with a few clicks. More than ever before, restaurants need to understand diverse lifestyles and viewpoints and be involved in the dialogue of what matters most to their consumer base. Restaurants can do that by engaging online—because as we'll see in the next chapter, restaurant patrons are increasingly unlikely to go anywhere for their meal beyond their own front door.

Chapter 3

DELIVERY IS THE NEW DRIVE-THRU

Jackson clung to the headrest of the driver's seat, reaching out to it like he was clinging on to his favorite cuddly toy. "Sit back down and put your belt on," chastised his father, Andrew, knowing how excited his son got in these moments. Jessica and Andrew were having another one of those weeks. Not enough time, and another Saturday lunchtime rolled around when the easiest thing to do was to head to the drive-thru. Jackson had been on about it all week too— something about the latest cartoon character toy set that all his friends had received when they visited this same fast food chain.

Jessica and Andrew were in that complicated stage of life where the demands are endless and there just isn't enough time in a day. As a mom, Jessica felt guilty joining this long line of cars—but in some ways, it was a respite. They had spent all morning at Jackson's soccer tournament, and the household chores waited for them at home; the last thing she wanted was to add making lunch to the day's list of to-dos. Jessica felt better when thinking of her own mother and how kids' meals were used as a treat for her at times when other priorities had surfaced. At least Jackson was more interested in the toys than the less-than-healthy food many of his friends devoured in these moments. Another twelve minutes in this line, she guessed as she looked at the cars in front of her. And then she spotted her sister—waiting in a parking spot right in front of the restaurant itself.

Samantha was fiddling on her phone, unaware that her sister was sitting in another vehicle just a few yards away. "Slot Number 2," she selected and was advised that her order would be out momentarily. "Suckers," she laughed to herself, looking over her shoulder at the long drive-thru line. It was crazy that people would waste so much time lining up for what was supposed to be food that was fast. *This app and curbside pickup is far better than drive-thru*, she thought. Moments later, her food arrived and Samantha pulled back on the road. Meanwhile, Jackson was wriggling out of his seat again, getting more and more restless as his family continued to wait in the drive-thru line.

One of California's earliest drive-thrus appeared in a Los Angeles suburb in 1948. It lured passing motorists with a sign assuring "No Delay" and a name that promised exactly what it delivered: In-N-Out.[1]

America's love affair with drive-thrus was nudged along by the Interstate Highway Act of 1956, which opened the door to automobile ownership. Each decade between 1950 and 1970, America's vehicle population doubled. For a generation that was becoming accustomed to driving as a central facet of modern life, drive-thrus offered the pinnacle of convenience. Then in the 1970s, women entered the formalized economy in greater numbers and found themselves crunched for time. The solution? The drive-thru.

It may seem far-fetched to look back half a century or more in order to get a handle on the future of restaurants, but the entire industry can learn a number of lessons from the influence and evolution of the drive-thru.

The newfangled drive-thru idea took a while to catch on. The first Jack in the Box restaurants featured a sign that warned unwary customers, "Jack will speak to you," preparing them for the novel experience of ordering through a two-way speaker.[2] Early drive-thrus looked nothing like today's facilities, with their video-screen menu and microphone interface, five-car stack between order and delivery point, dedicated food production line for drive-thru customers, and double lanes for especially busy locations.

The concept would go on to change quick service restaurants (or QSRs, the industry term for fast food) forever. However, it was far from an instant success. In order to succeed, drive-thrus needed consumers and restaurants alike to change their expectations and ways of doing things.

For restaurateurs, drive-thrus aren't cheap. The capital investment and municipal requirements mean that a restaurant can't just switch on a drive-thru facility overnight—if it's possible at all given the location, existing structure, and parking lot size. To do it well, the restaurant also needs to optimize the kitchen for the additional channel, introducing a second make-line so the demands of the drive-thru do not disrupt the dine-in patron service, calling for more staff and new processes.

For customers, the new behavior required some adjustments too—and a spirit of adventure. Early adoption was boosted by Southern California's cruising culture: groups of teenagers out for a fun evening were among the first to take to the grab-and-go style of eating. Later, novelty gave way to convenience as the key appeal of drive-thrus. Blue-collar workers found it a handy way to grab lunch on the road, and busy moms (often working and/or single, ferrying kids to after-school activities) welcomed a fast and easy way to feed the family.

Possibly the most famous drive-thru restaurant in America, McDonald's, didn't open its first drive-thru until 1975, when the brand already had three thousand restaurants.[3] Why did it take them so long? It took time for consumer adoption to spread. It took time for an established chain with a great business model to develop a version of drive-thru that was additive to its existing business. And it's possible that successful restaurants like

McDonald's resisted the change to a new channel that appeared at first glance to be less attractive than their current business.

Today, there are over 150,000 drive-thrus in the United States. Americans make more than twelve billion drive-thru trips each year, or about one hundred visits per household—that's one visit every three or four days![4] Seventy percent of fast food business now occurs through the drive-thru window.[5] Of those drive-thru sales, half are consumed at home or office rather than in the car. You could say that consumers are performing "self-delivery"—and they've been doing it for decades.

As drive-thrus became more common across the American landscape, they shaped consumer expectations for restaurants. Fast food was what Americans wanted, but how could it be made even faster? Recognizing that convenience mattered most, QSRs spent their time and effort on improving speed and accuracy. Today, we think nothing of getting our food two minutes after we order it. In fact, we are annoyed when it takes more than four minutes to receive our order. Each year, *QSR* magazine ranks the major chains for performance on speed and accuracy, and the brands compete with one another to improve each metric, with just seconds moving the needle.

Although drive-thrus utilized the latest technology of their time, they didn't nail the speed and accuracy equation—at least, not at first. The earliest drive-thrus just slapped a window into the kitchen on the side of a small building that had been designed to handle walk-up or dine-in orders. The parking lots were barely large enough to hold parked cars, much less create a lane for cars to drive around the building to the drive-thru window. Before the remote order point was created, drivers placed their order at the same window where they then waited, paid, and picked up their food. If another customer wanted something, they had to wait for the car in front of them to receive their food and leave.

Even Starbucks, which rolled out its first drive-thru in 1994,[6] benefiting from nearly fifty years of drive-thru innovation from other brands before it, followed the same pattern. Restaurant engineer Brian Reece recalls about his time at Starbucks:

> At first they just punched a hole in the wall and had cars drive up and order coffee. Cars were backing up into the street. We calculated the bottleneck at the window: if we could reduce the time at the window by one second, that would be worth $2 million to the business. We configured different drive-thru engine setups in a lab to test them, and then we brought in a bunch of digital elements—like an order confirmation board. It created a better customer experience and reduced the bottleneck at the window because people weren't sitting in their car verifying their order at the window.[7]

These innovations came with time as restaurant companies honed the business model to fit the consumer need. Now, drive-thru standards are shared across most of the industry. The lines are timed to ensure that the production time precisely matches the time a car spends between order point and pickup window. Most major QSR chains have increasingly sophisticated software calculating times and using artificial intelligence-reviewed video to eliminate bottlenecks. The goal? Each step in the process should be ready at the moment each driver arrives at that step. All of this innovation has led drive-thrus to grow from 0 percent to 70 percent of the revenue of a typical QSR.

The high volumes generated by drive-thrus led to an almost maniacal focus on process. Customer demand reached a point where it was putting customer experience and operational effectiveness at risk. QSRs invested in hiring engineers (like Brian Reece) to optimize the experience, developing processes, technical solutions, and equipment that could carve off a second from the average transaction.

"What does an engineer do in food service? Lots," says restaurant engineering consultant Jane Gannaway.[8] She has been an engineer for several major global brands. In fact, her team's innovations at Taco Bell in the late 1980s and early 1990s enabled the brand to become a national restaurant chain. Despite her focus on processes, Gannaway affirms that restaurants are, as they always have been, "a people business." However, she points out that to an engineer, people are a problem to be solved: "Most engineers like to isolate variables, and people are variables." With thirty employees at every Taco Bell location, eliminating the variables wasn't possible—"We created a system to take out work content and deliver consistency." Gannaway and her team did that by shifting much of the food preparation to outside vendors. By buying cooked and seasoned beef and preprepared vegetables, Taco Bell restaurants could shave labor costs by eliminating much of the time-consuming work of chopping and cooking. Known inside the brand as "K-minus," (literally Kitchen Minus), the system transformed Taco Bell restaurants into mini manufacturing plants that could churn out high volumes inexpensively and with consistent quality.[9]

In 2017 the American consumer had an epiphany: delivery was even easier than going through the drive-thru. Drive-thrus and food delivery services share a number of qualities in common. The novelty factor, for one: with drive-thru it was the two-way speaker; with delivery it's the idea of having a meal arrive on your doorstep. In both cases, a new piece of technology—automobiles and smartphones—enabled a different type of interaction with food. For restaurateurs, some of the pain points are similar: balancing the desire to serve the patron on table six with the customer waiting at the window or the delivery driver hovering by the door. It's a hospitality instinct to serve the person seated in your establishment, but with both drive-thru and delivery, you have a commitment to someone outside the door—maybe even several miles away.

What fast food perfected, other kinds of restaurants are now emulating in an effort to give consumers what they want: convenience. About half of all types of restaurant sales—fast food, casual, family style, and fine dining alike—are consumed "off-premise": drive-thru, delivery, or takeout. The future, it seems, is already here. Delivery is the new drive-thru and will increasingly be more so as the restaurant industry innovates to give consumers what they want.

QSRs are convenient first and foremost because of the restaurant location. McDonald's real estate website states they look for "the best locations within the marketplace to provide our customers with convenience."[10] In a world where consumers are out and about—working, shopping, having fun—being nearby and well designed is a huge competitive advantage. But what is even more convenient than a well-located QSR? Not having to be out and about in the first place.

Convenience is also about speed. The fact that a restaurant can take a consumer from idea to satiation in a half hour is incredible. Once the most convenient location is uncovered, a QSR designs its footprint for even greater convenience. The entire restaurant is designed around expediency—where cars enter and exit the parking lot, how the drive-thru wraps around the building, and the layout of the mini manufacturing plant inside. But what's even faster than a well-designed QSR? Not spending the time to drive to and from the restaurant.

No doubt some restaurants will never embrace delivery because it appears not to sit well with their brand. Some cuisines and menu items don't travel well. Steak, for example. Would anyone pay $80 for a prepared filet mignon dropped in a box on their doorstep? Fine dining doesn't seem like a candidate for delivery, though some of the most innovative chefs are converting their menus to eat or finish cooking at home. The limited-seat, $300-a-plate n/naka in Los Angeles, for example, has created a $38 bento box that has been wildly popular and greatly extended their ability to reach consumers.[11]

Overall, there are far fewer genuine barriers to food delivery services than to drive-thru, so it stands to reason the potential is far greater. It's hard to imagine as we write this book in the quarantine life of 2020, but the United States is only in the early stages of restaurant delivery adoption. Prior to COVID-19, non-pizza, non-Chinese restaurant delivery sales made up a mere 10 percent of total industry sales. In more developed delivery markets such as China and India, that number ranges from 30 to 70 percent. (And in Chapter 6, we'll ask what it will take for the US to reach that level.)

Every trend—whether food or consumer goods or lifestyle behaviors—follows a similar s-shaped adoption curve, as first described by Everett M. Rogers describing the adoption of agricultural practices[12] and popularized by Malcolm Gladwell in his book *The Tipping Point*. A small group of early adopters gives an innovation its slow start; rapid uptake occurs when the message gets through to the mass market; and finally, the more risk-averse consumers come on board.

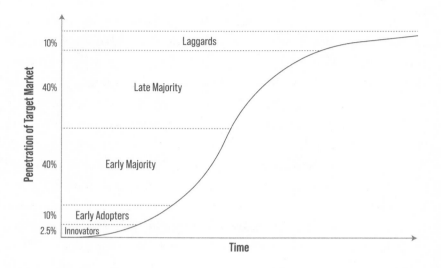

3.1 The Adoption *S*-Curve

In the case of digital delivery of restaurant food, the *early adopters* were technology mavens who lived in big cities—specifically Chicago (where Grubhub was born), New York (where Seamless was born), and San Francisco (where DoorDash and Postmates were born). These early adopters were savvy Internet users who kept up on the latest life-enhancing technologies. They were willing to try new things, even if some uncertainty lingered around the exact offering—who was bringing the meal? In what condition would it arrive? When would it arrive? The perceived benefits of the new platforms far outweighed any concerns.

The *early majority* came next, recruited with the help of increased availability and awareness. The delivery companies made big pushes to cover additional cities: buying up fledgling competitors, hiring MBAs to launch new locations, and taking on investors (like Grubhub's $200 million from Yum!)[13] to help cover the costs of expanding geography. In addition to *where*, the delivery companies expanded *what* they offered as well. The companies put together major marketing campaigns to teach restaurants about the new opportunity of delivery services, hired sales forces and customer success teams to get restaurants on board, and temporarily reduced fees to restaurants to seal the deal. With more restaurants in more places, it made sense for more consumers to download and use an app. The delivery companies capitalized on this momentum by pouring millions of dollars into "customer acquisition"—convincing consumers that this new format was worth a try.

For the *late majority* to adopt and for other cohorts to increase their frequency of use, cost must (and will) come down: the burger must cost the same over the counter as it does when delivered. Late adopters may also insist on a better overall experience—order-to-delivery times, accuracy, and quality should all improve. Retailers first viewed online shopping as an inferior channel but later realized it was actually the most profitable as they redesigned their systems to optimize for it. Restaurants will optimize for delivery and will find that in doing so, they are able to deliver more efficiently and effectively. Already, Chipotle has announced they expect digital sales of $2.4 billion in 2020, nearly half their total systemwide sales.[14] As the more flexible traditional restaurants double down on making the delivery experience outstanding, more and more restaurants will follow Chipotle's lead. The consumer will ultimately benefit from lower prices and enjoy a better experience.

The delivery companies will also get better. As usage of platforms increases, these companies will be able to increase their delivery density—making their networks more efficient—and will likely find ways to lower the cost of the service as they go. As the price of delivery platforms decline, usage will increase further, leading America into a "virtuous cycle" of delivery adoption growth.

S-shaped adoption curves don't happen in a vacuum. Consumers, technology platforms, and restaurants all play a role in determining how high ultimate penetration goes and how quickly it gets there. For food delivery, the COVID-19 pandemic accelerated inevitable change for the entire restaurant industry. As Bill Gates puts it, the pandemic "crammed ten to fifteen years of digital adoption into one to two years."[15] The pandemic may have even pushed the ultimate adoption point higher. Before, certain demographic groups may have never considered delivery. After the pandemic, every demographic group has tried it.

For restaurants of all kinds, the upside that delivery represents is equivalent to the upside that drive-thrus offered for QSRs. In retrospect, we can easily see that drive-thru hasn't cannibalized dine-in business. Rather, drive-thru occasions grew the overall restaurant industry, and delivery is doing the same. Drive-thru has been seamlessly built to work efficiently alongside dine-in; it isn't seen by restaurateurs as a cannibalization of dine-in nor as a major drain on profits.

The challenge is not to drive consumers back to what the industry defines as most profitable. The challenge is to figure out how to serve consumers what they want profitably. The big chains spend millions of dollars each year innovating to stay relevant with consumers, then advertising those innovations to stay front of mind. The craveability of QSR menus ensures consumers will want the offering. Consumer cravings aren't just about *what* the restaurants are selling. Cravings are also about *when* and *how* a consumer can get what's on offer. IWWIWWIWI (I Want What I Want When I Want It) captures the immediacy of the modern consumer. The expectation, enabled by technology, is instant gratification of any desire. Here's where digital food delivery really excels.

At first glance, the value proposition that delivery offers customers is less obvious than the craveability factor. Today, restaurant delivery is more expensive than takeout or dine-in—at least comparing the same items at the same restaurant across different channels. Many restaurants increase their prices on delivery platforms or charge delivery fees. Even pizza, once famous for its free deliveries, now has market leader Domino's charging $4.99 for the service. But most consumers aren't considering "Should I go to TGI Friday's tonight or have TGI Friday's delivered?" Most consumers are considering the cost of an evening's experience. If they are comparing delivery to cooking at home, for example, a consumer is likely thinking about the value of their time, the pantry staple ingredients they have to buy in far larger quantities than one meal requires, and the spoilage of goods they purchase before they are able to use everything up. If they are thinking about a date night, they are comparing the cost of delivery to the cost of a babysitter, marked-up wine, and an Uber.

The consumer understanding of value is not about service fees and delivery fees and restaurant markups. The consumer defines value compared to the next viable alternative. As we shared earlier, Census data shows that Millennials spend $1,000 a year less on groceries compared to the same cohort ten years ago.[16] These statistics suggest that, prior to COVID-19, delivery sales were more likely to eat into cook-at-home occasions than restaurant occasions. Incremental—just as history of drive-thru suggests.

The adoption of food delivery services is occurring against the backdrop of growth pressures on restaurants. Before COVID-19 threw the entire industry into a tailspin, it was already facing increased competition and rising costs. Since the Great Recession in 2008, restaurants have relied on price hikes to battle some of these pressures. Restaurants' ability to raise prices through that time is likely due to the long economic expansion coupled with the sociological shifts in American eating patterns. In fact, since the recession, restaurants have been able to increase prices at about twice the rate of grocery store price increases.[17] Typically, when restaurants increase prices in excess of grocery, consumers shift back to cooking at home. This has not been the case for the last ten years. Instead, consumers have actually been spending more in restaurants. In 2014, restaurant revenues surpassed that of grocery for the first time in American history.[18]

Independent restaurants have been hit especially hard by the challenges to operate profitably. Over the last five years, independents have declined at a rate of about 2 percent per year, losing out to big brands who can leverage their scale in marketing for top-of-mind awareness and in supply chains for the lowest cost ingredients.[19] Even real estate is cheaper for a big brand, as landlords trust they will stay in business and pay their rent, leading them to charge little or no initial deposit and often lower ongoing rent. And although the restaurant industry is sensitive to minimum wage—which all brands regardless of size must pay—the large brands are able to afford the kinds of engineering described above to reduce the number of labor hours needed to service the same revenue. The net of all this? We have seen a total reversal in American food culture, where independent restaurants made up the majority of the restaurant industry as recently as 1990.

The COVID-19 pandemic fast-tracked this change. Estimates from local business groups, the National Restaurant Association, and industry analysts such as the Restaurant Finance Monitor are that 20–30 percent of the restaurant locations that closed during the pandemic will never reopen. In localities where real estate is more expensive and the economy relies on daytime workers, tourism, and evenings out, estimates for permanent closures are as high as 50 percent.

When a consumer places an order that results in 30 percent of revenue going to someone other than the restaurant—as can be the case with delivery—many worry that big brands are more likely to overcome delivery challenges more effectively than independents. But what if delivery is the innovation the industry needs? What if it unlocks an era of exponential growth enabled by lower real estate costs, lower labor costs, and benefits that are available to all restaurateurs, regardless of size?

"Off-premise" (catering, delivery, and takeout) is the highest growth channel in the restaurant industry. Its growth is not surprising. If consumers love value and convenience, and a better value and more convenient convenience comes along, they will flock to it. What offers what a drive-thru does, but better? Delivery.

Restaurant delivery is meeting the needs of a new generation, just as drive-thrus did for Baby Boomers. What began with 1950s car culture turned into an American dream defined by large suburban homes surrounding a "daily needs center" with grocery stores, drug stores, and drive-thrus. The shift toward dual-income couples accelerated the use of drive-thrus, as working parents sought convenient ways to feed their families. But as demands on our time increase, and as our homes become our places of work, too, our need for greater convenience increases. For Millennials and Gen Zers—the digital natives who inherently interact with the world through technology—delivery is the new drive-thru. And the rest of the population is not far behind.

Once Americans fully understand the ease of having food brought to them, there will be no turning back the clock.

Chapter 4

THE DIGITAL DISRUPTORS

"But I want this one," Jackson whined, pointing to his smartphone, which displayed the menu for a restaurant known for their cartoon plates and kid-friendly meals. Jackson's grandparents exchanged glances, both thinking how much he reminded them of Andrew at that age. Except when Andrew was young, there were no smartphones. Andrew would have been waving a pizza flyer in the air. Back then, every Friday night, Andrew and his parents would have gone through the special folder in the kitchen drawer that contained the pizza and Chinese food menus they had received in the mail. It was one of those regular family moments when Andrew, his sister, and their parents discussed what dinner they'd choose to celebrate the start of the weekend. Discussions would sometimes lead to fights, as each child jockeyed for their favorite restaurant. Once selected, the family would have to agree on a specific pizza or dish. They would read menu descriptions of no more than eight words in length, designed to fit on a one-page flyer. Andrew's father, Michael, would then dial the restaurant and head out to pick up the order.

On this particular evening, now-retired Michael and his wife Elizabeth looked down at their grandson, wondering what it was about these smartphones that had transfixed the attention of such young children in such a short period of time. Jackson was teaching his grandparents about the new technology and all of the conveniences it brought with it. After watching his parents order once, Jackson was now an expert on food delivery apps.

On the other side of town, Andrew and Jessica were finalizing their date-night order on the very same app that Jackson was appealing for his grandparents to consider.

Consumers have wanted the convenience of restaurant delivery for a long time. Beginning in the 1980s, local services sprang up all over the country to satisfy this demand. These services would collect restaurants' paper menus, collate them into a book, and accept orders over the phone. Their drivers (all employees) would pick up the food and take it wherever it needed to go. The model was expensive, slow, and cumbersome, so its users were mostly late-night office workers and the occasional catering order.

One such regional delivery provider was TakeOut Taxi. Founder Kevin Abt recollects his vision for the potential of off-premise sales, if only restaurants would consider them in the right way: "If a restaurant viewed this as an incremental sale, this incremental sale could be a profitable one. If they understood that their only variable costs with my sale are their food costs and their packaging, they're able to squeeze more product out the door."[1] Abt started his business on June 22, 1987, and believes there were no other delivery services anywhere in the country doing what he was doing. That wouldn't be the case for long.

Many similar regional businesses started to emerge. Michael Caito, a former busboy who had worked his way up in the restaurant industry, cofounded Restaurants on the Run in 1993. At first it was a side hustle for Caito and his two partners. "We worked at night in restaurants and hotels, and once the business got some traction, we were able to quit our night jobs and work all day in the business," recalls Caito. "I had been a manager at Pick Up Stix. There I saw the future was a small box that was primarily takeout."[2]

Restaurants on the Run started with landline phones and two-way radios. "We lived through the phone to Internet conversion," Caito remembers. "Restaurants were super slow to change. Technology is not a restaurant's core. Their core is feeding hungry people coming into the restaurant."

Abt grew TakeOut Taxi through franchising and established a presence in seventy-five cities across the country. "We were doing almost three hundred million a year in system sales with no Internet." However, it wasn't all plain sailing. Abt concedes, "I made one telltale mistake. I did all this on a $3 million venture capital investment." The investors wanted a more employee-driven growth plan versus a franchised approach, which led to Abt selling out his interest in the company.

Restaurants on the Run, in contrast, grew through acquisition. "We had made ten to twelve acquisitions into new markets by the time Grubhub came on the scene," Caito remembers. In 2015 Restaurants on the Run needed more cash to continue their acquisition spree, but "as a twenty-year-old company, we weren't getting the same buzz." The attention was on Grubhub, DoorDash, Postmates, and Uber Eats. However, "strategic buyers saw us as sexy." The proof came with an offer from Grubhub to buy Restaurants on the Run. "I was playing cards with my family when the offer sheet came in. It was a lot more than we thought."

Grubhub acquired many similar businesses in its bid to become a national online restaurant aggregator. Founded in 2004, Grubhub was the earliest of the modern delivery aggregators. From 2007 to 2011, venture capitalists poured $34 million into the start-up.[3] The idea was compelling—give consumers what they want, and give restaurants incremental revenue by bringing the two together in a frictionless way.

Grubhub's rise from two hungry twentysomethings with an idea to the leading delivery platform in the US required a series of acquisitions of both regional delivery networks (such as Restaurants on the Run, Seamless, DiningIn, Delivered Dish, LAbite, Eat24, and OrderUp) and capabilities (such as LevelUp and Tapingo). In 2011, it culminated in Grubhub receiving $50 million of additional venture capital. That $50 million funded the capstone acquisition Dotmenu, the parent company of AllMenus and CampusFood.[4]

In 2013, Seamless and Grubhub merged. Seamless had previously purchased MenuPages, so the two companies together created a national presence with coverage in all of the major US markets. By 2015 Grubhub operated in fifty US cities, adding another twenty-eight the following year.[5]

In the early days, Grubhub operated solely in Chicago and San Francisco. They now deliver nationwide in more than four thousand US cities, serve more than thirty million active diners, process more than half a million orders each day, and in 2019 accounted for about 1 percent of total US restaurant sales.[6]

Grubhub took leadership early in the game. At the time of the Seamless–Grubhub merger, DoorDash was just starting out in a Stanford University dorm room.[7] Uber didn't focus on restaurant delivery with Uber Eats until a year later in 2014.[8] Postmates is a bit older than either of them, starting in 2011, but their business model was more broad-based delivery, with restaurants just a part of it.[9] As the elder statesman in the food delivery space, Grubhub long maintained the highest market share among online food orders. Even as recently as 2018, Grubhub held an astounding 50 percent market share, with the newer players fighting over the other half.

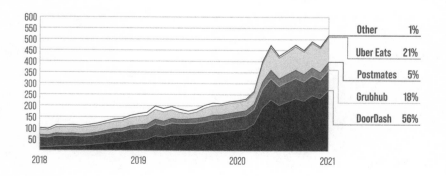

4.1 Meal Delivery by Third-Party Provider 2018–2020.[10]

By 2020, the story had reversed. While Grubhub held on to its sales, it failed to keep up with the rapidly growing market. The new entrants—DoorDash and Uber Eats—had surpassed Grubhub's share. Credit card analytics firm Second Measure estimates that DoorDash now leads with 52 percent of the market, and the combined Uber Eats–Postmates entity is close behind at nearly 30 percent.[11]

While Grubhub raised $84 million before it went public, DoorDash raised a total of $2.5 billion.[12] More than an order of magnitude higher than Grubhub, DoorDash had the money to invest in three important things that Grubhub has not been able to keep up with:

1. Access to technology
2. Customer acquisition
3. Logistics solutions

These are the three core competencies of a digital delivery platform and the value that they bring to the industry. While many restaurants might fear the emergence of a platform that gets between the restaurant and the consumer—and charges a fee to do so—platforms in every industry have disrupted their host industry through these three keys.

1. Access to Technology

There is no question who wins when a platform enters an industry: the consumer. Long term, an improved consumer experience benefits the industry as consumers use the industry more. Who benefits from the *growth* of the platform, though, is a different story.

What Uber did to taxis is a great example. Uber made rides cheaper, easier, and more available. Consumers took more rides as a result. The industry grew to the point where Baby Boomers now lament that their grandchildren have no interest in getting a driver's license. But the previous provider of rides—taxis—did not grow. In fact, taxis have been hard hit by the emergence of Uber and Lyft. In San Francisco, where these services were founded, taxis went from a near-monopoly on rides to providing only about 8 percent.[13]

Taxis have fared better (not well, but better) in other cities. For example, in New York City prior to the COVID-19 pandemic, taxis still made up 30 percent of rides.[14] New York City taxis have performed better than in other cities because they followed the consumer: in 2015, the Taxi & Limousine Commission launched its own app, Arro, to help consumers hail yellow cabs.[15] The app is now available in several major cities and makes using a taxi as easy as using an Uber. For consumers who value the background checks and street knowledge of a taxi driver, making a taxi competitive on the ease-of-use front levels the playing field with Uber. The specter of what happened in taxis, travel, and online shopping looms large in the restaurant landscape.

How is it that platforms seem uniquely able to shake up industries so completely when consumers are clearly communicating their desire for change? Why do we so rarely see change initiated from inside an industry? It's true that some industries have tried to come together to provide consumers what they want in a way that is less disruptive to the existing businesses. For example, the airline industry created Orbitz in reaction to Expedia but ultimately spun it out into its own entity—which, ironically, Expedia purchased in 2015.[16] Even so, in industry after industry, the pattern is the same. Established businesses with a proven and historical business model have existing profit streams to protect. Upstart companies with an idea and a fresh perspective have nothing to lose. And in the most compelling cases, venture capital funds the change they seek to deploy. Established businesses either adopt the new model or find their path to success much less traversable than before the disruption.

Aaron Cheris, Head of Bain & Company's Americas Retail Practice, says, "It is always easier to disrupt someone else than to disrupt yourself. Disrupting yourself is really hard. Kodak knew down to the day when digital cameras were going to take off, and yet they couldn't get themselves to disrupt themselves and their existing profit stream."[17]

The same is happening in restaurants now. Only Domino's has successfully disrupted itself, spending millions on pushing pizza from a phone order system to an Internet order system before anyone else. Domino's was able to do this because at the time, they had less to lose: they were in a turnaround situation when they began to make their technology investments. Technology was their way out. Every other restaurant has been subject to the impact of venture capital investments in the space.

Platforms are not cheap nor easy to build. The first iteration of consumer technology can cost tens of millions of dollars to create. It is rare for an existing business to be able to make the case to invest the funds. Even if they have the cash on hand to fund the undertaking, they are loath to invest in a future that directly counters existing business models and investments. Platforms spread these development costs over many parties within their ecosystem: each member of the supply side of the marketplace contributes to the development costs through the fees they pay when consumers buy their goods on the marketplace. In addition to the expense, the intellectual property and ability to bring all participants of the market to the same table is difficult, if not impossible, for a single restaurant to do.

DoorDash Head of New Verticals Fuad Hannon says:

> The ability to build technology that can tell you minute by minute where your Dasher is, or update prep time based on how busy the restaurant is—it is unlikely a single restaurant could develop that. We are able to make the investments that "uplevel" the industry in a way that no one restaurant could. Third-party marketplaces like DoorDash also benefit from local network effects and economies of scale to create a virtuous cycle that enables a more efficient, cost-effective system that's attractive to consumers, merchants, and drivers.[18]

Ultimately, platforms come to act as a reference design for the rest of the industry. "You can show consumers and restaurants the future, what's possible," says Hannon. "When I started at DoorDash in 2015, the idea that somebody would get Taco Bell or McDonald's delivered was laughable. But there was this untapped demand—we could help brands find more consumers in their vicinity and serve them at more locations." Both of these brands now offer online ordering on their websites.

The advent of platforms has caused major chains to reinvest in their technology infrastructure—everything from POS (point of sale) systems to consumer-facing apps. Most large chains in 2020 charge their franchisees a "technology fee," something that was unheard of in a Franchise Disclosure Document just five years ago.

But it's more than just big chains who benefit from this technological evolution. The beauty of a platform is that it levels the playing field: it is equally available to a large chain and a local independent. The nature of the economic relationship—a percentage fee rather than a large upfront investment—makes the technology accessible to all. An independent restaurant may even be able to compete more effectively on a platform. Where previously national TV adverts and location were the two major drivers in consumer restaurant selection—and only the largest could afford prime ad spots and real estate—the platforms highlight order-to-delivery times, customer ratings, and highly localized ad spend. "It used to be location, location, location then good food," says Bain & Company's Cheris. "Now it's good food, packaged well, arrives to you nicely. The basis of competition has changed. Platforms enable hitchhikers—brands that could be cute local gems but now have wider access and availability."

"Platforms simplify innovation for a lot of people," says Amir Nahai, CEO of Lifestyle Brands and Global Food & Beverage for Accor Hotels. Having watched how the entrance of marketplaces affected the travel industry, Nahai could easily predict how they would play out in food:

> When you have a platform, a lot more companies can benefit. For your average mom and pop restaurant to deliver without a platform would have been super hard. Same thing for hotels. Booking.com is way better than most hotels' online booking. Platforms enable innovation. Maybe they are the lowest

common denominator, maybe they are not best of breed, but they give access to a huge number of people.[19]

2. Customer Acquisition

Once consumers have been shown what's possible, they shift their behavior rapidly. Delivery platforms accelerate adoption by spending a phenomenal portion of their venture capital cash on marketing and subsidizing the cost of the service. DoorDash highlights several practices in its S-1 filing for initial public offering (IPO) that convey a strong intention to lose money in order to change consumer behavior. Even after charging a restaurant up to 30 percent of sales to reach a consumer, DoorDash loses another 5–10 percent of sales on new customers (those in their first year):

> Contribution Profit (Loss) as a percentage of Marketplace GOV (Gross Order Volume) for a cohort is generally negative in the first year that the cohort is on our platform, due to the investments we make to acquire the consumers in the cohort and encourage their repeat use of our platform . . . In the near term, we expect to continue to make substantial investments to increase consumer adoption and extend our leadership.[20]

In fact, according to the P&L published in the S-1, DoorDash has spent more on sales and marketing than it has on actually delivering food in 2019 and 2020 (excluding any promotional discounts that offset revenue).

Where are these new consumers coming from? Before the COVID-19 pandemic, most consumers were already changing behavior from cooking to dining out, as evidenced by an increasing shift from Food at Home (grocery) spend to Food away from Home (restaurant) spend.[21] Some consumers were also switching from dining in to off-premise consumption, as evidenced by an increasing shift from dine-in to off-premise spend. The National Restaurant Association, in partnership with research firm

Technomic, found that 60 percent of all restaurant occasions in 2019—before the COVID-19 pandemic—were off-premise occasions.[22] The following year, off-premise skyrocketed as dining in was restricted or prohibited.

In addition to capturing consumers who are new to ordering in, the platforms also help restaurants capture consumers who are not already active users of a particular brand. Rob Lynch, CEO of Papa John's, puts it this way: "Our approach and our rationale is that we are going to be consumer-centric. If people are going to order Papa John's all the time, they are going to figure out that it's a lot more conducive for them to order it through our app than it is to order through DoorDash or Uber. If they don't order Papa John's all the time, then by definition they are incremental, and we've determined that about 65 percent of the transactions that we do through that channel are incremental."[23]

3. Logistics Solutions

With all these benefits, why did it take so long for online food delivery to go mainstream? Restaurant platforms are one of the last categories to launch—a full twenty years after travel platforms came on to the scene. Yi Sung Yong is Founder and CEO of Grain, a delivery start-up in Singapore. He says, "Food is the second hardest thing to deliver after organs. It is time sensitive. It is fragile. It is temperature sensitive. There are a lot of things to get right. It's very hard."[24]

Restaurant platforms are unique in offering both front-end (ordering) and back-end (fulfillment) services. In travel, for example, the platforms enable online booking, but once the order has been placed, the platforms don't really need to be involved. Consumers get themselves to the airport or hotel, and the airline or hotel fulfills the booking. In this respect, restaurant platforms are more like the Amazon Fulfillment Services model, where businesses can list their wares on Amazon for e-commerce ordering but then also use the Amazon logistics network to get the order to the consumer.

Considering the volume of fragmented competition that requires constant innovation and menu changes, the restaurant ecosystem is far more demanding of platforms than other industries. Not only does it require advanced software algorithms, sophisticated consumers trained through other interfaces in simpler industries, and significant venture capital—restaurant platforms also need an extensive logistics network. Fuad Hannon of DoorDash says,

> It is very difficult to build a last-mile delivery network that covers all portions of your trade area. The reality is that because you are only picking up from a single merchant, your cost structure is definitionally higher. It's a one-to-many distribution model. Because we are pooling demand, we are able to have a structurally lower cost basis, which allows us to reduce the cost to the merchant, reduce the cost to consumers. The only business who really has their own national delivery fleet is Domino's. We've enabled any restaurant to have access to that.

It is no accident that DoorDash takes such a restaurant-first stance. After all, the company was founded with the mission of helping small businesses reach consumers. "Tony Xu, Evan Moore, Andy Fang, and Stanley Tang had been working on a project to help small, local businesses grow," recounts Hannon. "They had been going door to door talking with small businesses, asking them about their pain points. There was a macaron shop near Stanford. The owner said she had a list of customers waiting for her to offer delivery. Outside of pizza or really dense locations, having your own delivery fleet was just too costly." They decided to create a three-sided marketplace—the merchant, the consumer, and the ordering platform, with logistics on the back end. "They put eight PDF menus on a website and turned it on to see if there was demand," Hannon says.

"Forty-five minutes later, they got their first order. They ate lunch at 4:00 p.m. and dinner at 10:00 p.m. because they were the delivery drivers." The business started in January 2013 as Palo Alto Delivery, then a few months later changed the name to DoorDash.

DoorDash isn't the only start-up founded by college students posting PDFs online, but it is the only one that turned into a multi-billion-dollar enterprise with more than 50 percent market share. Between four guys in a dorm room and a $68 billion IPO valuation, Hannon says, is "a series of micro decisions that compounded over time." He explains how DoorDash has stood out from the crowd.

Firstly, "DoorDash since its earliest days has been a merchant-first company." He uses their Drive product as an example, referring to the company's white-label delivery solution that merchants can use to deliver meals or other items that are ordered outside the DoorDash platform. "Why would you take the asset you've developed—the logistics engine, the driver fleet, the technology—and offer it to merchants?" Hannon asks rhetorically. "The idea was that to enable merchants to reach their own customers would help the merchants to succeed, and then it would be mutually beneficial. We are obsessed with solving our customers' problems. We want to build in a way that is accretive to our restaurant partners."

Secondly, Hannon continues, "There is a tremendous amount of operational vigor that this business requires. It's a physical digital business. The experience might start online, but it is fulfilled in a kitchen and then by a driver." The decision to put restaurants first and then to help the ecosystem with logistics puts DoorDash in a unique place among platforms. "We are agnostic between a marketplace [third-party] or a direct [first-party] order. If you order on Wingstop.com or Chipotle.com, we deliver the order via Drive." Drive is a DoorDash product that powers direct delivery fulfillment for a restaurant's owned channel. In 2020, the company has also developed a product called Storefront. With it, a restaurant can offer the same technology DoorDash has, but on their own website skinned in their own brand—much like what Shopify has done for Internet sellers. Again, it's the consumer who wins: "If you love a particular merchant and know what you want to buy, fantastic. Order on their website," Hannon says. "But if you aren't sure what you want, a marketplace makes more sense."

We can see that platforms bring technology, customers, and a logistics network to restaurants—and yet, many restaurateurs still feel that platforms are not the ally of the industry that they claim to be. Zach Goldstein, CEO of Thanx, believes that some of this anger from restaurants toward the platforms is perhaps more to do with not truly understanding the customer desire for eating food through off-premise channels. After all, why would restaurants choose a long-distance relationship rather than being up close and personal? Customers are sold on the benefits of off-premise dining, but for restaurants, it remains something of a love-hate relationship—for now.[25]

Chapter 5

WHY PIZZA WORKS

Andrew packed up the cones and balls at the end of Jackson's weekly soccer practice. The kids shivered on the side of the field in eager anticipation of what was to come. They knew when Jackson's dad led practice, pizza would follow. All the parents recognized that by the time their children got home, it would be too close to bedtime for them to eat dinner, so Andrew's routine was to click through the order around fifteen minutes before the end of play.

Although Andrew ate mostly vegan and they tried to keep gluten and dairy out of Jackson's diet, sometimes pizza was the best option. The pizza guy would meet them right at the edge of the sports field, carrying a delicious hot meal. Jackson wasn't gluten-free and dairy-free by choice, so he loved the treat. After all, pizza contains everything a little boy likes to eat: fluffy bread with a crispy crust, gooey cheese, and red sauce.

Jessica would probably frown at Andrew's health choices, but she, too, would gleefully eat the hot, tasty treat—if there were any leftovers, that is. She would probably make a side salad to demonstrate her dedication to vegetables, but she would secretly love the pizza.

Best of all, the entire thing would cost less than $50. To feed a group of hungry boys, it was the cheapest form of group dining. The value was amazing. They could all share cheese pizzas, so by the time Andrew added a tip, dinner would cost less than if he had gone to the grocery store, purchased ingredients, and made a picnic meal right there for Jackson and his fellow athletes.

The evolution of the pizza industry foreshadows what's to come for other cuisine types. Pizza has nailed delivery—and everything that is involved to make delivery a great experience. A typical delivery pizza is completely optimized for off-premise consumption: where it's made, how it's made, what the packaging is like, digital consumer acquisition, consumer interaction with the restaurant, and delivery fulfillment. Leading pizza delivery restaurants and the industry as a whole continue to innovate ways to make the delivery experience better and better.

According to PMQ's *Pizza Magazine*, Americans eat nearly $50 billion worth of pizza every year, making it one of the most commonly eaten foods in the US.[1] The United States Department of Agriculture (USDA) estimates that 13 percent of Americans eat pizza on any given day—that's one in eight Americans.[2]

"Why pizza?" asks Mandy Shaw, CEO of Blaze Pizza. To her, the answer is obvious. Shaw was raised around pizza, with her father working his way up from an hourly role to operations leadership in the Pizza Hut system. Those childhood influences stuck with Shaw, and she, too, made her career in restaurants, serving in senior technology and accounting roles at Bloomin' Brands and Blaze Pizza before taking the top job of the high-growth fast casual pizza chain.[3]

Shaw explains the wide appeal of pizza: "Your brain is happiest when your senses are overloaded, and that's what pizza is. It's sweet and acidic. The crust is crunchy and chewy. The umami of cheese. It's good." Beyond the flavor, it's fun. "Pizza is family friendly. It's sharable."

Rob Lynch, CEO of Papa John's, agrees: "Pizza is the most communal food. At home, people are looking for food that is easy, relatively inexpensive, and feeds a lot of people."[4] Few items can compete with the popularity and price per serving of pizza. The appeal becomes obvious the first time you organize food for a child's birthday party. What will most kids like? Pizza. How much will it cost? Perhaps a dollar or two per child.

Pizza is also adaptable to any occasion. Although most pizza ordered is cheese or pepperoni, "You can put any recipe on it as long as you can hold it in your hand," says Lynch. Indeed, pizza is so flexible that it's getting difficult to define what exactly pizza is. Traditionally a wheat dough topped with tomato sauce and cheese, pizza is now available with cauliflower crust, white and pesto sauces, and vegan "cheese." As long as it's a flat, edible surface, covered in toppings, baked in an oven, anything goes. "Pizza can evolve," says Fired Pie Cofounder Fred Morgan. He is a longtime pizza veteran, having spent his career at toppings innovator California Pizza Kitchen prior to starting his own chain:

> You can put anything you want on top of it. Vegetarian. Meat eater. Even gluten free. I just rolled out Nashville Hot Chicken Pizza, and it took off like crazy. We have plant-based chorizo—I never would have thought that would be on the menu. Twenty percent of our pizzas are cauliflower crust. Even the Big 3 [Domino's, Pizza Hut, and Little Caesars] have changed their menus. Even frozen pizzas are better than they ever were.[5]

Americans like pizza, but they also increasingly want to make better health choices. Oath Pizza was founded on this insight. Chief Marketing Officer Stacie Colburn Hayes describes the modern consumer's thought process this way: "If I have a choice between something that's better for me or not, I'll go with the ingredients I can pronounce that aren't totally processed." Most of the newer pizza brands embrace this trend toward simpler, healthier food.

Pizza is also easy to operationalize. According to PMQ's *Pizza Magazine*, there are about forty-two thousand independent pizza restaurants in the United States—and it's little wonder. All it takes to start a pizza restaurant is an oven and preprepared ingredients. The speed with which a restaurant can assemble and cook a pizza makes it highly attractive as an off-premise solution. Large and small pizza restaurants alike prep a "make table" filled with ingredients ready to be piled onto a pizza, so that the actual cook time is rapid and predictable. Cofounder of Blaze Pizza Elise Wetzel says, "We can fulfill an order in twelve minutes, or less."[6] Such a speedy turnaround improves the way the third-party platform algorithms rate their performance: "The more we do that stuff better and better than everyone else, the higher up they put us on the page."

While making an excellent pizza is an art form, making a decent one is pretty straightforward, and that enables the supply of pizza to proliferate. For restaurants who want to offer better than decent, many of the techniques that make for a great pizza occur well before the pizza is assembled and cooked. Blaze prepares their dough in such a way that it tastes great and is easy to digest, so it doesn't give you that bloated "pizza belly" feeling. Papa John's makes fresh dough daily and uses its own proprietary tomato variety for its sauce.

Good. Check.

Communal. Check.

Flexible to accommodate trends. Check.

Fast. Check.

Predictable. Check.

And deliverable. Blaze's Shaw says pizza "is one of the easiest things to deliver, and it delivers really well. It also reheats perfectly. You can put it in a cast iron skillet. You can put it in the oven. And it tastes [only] marginally different from the restaurant experience." Papa John's Lynch agrees: "It travels really well. Traditional QSR—burgers and fries or sandwiches—by the time thirty minutes goes by, they degrade. Pizza holds up better. It's easy to transport. Quality maintains itself."

The ease and quality of delivery make pizza the number one delivered meal in America. Of course, prior to the launch of the digital ordering platforms, pizza was nearly the *only* delivered meal in America. Today, make-your-own pizza is the fourth most ordered item on the DoorDash platform alone, so when you add the first-party ordering at the Big 3 pizza chains, pizza continues to be the most delivered meal—even after so many competing cuisine options have been enabled by the platforms.[7]

It wasn't always this way. Shaw recalls the Pizza Hut her father worked at when she was a child: "Pizza Hut was this romantic, amazing dine-out place where you went and had great handmade pizza. They used to make the dough from scratch. They ground up the tomatoes and let it sit overnight before it became sauce. Everything was fresh. Pizza Hut had not yet started delivery." No one really had. Ask any Gen Xer or older, and their childhood memories of pizza will be like Shaw's: it was a special night out at a restaurant that, for dates, was dark and romantic, and, for families, featured tabletop Ms. Pac-Man, a jukebox, or a pinball machine. Instead of recalling brands known for their delivery, like Domino's and Papa John's, anyone above the age of forty will recall Round Table Pizza, Godfather's Pizza, and Shakey's.

And then the Domino's effect came along and knocked the world of pizza sideways. Although some restaurants had offered their product for takeout, pizza delivery didn't really take off until Domino's designed their business entirely around the idea that the pizza would be eaten off-premise, and the product needed to survive the transit from point A to point B. This was a key pivot point: Domino's designed *everything* they did around delivery. They then spent forty years innovating in one consistent direction: a better delivery pizza.

The most industry-changing innovation of all? The humble pizza box. Prior to Domino's spending serious time and effort on perfecting the modern-day corrugated pizza box, takeout pizza went out the door on a corrugated base slid into a paper bag—much like how a Danish kringle is sold at Trader Joe's today.[8] Pizza boxes protect the integrity of the pizza, keeping it warm and orderly, while simultaneously allowing steam to vent out. Trapped steam, as anyone who has reheated their pizza in a microwave knows, ruins the crust by rendering it chewy and unpleasant to eat. Domino's Pizza slides their boxes into an insulated bag, which they patented as the "Heatwave" bag, to ensure that the product inside arrives at its destination piping hot.[9]

The box and heated bag were not the only innovations that Domino's brought to pizza. In their quest to make pizza deliverable, Domino's radically changed the whole idea of what a restaurant is. A typical Domino's location is off the main drag, has no dine-in seating, and measures about one thousand square feet. This little restaurant kitchen, designed exclusively for the ordering and baking of off-premise pizza, makes much more financial sense than an amazing, romantic, dine-in place. So much so that in 2018 Pizza Hut announced: "In contrast to the current asset base, which has a heavy reliance on dine-in, we expect at least 90 percent of our net new unit openings this year to be the Delco Model, which generally bodes healthy paybacks and strong unit level economics."[10] Delco, short for "delivery/carryout," is a smaller layout designed for off-premise pizza consumption.

Off-premise units are so small and so cheap to operate that a typical pizza restaurant can thrive with sales well below a million dollars a year—a feat few other restaurants can accomplish. At the same time, pizza is so popular with Americans, $700,000 of pizza a year can be sold to a trade area about two miles in radius. A QSR needs at least a four-mile radius and well over a million dollars of sales to make their model work.

Pizza joints commonly offer bundles of pizza, salads, breadsticks, desserts, and drinks. The demand for these meal combos pushes the delivery density (volume of demand) high enough that having an internal team of drivers and order-takers makes sense: enough pizza is going out the door to keep phone operators and delivery drivers fully utilized. This in-house ordering and delivery team is cheaper than paying a third-party platform 20–30 percent of sales.

Delivery density is often so high that multiple pizzas going to different houses can go out the door with the same driver. Batching orders in this way makes delivery networks more economically viable. Batching is an elusive goal for the delivery platforms, which currently engage in point-to-point logistics: each order goes direct from the restaurant to the customer's home, which is an incredibly inefficient and expensive way to deliver anything.

A barbeque restaurant wanting to convert their business to a full delivery model, on the other hand, would likely struggle. The ability to drive sufficient sales in a tight radius doesn't exist in most places—Texas and other barbeque-loving locations excepted. What can other restaurants do to emulate the delivery density of pizza? Focus their marketing to drive volumes in particular locations. The Newport Rib Company did this at the start of the COVID-19 pandemic through yard signs. On Wednesday, they would put a yard sign in an area of town saying, "Delivering to this neighborhood tomorrow. Order today!" On Thursday, they would move the sign to another part of town. Through this simple mechanism, the Newport Rib Company drove concentrated sales in specific neighborhoods that they could then deliver all at once. Other restaurants achieve the same goal by partnering with local hotels to provide room service or specific condo buildings to become the default dinner supplier for unit owners who don't want to cook. The digital equivalent is focusing digital promotional offers in specific quadrants of town for specific days and times.

The other facet of the Domino's effect was that they valued technology and process as much as they valued the food they offered their customers. Although Papa John's was first to launch online ordering in the US—back in 2002, [11] a time when many retailers were just starting to experiment with going online—Domino's was busily laying the foundation for their future e-commerce growth. They started with point of sale (POS). In 2002, Domino's created its own internal POS, which 100 percent of franchisees worldwide ultimately adopted (after a 2007 lawsuit to the contrary). Called Pulse, this POS allows Domino's to consistently roll out all kinds of technology that plugs directly into the restaurant. In contrast, most large restaurant chains have to deal with multiple expensive integrations to bring any kind of consumer-facing e-commerce initiative to life in the restaurant and ultimately fulfill online orders.

One element Domino's had in its favor was a near-bankruptcy. Three consecutive years of negative same-store sales, combined with a debt balance of nearly $2 billion, drove the entire system into an existential crisis around the time of the Great Recession. Franchisees left the system, and restaurants closed. The stock fell to less than $3 a share in 2009 (in 2020, the share price hovered near $400).[12] Nearly going out of business doesn't immediately seem like an advantage, but the Domino's leadership team made it one. With nothing to lose, Domino's was able to bet the house on a future that most considered at best unlikely to materialize—and, at worst, detrimental to the existing business model.

Domino's launched Order by SMS text in the UK in 2007, the same year the iPhone launched. Also in 2007, the company rolled out online ordering in the US. Two years later, Domino's introduced the pizza tracker, helping online shoppers keep tabs on their orders. In 2010, Domino's UK launched their first iPhone app, quickly followed in the US in 2011.[13] Smartphones existed prior to the iPhone, but it was the iPhone—with its ease of use, sexy marketing, and support for app developers—that converted the telephone into a handheld computer. As iPhone adoption by consumers grew, mobile ordering for pizza simply made sense.

More than a decade on, consumers value the frictionless ease of ordering almost as much as they do the food. Pizza chains continue to take share from independents, according to PMQ's *Pizza Magazine*, and one of the main reasons is that the large chains make it so easy to order a pizza.[14] Many of Domino's original innovations are now considered table stakes for pizza chains, features like Easy Order, which enables repeat customers to get exactly what they got last time. Domino's and other large chains innovating their digital consumer relationships also make a point of telling the consumer about their innovations just as much as telling them about the food. "Having the marketing department be one of our biggest cheerleaders and proponents is incredible," then-CIO Kevin Vasconi said in an interview with *Nation's Restaurant News*. "It's something that doesn't happen at every company." *NRN* notes that more than half of Domino's 2016 marketing spending focused on the chain's digital efforts.[15]

The innovation hasn't stopped. Domino's has created an inventor space called the Innovation Garage, where cross-functional teams come together to solve problems. They've partnered with Xevo to bring in-car ordering to new car models, enabling drivers to order pizza with a few taps on a touchscreen. They've partnered with Nuro to explore autonomous vehicle pizza delivery, dispatching hot pizza in a robot vehicle about half the size of a sedan.[16] Meanwhile, upstart competitor &Pizza—with only thirty-six locations to Domino's sixteen thousand—is working on mobile pizza baking to bring the store to consumers.[17]

Not every restaurant is going to invest in technology to the extent that Domino's did. Nor does it make sense for every restaurant to do so. Each passing year brings innovations not just in the third-party delivery platforms, but in technologies that restaurants can access for a monthly fee. The millions of dollars that Domino's invested in a proprietary, system-standard POS, online ordering, and continuing frictionless innovations are no longer required for a restaurant to compete effectively for consumers who want online ordering and restaurant delivery. As Papa John's Lynch says, it's about being "consumer-led." The goal is to offer consumers what they want—easy ordering and delivery—not to invest in technology for technology's sake.

Papa John's and Domino's are following different strategies, and each has been enormously successful. In stark contrast to Domino's refusal to work with third-party platforms, Papa John's is happy to let some consumers access the brand through third parties as well as offering a first-party ordering experience. "If marketplace consumers like our product enough, they'll order from us more often, and eventually they'll transition to our own ordering channel," Lynch says. Papa John's then executes differently on each ordering channel so that each consumer can self-select into the channel that makes the most sense for them . . . with some encouragement toward first-party. Like Domino's, Papa John's drives frequent consumers to order first-party through its loyalty program, offering "Papa Dough" that can be redeemed for anything on the menu. "In pizza, there is typically some level of discounting through direct channels. In contrast, the aggregators sell it at full price," Lynch explains.

This differentiation in channel pricing enables Papa John's to be profitable on every order, regardless of the source. "Our customers naturally select the ordering platform and value proposition that work best for them."

To become as deliverable as pizza is, the rest of the restaurant industry must go through the same transition that pizza has gone through over the last fifty years. The industry will likely bifurcate into two separate modes—dine-in and off-premise—just as pizza did. Off-premise might be served out of dine-in kitchens, but more likely it will be served out of the Delco (delivery/carryout) model of the future: perhaps a ghost kitchen, a large commercial kitchen, or a small, out-of-the-way unit. Packaging innovation will be a critical component to operating a great Delco restaurant. Online ordering will continue to get easier for both the consumer and the restaurant. Digital marketing will acquire new users, and sophisticated loyalty programs will drive them to return.

Wingstop offers a vision of what the pizza model might look like when applied to another category. This runaway success of a restaurant offers made-to-order chicken wings, unique clean-label sauces, and hand-cut fries in a model very much like a Delco. CEO Charlie Morrison, who has led the brand through its digitization efforts, says about the chain, "I saw something quite similar to what I experienced in the pizza industry. An operating model that was primarily off-premise. A business that behaves a whole lot like the business I was raised in." Morrison spent his formative years first at Pizza Hut and later at Pizza Inn. "The experience in pizza really framed my perspective on the importance of digital and delivery as being two key drivers for restaurants."[18]

"For the last twenty-two years we've been the same brand. Combos, family packs," Morrison says about the menu structure, which seems custom-made to support digital delivery occasions. Like pizza, wings are a communal food, often consumed in a party setting. Wingstop's menu reflects this consumer behavior.

Morrison has announced an intention to take the brand to 100 percent digital sales. "Digital sales were 62 percent of our business in the US—second only to pizza. Digital is a necessity. It delivers on things we knew our guests wanted from us." Morrison carefully separates digital ordering from delivery fulfillment:

> We didn't see [third-party delivery] as a panacea. It wasn't something you could just jump into. In hindsight, that was very important. I was constantly challenged by analysts: "Why aren't you moving faster?" And our answer was pretty consistent—"We want to understand how it works." We wanted to make sure we didn't disappoint. If we were going to hand over our product to someone other than our guest, we needed to trust that they were going to treat it the way our guest would. The delivery experience had to be the same or better than carry out.

First, taking another cue from pizza, Wingstop put strict standards on how far an ordered meal can travel. "You cannot expect a driver to go beyond a fourteen-minute drive time," he says. Second, Morrison explains, "The technology with DoorDash is fully integrated into our system. The experience is seamless for everybody involved, including those inside our restaurant."

"Delivery is now 25 percent of our business," said Morrison in 2020. "It seems like it happened overnight, but we spent two years testing and perfecting it."

Chapter 6

THE MATURITY OF MARKETS

itesh began in the morning, leaving his village on his bike, taking the local train to the city and then a hand cart to the office. It was 100°F, humid, and far from comfortable, but he completed a similar journey every day. This was his job—but he had no boss telling him what to do.

Later that day, his colleague completed a similar trip in reverse. He returned to the same office, left via a different hand cart, took the local train, and biked to a village. He also didn't have a manager. And yet these two colleagues who didn't know each other were part of something pretty unique. Around them both, in a geographical area just slightly bigger than Chicago, two hundred thousand repeat trips like theirs were occurring that very same day.

Ritesh was not an office worker, nor was his colleague. In fact, much like the forty-five hundred others undertaking these trips, his colleague was completely illiterate. Even so, they were part of the most advanced food delivery system in the world—a system without any carbon emissions or private car usage and with no digital technology within its infrastructure. The system holds Six Sigma certification, meaning it has an error rate of one in six million trips.[1] It has been used to deliver dabbas (lunchboxes) by walas (people who carry lunchboxes) to thousands of workers across Mumbai for over 125 years.

A trip in a jam-packed metro in New York City feels like spacious luxury relative to the crushing commute in India's most populous city (twenty million people). It's for that reason, combined with the desire for a home-cooked meal, that many people simply can't carry their lunch with them on their journey to work.

The Honorable Mahadeo Havaji Bacche developed India's dabbawala system in the 1890s. His great-grandson Ritesh Andre was a wala in Mumbai, just like his great-grandfather before him. Unlike his great-grandfather, who left school at a very young age, Ritesh recently studied for an MBA. Today, he acts as spokesperson for the entire organization that is lauded around the world. In 2005, three dabbawalas attended Prince Charles's second marriage in the UK, a reflection of the Prince's appreciation for their acumen, accuracy, and work ethic.

"Most people think it's a catering service," Ritesh explains. But it's not—it's a home-cooked lunch delivery service that uses "tiffin boxes" containing a three-course meal specific to the recipient's desires. The meals are made at the recipient's home, collected by a member of the dabbawala system, and delivered by train and bicycle or hand cart precisely in time for lunch at 1:00 p.m. Not just that, the empty tiffin box is then collected and returned to whence it came—often before even the person who ate from it gets home from work.

The dabbawalas believe serving people is how they serve their God[2]—it is a form of worship without any need to go to a temple. In that sense, Ritesh says, the "customer is seen as a god."

Part of the efficiency of the process comes down to an intricate coding system. The dabbawala coding system is much like a barcode system, but where a barcode is designed to be read with a laser scanner: "In our scanning system, you can scan it with your eyes," explains Ritesh. The code on a tiffin box comprises a series of numbers, letters from two languages, signs, and a series of colors. Dabbawalas require three

> months of training to interpret the code. It enables the dabbawala to understand who should pick it up, the pickup location, the starting and final train station, the destination building name and floor number, and the name of the recipient.

Around the world, food delivery systems appear in many forms and enjoy varying levels of adoption. Some rely on urban density for their success, others are distinguished by their integration with other apps and platforms, while yet others could not succeed without a deeply ingrained preference for at-home eating over dining out.

In some of the nations described in this chapter, adoption of delivery can be as high as 70 percent of restaurant sales. Compare that to the US rate, pre–COVID-19 pandemic running at just 10 percent of non-pizza and non-Chinese food sales. Thanks largely to its density, New York City has the most developed food delivery market in the nation at about 40 percent. Judging by overseas figures, US restaurateurs need not expect to hit a ceiling in demand for delivery any time soon. Instead, they should consider what it would take to grow digital delivery sales by four to seven times its 2019 rate of penetration.

India: Hyper-Growth Delivery Tech in the Third World

India has a population of 1.3 billion people—over four times that of the United States. Online food delivery platforms don't cover the entire nation, but in the 550 cities where they are active and accessible to 250 million people, they are a growing powerhouse.

Zomato, the Zagat of India, opened its doors in 2008 with the intention of creating an Internet directory for restaurant menus. As it grew, it offered online reviews and referral table bookings for restaurants across one hundred of India's largest cities. When food delivery was requested, Zomato handed that task over to the restaurants themselves to manage fulfilment. It wasn't until 2014, when Swiggy entered the market with the sole intent of being a marketplace for food delivery, that consistent order fulfilment became a reality in Indian cities.

When Vivek Sunder joined Swiggy as their Chief Operating Officer in the summer of 2018, he saw food delivery at a point of inflection: "Urban cities were becoming a nightmare, and therefore traffic was becoming a nightmare, and both partners at home were working couples—and with this raw material, you're talking about an explosion of the category."[3] The same could be said of the US delivery market's potential at that same time, but in India the concurrent shift in technology adoption was much more rapid.

India went from having one of the most expensive mobile broadband costs in the world (118th) to the cheapest in a few short years. Telecommunication broadband infrastructure skipped entirely to the more recently introduced 4G cellular connectivity. Jio, now India's largest mobile network operator and third largest in the world, launched in 2016 with a 4G-only service, picking up 100 million customers in just six months.[4]

Fueled by low-cost, near-universal connectivity, digital food delivery in India has grown exponentially. Swiggy is one of the primary players in the market, and their rival, Zomato, has now entered the third-party platform arena. In aggregate, the two companies have raised over $2 billion.

Like their American counterparts, Zomato and Swiggy have invested much of their early effort in attaining representation in cities across India. It hasn't exactly been easy. Unlike in the United States, in India, Google didn't know the small towns: there was simply not enough geographical data for accurate mapping. Swiggy's Sunder says there's a "fat chance" Google can tell you which are the best restaurants in India. Swiggy solved that problem by crowdsourcing restaurants. First, they enabled users to show their interest by downloading the Swiggy app. If the platform was not yet live in their city, the registration count would help Swiggy focus on locations where customer interest was highest. The company would then reach out to those registered users and ask them which restaurants they would like to see on the platform, thus generating a lead source for their remote sales teams. Similarly, they engaged university students across the nation to "be the CEO for a city or campus," helping to sell the platform to restaurants ready to be on it. After all, students represented a relevant and active consumer base for delivered food. It was entrepreneurial efforts like this that enabled Swiggy to overtake Zomato's market share dominance.

But the Indian food delivery market faces significant challenges. Part of the reason is that there are far fewer restaurants than you might expect. In India, a restaurant isn't seen as a place for refueling—it's a place to delight in gluttony. "The kind of food at restaurants is not street food, it's treat food," Sunder explains. "That means it is not really healthy." Consumers believe that too much restaurant food is bad for you. "Even in Swiggy's cafeteria, only 10–15 percent of our employees will order via the platform using our discounts, but half would be bringing their lunch to work," Sunder says. He breaks down the numbers like this: "If you assume every urban Indian is having one hundred meals or so a month, seven to ten of those will be in a restaurant, and maybe one or two are eaten via Swiggy or Zomato."

The home cooking dynamic is also different for many families, especially those with dual incomes, Sunder observes. "The number of such working women who have home cooks is pretty close to 100 percent; you have a situation where very few Indians actually eat out."

Even so, before the COVID-19 pandemic in 2020, Swiggy achieved forty-five million orders a month. It's an impressive number—until you realize that unlike the US, where orders average around $16, in India the average order value is about $5.50. While India's delivery mechanism through bicycles and motorbikes makes logistical costs more palatable, restaurants still pay fees in the 15–25 percent range. Swiggy recognizes it has to offer more value to restaurants so that it can remain competitive and help restaurants do the same.

The company's executive team believes the solution lies in being more than just a platform for its restaurants. That starts with funding working capital through their "Capital Assist" financial program or through "Raw Material Assist," which matches the food sold to the most efficient, practical and delivery-ready packaging, or even "Labor Assist," where temporary labor providers (on-call staff) get connected to those needing staff quickly. Swiggy's huge data science team also uses empirical data (both past and real-time) from restaurants, extrapolating it through artificial intelligence to improve delivery timing while supporting restaurants with recommended menu improvements for sales or production optimization.

Pulling something together like this is almost like a SaaS (Software as a Service) model for independent restaurants. Sunder explains it is a "long, long tail of restaurants, because only ten to twenty brands in the country have perfected [utilization of data for performance improvement] down to an industrial art. Everyone else operates in an artisanal manner."

China: The Everything Store of the East

China boasts one of the most mature food delivery networks in the world. Like India, it's driven by a duopoly: Ele.me (meaning "hungry yet?") owned by Alibaba, together with Meituan (meaning "beautiful together") owned by Tencent. Together, they are responsible for 90 percent of the market share for food delivery—and they take China's food delivery customer experience to an entirely new level.[5]

"Meituan has developed an almost unreal system,"[6] says Abey Lin, a fourth-generation Chinese-American from San Francisco who studied in Beijing. The first thing that hit Lin when his Beijing friends told him about Meituan was the sheer level of choice. "There were fifty categories of food with a minimum of seventy restaurants per category," he explains. "Not only that, but the restaurants would give you free delivery, and they'd be there in less than thirty minutes." Relative to Lin's food delivery experiences in the Bay Area, this was mind-blowing.

The biggest difference that he noticed, however, was cultural. "Especially among the youth in China, you only eat out for either social events or business . . . Nobody goes out to eat if they just want to get a specific type of food. If they want a specific type of food, it's almost always available on delivery."

Intriguingly, Meituan's food delivery arm—representing about 60 percent of the market—is one of very few platforms worldwide that is in profit.[7] They receive twenty-four million orders a day through a user base that reached over 353 million in 2019. More surprising still is that most of their seven hundred thousand drivers are employed and salaried, with a fleet made up of e-bikes rather than cars. Third-party riders are part of their fleet, but typically only in rural areas or smaller cities.

Meituan CEO Wang Xing is very clear on one thing: his company is not in the food business. "The mission of Meituan is to help people eat better, be better. We don't grow food. We don't cook food. We don't prepare food. What we do is to deliver food. So essentially, Meituan is a mobility company. That's what we do. We deliver something. So [the] vehicle is important for us."[8]

It explains why his company has invested over half a billion dollars into Li-One (also known as Lixiang), an electric/hybrid vehicle manufacturer with autonomous driving functionality as a core feature.[9] Riders represent a huge cost burden to the company, so Meituan is investing in a future of autonomous vehicles, improved mapping technology, and voice-to-car instructions that will drive further efficiencies.

Meituan's dispatch system is also impressive. It calculates 2.9 billion route plans every hour and enables riders to pick up and drop off up to ten orders at once in the shortest time and distance. That has helped reduce delivery times by 30 percent since 2015. It also has allowed riders to complete around thirty orders a day.[10] In comparison to the busiest Dasher in New York, that's about three times the volume.

Reflecting Meituan's confidence with their algorithms and back-end technology, they regularly refund fees or provide credit if deliveries aren't completed within thirty minutes. How's that for a customer promise? Just as the US early market leaders did, Meituan provided very enticing subsidies to its first customers to encourage adoption—but even today, consumers only pay a moderate marginal cost. Hans Chung, an analyst at KeyBanc, explains, "Typically, the delivery fee is 10 percent of the meal price, often 5 percent with a coupon, and there's no service fee, no tips."

Unlike comparable platforms in either the US or India, Chung points out, Ele.me and Meituan had big on-ground sales forces to develop the restaurant merchant ecosystem. "Success in the supply side [was] critical to the platform."

Apart from refunds and moderate costs, Meituan users also enjoy a remarkable level of integration through the interface. Imagine having one interface for Booking.com, Fandango, Bird, OpenTable, and Airbnb. Meituan users utilize WeChat as a primary means of digital communication and payment, making the whole transaction incredibly frictionless. There's plenty of choice with Apple Pay, Meituan Pay, and the digital payment services that Chinese banks provide as an option too.

With access to details of where you order your food, what's in your basket, what you watch, where you stay for your vacations, and your payment history, Meituan amasses a level of consumer data only rivaled by the likes of Google, Amazon, and Alibaba. This capability allows the platform to tailor its feature set and products to the users that it serves, and perform the role of a platform across numerous verticals. "Our strategy in integrating different businesses," says Xia Huaxia, Meituan's Chief Scientist, "is to attract a large volume of users with high-frequency services, and then push forward some low- and medium-frequency ones like haircuts and marriage services."[11]

When he completed his Beijing studies, Abey Lin returned to San Francisco—and had to get used to doing without the super apps that his experience in China unveiled to him. Although those services may not be available to Abey here yet, the Far East foreshadows the potential dawn of revolution in the restaurant industry's Western skies.

Britain: The Great British Takeout

Takeout has been part of the British way of eating for generations. The local "chippy," where fish and chips are served up wrapped in newspaper for the sole purpose of takeout, is as much a part of life for Brits that grew up in the early twentieth century as for those born in the twenty-first century. As in India and China, eating takeout food or food prepared at home is far more ingrained in the culture than in the US, with just 2.5 percent of Brits visiting a restaurant once a week or more.[12] That's not to say the UK doesn't have a powerful thirst for food convenience. Ready-made meals, which are only just starting to hit grocery shelves in the US, have been a staple of UK supermarket aisles for many years, affording great value, choice, and quality. Grocery online ordering also started far earlier and with more significant effect than in the United States. Tesco, the UK's largest supermarket chain, launched "Click and Collect" for grocery food pickup in 2011—a feature that only became mainstream in US grocery stores during the COVID-19 pandemic.[13]

Even before that, the British consumer was adopting online grocery delivery functionality through new businesses such as Ocado, founded in 2000 and now enjoying a 15 percent share of the UK online grocery market.[14] Why were the seemingly tradition-bound Brits so ready to embrace these innovations? The UK packs sixty-seven million people into its space.[15] That's equivalent to the population of California and Texas, but in a landmass only a quarter the size of those two US states combined.[16] This density creates a society quite on top of itself, so essential services are situated very close to residential areas, relieving pressure on transportation infrastructure. The proximity of British people to their food reduces the value associated with having something delivered, albeit the convenience remains a huge plus. But as a result, takeout (or Click and Collect) remains a very viable mechanism that doesn't require a massive shift in consumer behavior.

Brands also play a different role in the UK restaurant industry. In a list of the UK's most popular dining brands, leading the way is a takeout bakery named Greggs.[17] (McDonald's was third on the same list, followed by several American franchise/QSR staples.) Founded in 1951, Greggs owes its popularity to a shrewd blend of tradition and a recent pivot to position the brand as a "grab-and-go" bakery rather than a "take-home" bakery. The UK consumer has a strong affinity to independents and, in particular, ethnic cuisines (and the chippy). The "local" is an alternative name for your nearest pub or ethnic takeout restaurant. Consumers tend not to favor a restaurant because of its brand or under the influence of a costly advertising campaign. Many people may not even remember the name of the chippy they frequent—they choose it because it is a short walk from home.

The potential of digital food delivery is truly global. Many of the most powerful food delivery services reach well beyond the borders of the nation in which they were born.

Across the North Sea from the UK, Just Eat was founded in Denmark in 2001. Five entrepreneurs saw an opportunity to help "local" restaurants with low brand resonance grow sales by providing them a platform to broadcast their reach in a way that no individual restaurant could manage. Former CEO Klaus Nyengaard said that their platform had a "clear local focus (postcode by postcode, etc.)."[18] The initial business model was to offer a platform for takeout food options. Just Eat charged restaurant partners a commission for each order through their platform but were not responsible for the physical delivery of the orders. In their first business plan, the founders openly acknowledged that "the idea behind the business concept is easy to copy. Many people have had the idea . . . but they have failed to solve the problem of signing with enough restaurants."[19] The UK arm of Just Eat was launched in 2006 when one of the founders bought out the company and moved its headquarters there.

Deliveroo is the other main British delivery company. It opened its doors in the UK in 2013, many years after Just Eat. Initially, they may not have seen themselves as direct competitors. Deliveroo was a platform for delivering while Just Eat was "just" a platform for takeout. Deliveroo, which by then had started making serious inroads into the UK market, secured brands like Five Guys and Café Rouge and were gearing up for bigger things. Meanwhile, their PR team was busy polishing their collection of industry awards such as Best Start-Up Founders from TechCrunch and being listed at the top of Deloitte's annual ranking of fastest-growing tech companies, helping them toward securing $275 million in Series E funding in 2016 and $483 million a year later.[20]

Deliveroo, however, did not try to acquire restaurants in bulk, as we've seen in other operators and other markets. A former Deliveroo executive who led their international expansion told us, "When Deliveroo came in, they pitched themselves with the intent to get the high-end offers."[21] Much like Swiggy, Deliveroo also tried to secure exclusive deals with restaurants to tie them to one particular platform. Over time, it became clear that wasn't a realistic option—Deliveroo's executive team realized that restaurant acquisition and consumer adoption were paramount. The company now operates in two hundred locations across the United Kingdom, the Netherlands, France, Spain, Australia, Singapore, Hong Kong, the United Arab Emirates, and Kuwait.[22] Just Eat has similarly built operations in a dozen other nations, including the Netherlands, Ireland, Mexico, and Australia.

In 2016, Just Eat acquired Canada's leading delivery service, Skip the Dishes, for $200 million, and spent the next few years incorporating that delivery capability into the UK market. In doing so, Just Eat's margins shrank considerably—from 28.3 percent in 2017 to 15.4 percent in the first half of 2019—demonstrating the sheer cost and complexity of managing a driver fleet.[23] But in the same way Just Eat started delivery operations, in 2019 Deliveroo announced functionality for restaurants to accept takeout orders, further demonstrating that ubiquity of choice and functionality were more pertinent than differentiation from the competition. A former Deliveroo executive told us the company moved away from only working with higher-end eateries—as he calls it, "snobbery around food"—to "going down the path of market share. It doesn't matter what it costs—you get people to download the app, and that gives you credibility."

So what can we learn from these other, often more mature markets? What are the patterns that can be replicated, and which would never succeed in our own market?

1. Consolidation Is King

The US market is slowly becoming dominated by two key players: DoorDash and Uber Eats, which occupy over 70 percent of the market.[24] In China, it's Meituan and Ele.me; in India, it's Zomato and Swiggy; Just Eat and Deliveroo dominate the UK. All of these companies have pursued market share acquisition as a key strategy in their formative years, much to the chagrin of the restaurants they affected. Little surprise, then, that the biggest US platforms have chosen to focus on restaurant sign-ups and consumer downloads versus differentiation, and are now turning to non-organic means of winning that race.

The consolidation game continues beyond country boundaries too. Just Eat was acquired by Dutch food delivery giant Takeaway.com in 2020, which in the same year acquired Grubhub—the US's third-largest food delivery player—in a near $8 billion deal.

Decrowding the space of food delivery is one strategy that may shape a path to platform profitability, as shown by Meituan's financial results in 2019. Once customers are acquired onto a platform using an app, it appears they continue to use that app. McKinsey reports that 80 percent of UK food delivery customers have never or rarely switched platforms.

If restaurant and consumer acquisition investments decline, commission rates could become more competitive. However, with duopolies in place, competitive forces won't necessarily reduce rates—as demonstrated by Swiggy's 15–25 percent range. What incentives do platforms have to lower prices if customer retention is not a problem and competitive forces are minimized?

2. Smart Symbiotic Systems Boost Efficiency

The dabbawala system in India demonstrates the merits of having one coding system to manage deliveries and minimize operational deficiencies. If drivers in the US did not have to move between various platform apps, we would see similar benefits. As it is, the language of how and where to go (the algorithms and driver support services) varies significantly between platforms. Could one set of drivers be utilized across multiple platforms, for instance—each using a similar interface? We see in the dabbawala system that having a unified ordering system allows the couriers to interpret the procedures with high accuracy levels. The three months' training also supports that, emphasizing that simplicity matters when it comes to your driver force, but only if investment occurs upfront. The dabbawalas have only gone on strike once in their 125-year history and seem content and motivated in their work—another factor we'll explore more fully in Chapter 10.

3. Multiple Verticals Improve Network Economics

Consolidation is taken a level further in more mature markets where additional verticals are supported by the same platforms and where payment and communication are tied together in a seamless user experience. While the US saw both Uber Eats and DoorDash unveil products enabling their move into convenience and retail drug partnerships during the COVID-19 pandemic, it's likely that more will be identified in the future.

Vivek Sunder at Swiggy believes it's also key to utilize the driver force more effectively throughout the day:

> People are very rarely ordering groceries when they're eating food," he explains when describing the valleys of demand in between breakfast, lunch, and dinner. "A delivery partner costs us money because he doesn't have orders. If we can use an outsourced fleet that can do grocery orders in between times when they're ordering food, that helps. Swiggy getting into these services means we can give work during those valleys so we can get better utilization, and when utilization is high, costs come down—because we always have a minimum wage that we have to pay.

If the cost of a delivery network is reduced through layering in such verticals, it is not surprising to see Meituan employing their own drivers. Additionally, labor costs in China and India are much lower than in the rest of the world. Between better utilization and lower costs, it's easier for delivery platforms to draw a profit from operations. In India, drivers earn 47 percent above the national wage rate average, but that still amounts to just $300–$600 per month.[25] In his 2019 letter to shareholders, Grubhub chief executive Matt Maloney observed that "a common fallacy in this business is that an avalanche of volume, food or otherwise, will drive logistics costs down materially. The bottom line is that you need to pay someone enough money to drive to the restaurant, pick up the food, and drive it to a diner. That takes time, and drivers need to be appropriately paid for their time."[26]

4. Proximity and Density Drive Value

The significance of proximity, density, and batching (deliveries consolidated across verticals)—only enabled by concentrated order volume—stands out as the core lesson to be learned from other more established delivery markets. Having the food produced closer to the consumer addresses speed—both for the consumer to have what they want, when they want it, and for the driver to secure more jobs per hour. It also enables the value-conscious consumer to choose takeout when the journey to pick up is convenient. Many QSRs, including Burger King and Taco Bell, and fast casual concepts like Shake Shack, brought in new store designs in response to the seismic shift occurring through the COVID-19 pandemic. By providing lanes for drive-thru, driver pickup, and curbside pickup, they acknowledged the significant trend toward pickup in the US restaurant industry.

With higher volumes of customers ordering delivered food, batching will increasingly become more prevalent. Swiggy completes around 40 percent of their delivered orders via a batch delivery, where two food packages are picked up at one restaurant and delivered to two different but closely located customers. Batch delivery adds further efficiencies and is becoming a more significant part of the US system of delivery as well.

Consumers across the globe have demonstrated that they want food delivery to continue as a critical part of their lives. The businesses shaping that future have already made considerable strides to fulfilling that desire. Momentum peaked in 2020 with the COVID-19 pandemic pushing takeout and delivery to 100 percent of all food orders fulfilled. As we descend from that peak, where will the United States land—at 70 percent like the Middle East? Closer to 30 percent like the UK, Western Europe, India, and China? Or back at 10 percent for non-pizza, non-Chinese deliveries, just where we were before the COVID-19 pandemic?

We may not have a crystal ball, but from close analysis of the dynamics in the United States and elsewhere, we foresee digital food delivery following the *s*-curve of adoption. Here in the United States, we are in the early stages—growing fast but coming off a small base. We don't see delivery adoption reaching 70 percent because this nation lacks the preconditions of cheap labor and urban density. There is no question in our minds, though, that we will reach 30 percent, and even 50 percent is not out of reach.

A market for digital food delivery that is three to five times the size it is now? For most restaurant owners, that is a mind-blowing scenario. Think of it like this, though: if you equate the adoption of digital food delivery with the adoption of social media, in the US we are far more like MySpace right now. The equivalent of Facebook (with all its dominance and associated concerns) may be just around the corner.

Chapter 7

GOING DIGITAL ON YOUR OWN PROFITABLE TERMS

You guys all criticize me for how much I charge you for guests to come to your hotel. I think you're looking at it wrong. Look at us as the cheapest source of referrals that you could imagine. If they come through me, you pay me once, and if they come back to me again and again, shame on you. You should make them a loyal customer.

—DARA KHOSROWSHAHI, CEO, UBER (THEN-EXPEDIA CEO)[1]

Although delivery has been the highest growth channel for restaurants in recent years, it has also been the least profitable, creating a love-hate relationship between restaurants and delivery companies. Right now, neither restaurants nor delivery platforms are particularly happy with the economics that result from giving customers what they want. Restaurateurs struggle to understand how and why third-party platforms can charge what they charge, seeing it eat into their already thin profit margins. But for the platforms, the logistics of delivery comes with a hefty price tag, especially in the US, with its high labor costs and low population density. There's a great deal of potential and desire around the table to improve the value provided.

Consumers have it best right now. Venture capital investment is funding customer acquisition to drive adoption of food delivery and preference for one platform over another, even when the short-term result is a paper loss. Brian Nowak, Managing Director at Morgan Stanley, believes that while "promotions and deals play a role in 58 percent of diners' decision-making, it's also leading to negative earnings [for the platforms] in every region except New York."[2] Yet even while the platforms vie for their favor, customers must tolerate a less-than-excellent experience. They face a litany of choices of what to eat, to the point of search fatigue. Mostly, they have to pay for the cost of delivery. The experience of ordering is not as seamless as, say, Amazon's offering. Even after ordering, the food is not always delivered in time nor to the quality customers expect. The delivery vehicles are not kitted out with the appropriate equipment to ensure the safe, temperature-controlled, and integrity-focused transit that is afforded to many other packages delivered to our door. When their meal is on the table in front of them, customers do not get the same service or hospitality-rich experience that they may enjoy inside a restaurant. And when issues arise, they often have to channel them through platform chatbots rather than speaking directly with the restaurant's staff.

For restaurateurs, operational challenges remain plentiful, and third-party platforms provide more complexity than simplicity. A restaurant's mettle is tested by the fact that there is no single, consistent system that restaurants and third-party platforms work within. For example, a restaurant operator's choice of when to initiate "fire time" (preparation) for each order can impact the platform's ability to predict when the consumer will receive their food. One operator may begin preparing orders when the driver arrives, while another makes the item immediately and lets it sit until the driver turns up. Some delivery drivers will have to park minutes away from the restaurant because of parking restrictions, while others pick up orders from restaurants that provide "delivery driver only" parking right outside. Each third-party platform brings its own setup, usage protocols, and algorithms, intensifying the frustration for restaurant operators who are spending a significant chunk of their time and profit margin—only to achieve a sub-optimal experience for everyone involved.[3]

GrubHub Summary of March Deposits	
46 Prepaid Order	$1,042.63
Commission	($206.51)
Delivery Commission	($94.99)
Processing Fee	($38.52)
Promotions	($231.00)
7 Order Adjustment	($131.19)
Commission	$9.75
Delivery Commission	$4.88
Processing Fee	$1.49
Promotions	$20.00
Pay Me Now Fee	$0.00
46 Orders in March	$376.54

7.1 Grubhub Summary of March Deposits to Food Truck Owner Giuseppe Badalamenti

Restaurant owners argue that the fees they pay to third-party platforms are not sustainable. Chicago food truck owner Giuseppe Badalamenti's social media profile was flooded when he posted a photo of the Grubhub receipt for his business in March 2020. Along with the photo, Badalamenti told his consumers, "Stop believing you are supporting your community by ordering from a third-party delivery company. Out of almost $1,100 of orders, [the] restaurant you are trying to support receives not even $400. It is almost not enough to pay for the food."

Badalamenti includes in his payments to Grubhub seven order adjustments that were refunded. Putting that aside, his comments and sentiment reflect many independent owners' general resentment toward third-party platforms. They can't live without the third parties, but that doesn't mean they have to like them.

When restaurants were in complete control of how they cooked and who they cooked for, it was so much more straightforward, but those times have gone. The stark reality is that today's consumer demands this new channel of service.

One of the barriers to making fiscal sense of the fees is that restaurants often focus on the value of just one of the services the platform provides—typically the technology. Thirty percent of each order seems like an enormous amount to pay for a simple ordering interface. But the platforms are doing so much more. As we first discussed in Chapter 4, there are three "value levers" that restaurants receive from third-party platforms:

1. Ordering technology
2. Customer acquisition
3. Fulfillment logistics

Taken together, those three elements may well be worth 30 percent of each order to provide. While many in the restaurant industry would like to see the percentage come down, it is unlikely to drop substantially while consumers demand the channel and while platforms struggle to make money. Even the largest restaurant chains, which have been successful in using their scale to lower the percentage paid to the platform, have been unable to get the number below 15 percent. Most restaurant chains pay 20–25 percent, and independents struggle to get below list price (30 percent) without trading off exclusivity.

This fundamental change in economics is causing the industry to rethink the basic restaurant financial framework. Murad Karimi is Founder and

CEO of Epic Kitchens, a restaurant-as-a-service multi-concept operator. As he puts it, "The historical way that a P&L worked in the restaurant industry was pretty straightforward."[4] Now, Karimi believes an alternative perspective is needed: "To optimize the P&L, to make room for all of these fees, is an important endeavor given there's such a large growth rate in delivery versus the decline in dine-in."

Many restaurants break down their costs as a percentage of revenue, as in the example below. Percentages will vary for different types of restaurants, but most fall close to this type of breakdown.

Item	Percent of Revenue	Definition
Food and Paper	30%	Ingredient and packaging costs
Labor	30%	Staff operating the restaurant
Occupancy	15%	Rent, common area maintenance, utilities, insurance
Marketing	5%	Promotion of the restaurant
Profit Margin	20%	Pre-tax profit margin

7.2 Profit & Loss Statement (P&L) for a Traditional Restaurant

Based on this math, it seems obvious why restaurant operators are so upset by the costs of third-party platforms. At 30 percent, the third-party delivery fee is larger than the profit margin of a restaurant. On top of that, delivery food and paper costs are likely to be more expensive because of the packaging and product mix. Finally, marketing costs will also typically increase to achieve higher ranking on the third-party apps. The resulting profit margin doesn't look healthy, and for many restaurant operators it disappears entirely. Here's how many restaurateurs calculate the profitability of a delivery meal.

Item	Percentage	Adjustment
Food and Paper	35%	Incremental packaging for off-premise consumption and mix shift away from high-margin items (beverages, desserts)
Labor	30%	
Occupancy	15%	
Marketing	10%	More marketing spending is often required to acquire customers on third-party platforms
Third-Party Fee	30%	Fees are typically 20–30% for most restaurants. We'll use 30% to best exemplify the situation faced by those with less leverage
Profit Margin	-20%	

7.3 Profit and Loss Statement with Third-Party Fee

This representation above, however, is not correct. Incremental orders do not incur, for example, added rent, nor an additional manager to service them. The lights are already on. Incremental orders incur only marginal costs—costs that are added because the order was added—like food and paper costs. Looking at only the incremental costs, the profit margin for off-premise orders looks a lot more encouraging.

Item	Percentage	Adjustment
Food and Paper	35%	
Labor	0%	No additional labor is required beyond what was already there, servicing dine-in orders
Occupancy	0%	No incremental cost. Occupancy is fixed, and so with incremental orders, there is no additional charge
Marketing	10%	
Third-Party Fee	30%	
Profit Margin	25%	A higher profit margin for incremental orders

7. 4 Fully Incremental Off-Premise Order Profit & Loss Statement

This representation, however, skims over some potential added labor costs. Delivery orders may create potential inefficiencies for a restaurant designed for dine-in: e.g., the processes for managing third-party deliveries, bagging instead of plating, and expediting to drivers instead of servers. We also need to understand the output capacity of a kitchen to determine whether the restaurant incurs incremental labor costs. Let's say a restaurant kitchen has the capacity to produce sixty plates an hour on average. Three cooks produce those sixty plates. Each cook, then, has a theoretical twenty-plate output (recognizing the reality that orders per hour fluctuate depending on the time of day). If the restaurant served forty plates on average to its dine-in customers each hour, it has capacity to push out twenty plates at no incremental cost. However, if the restaurant were to find themselves producing forty plates for off-premise on top of their forty dine-in customers, there would be some incremental labor cost. There may be offsetting labor savings of an off-premise transaction. An off-premise dish doesn't incur the costs of dishwashing, expediting, servers, front desk, and cleaners. Therefore, 30 percent is too high a cost for incremental off-premise labor, so let's assume 15 percent.

When we calculate the breakdown in the blended scenario, the total restaurant profit margin drops to 18.5 percent. This reduction represents a common complaint that echoes across the nation's conference halls whenever restaurant industry attendees meet to discuss food delivery.

	Dine-in (40 plates)	Off-premise (20 plates within kitchen capacity)	Off-premise (additional 20 plates outside of kitchen capacity)	Blended margin
Food and Paper	30%	35%	35%	32.5%
Labor	30%	0%	15%—an additional chef	19%
Occupancy	15%	0%	0%	7.5%
Marketing	5%	10%	10%	7.5%
Third-Party Fee	0%	30%	30%	15%
Profit Margin	20%	25%	10%	18.5%

7.5 The Blended Capacity Profit & Loss Statement

True, the profit margin (profit as a percent of total revenue) drops, but cash profit (profit stated in dollars) goes up. To illustrate this, let's keep the numbers simple and assume the average dish price is $10. In the table below, you'll see that while off-premise profitability is strong when managed within current operational capacity, the cash profit drops when we add incremental labor costs.

The blended capacity perspective	Dine-in (40 plates)	Off-premise (20 plates within kitchen capacity)	Off-premise (additional 20 plates outside of kitchen capacity)	Blended Cash
Revenue	$400	$200	$200	$800
Food and Paper	$120	$70	$70	$260
Labor	$120	$0	$30	$150
Occupancy	$60	$0	$0	$60
Marketing	$20	$20	$20	$60
Third-Party Fee	$0	$60	$60	$120
Cash Profit	$80	$50	$20	$150

7.6 The Blended Capacity Cash Profit

Off-premise volume that fully utilizes a kitchen's output capacity is the crux of the opportunity for restaurants. Off-premise dining doubles, triples, quadruples the number of tables that can be physically served in the restaurant, so the limit is no longer table turns but the throughput the kitchen can produce. Or, to flip that concept around, the maximum throughput capacity from a kitchen is no longer capped by the restaurant's number of tables. Once kitchen utilization (or throughput of dishes per hour) is maximized, the value of incrementality becomes clearer.

Of course, that outcome relies on managing sales and scheduling closely so that the operator can understand when the incremental resource is required. In the example above, the incremental resource is not fully utilized. Jordan Boesch, CEO of 7shifts—a labor scheduling platform for restaurants—believes one of the most significant inefficiencies in food delivery right now is labor management. He says, "As we think about labor management as a whole, it's going to need to encompass and predict the volume of deliveries coming in to help staff accordingly. And it's a big pain point for the delivery companies—where [restaurants] shut off the [incoming order] tablets when things get busy."[5]

With that in mind, let's continue with our example. We have seen that the labor cost for sixty dishes ($600 revenue) is $120, or $40 per twenty dishes. Given the existing dine-in demands, another $200 of delivery orders need an additional labor cost of $30.

It's easy to see why many restaurants can't rely on third-party platforms alone to succeed. Third-party platforms can contribute to success, but are unlikely to be a panacea. Rather than perceiving the commission charge on delivery as an additional cost—similar to the cost of an extra server, say—it could be understood as a marketing cost to acquire new customers. That puts the commission in the same bucket as a newspaper ad or a printed leaflet. If a restaurant spends $1,000 on sending a flyer to a thousand people, and ten of them actually make a purchase, then the customer acquisition cost through that flyer is $100 per customer. If a restaurant gets ten new customers through a third-party delivery platform with an average ticket of $20 and fee of 30 percent, the customer acquisition cost is $6 per customer. There is a cost to acquire digital delivery customers, and acquiring them through the platforms is the most cost-effective way to do it.

There's a particularly strong argument that delivery platform fees should be considered as a marketing cost. Acquiring an incremental customer for just $6 seems pretty reasonable, but not if $6 is paid every time the customer returns. That is indeed what happens when restaurants depend solely on third-party platforms. This is why leading restaurateurs are wise to consider having their own digital channel.

With all its scale and negotiated efficiencies, Chipotle announced in the summer of 2020 their intent to test price hikes on third-party delivery platforms.[6] If major companies like Chipotle are trying this, it's no wonder the profit margin debate continues. The challenging question for all restaurateurs is whether increasing prices is indeed the right answer. After all, the consumer is already paying a convenience fee—how much will demand be eroded by a price increase? If guests are using third-party platforms to order from a restaurant's menu, it's because it has become their preferred method of ordering food online. Chipotle knows this, of course, and has built its own channel for processing digital orders to give their customer base an ever-better experience at a more affordable price—where service fees and delivery costs are lower than third-party charges, as the comparison below shows.

	DoorDash	Chipotle.com
Burrito Bowl	$8.20	$8.20
Pressed Apple Juice	$3.15	$3.15
Subtotal	$11.35	$11.35
Fees & Estimated Tax	$2.81	
Delivery Fee	$2.99	$1.00
Taxes & Fees		$1.86
TOTAL	$17.15	$14.21

7.7 Comparison of Chipotle through Third- and First-Party Ordering

Half of Chipotle's revenue now comes through digital channels ($829 million in Q2 2020), and their delivery sales quintupled between Q2 2019 and Q3 2020.[7] Little wonder, then, that their sheer scale and volume enabled them to invest in building their own platform—and that the platform attracted seventeen million users, as Chipotle CEO Brian Niccol announced to investors in an earnings call in 2020.[8]

But what of all the customers that have yet to use the Chipotle app? In testing this approach, the company runs the risk of customers shifting their understanding of Chipotle's price points because their only experience of Chipotle's pricing may be through the third-party platform menus. Customers won't necessarily understand or delineate between a third-party price and an in-store price, in the same way that they don't delineate between a corporate store and a franchise location. As Fred Morgan, former VP Operations of California Pizza Kitchen and Founder of Fired Pie, says, "It was always my strong belief that you did not want to raise your price, because 50 percent of our customers are still first-time guests."[9] If cheap, affordable food is part of the brand story, then anywhere the food is not cheap and affordable, the brand messaging will become mixed—and confuse customers.

Nevertheless, for independent restaurateurs and regional chains, the challenge remains. They can't compete with the millions of dollars invested in technology by third-party platforms and the major chains. Raising prices to compensate for third-party fees poses a much greater risk for independents because customers know that other competitive options are just a click away. So for restaurants without the size and scale of Chipotle, what are the alternatives? If restaurateurs can have their own digital channel, their own technology to provide an enhanced user experience and to retain customers (and their respective data), together with an outsourced logistics solution, then perhaps there is hope.

One man carrying the flag of that hope is Noah Glass. Glass is seen as one of the early proponents for restaurants to have a "self-owned" digital platform. As he recalls it, the birth of the smartphone was an early sign of things to come:

You could see how mobile phones were going to become the ultimate personal computing device. And the idea for me was when that happens and these things become ubiquitous, they're not just going to be content or communications devices; they will become commerce devices. You'll be able to order and pay from anywhere from this thing that's always on and available.[10]

While brick-and-mortar retailers were edging their way into e-commerce, Glass remembers:

Long lines at coffee shops in the morning and long lines for lunch in the afternoon. I thought if you could use the smartphone to place your order and pay ahead of time, have the prep happen while you were en route, and then when you got there, be able to skip the line—that would be a better experience for you as a consumer. It would be a better experience for the operation, because it would increase their throughput capacity.[11]

However, in 2005 Glass's vision was ahead of its time: "The iPhone didn't exist, Android didn't exist, and only 5 percent of the phones in the US were smartphones." Glass was then based in Johannesburg, South Africa, where he began working with smartphone software developers (known now as app developers). Starting with a text messaging interface, Glass set about making the off-premise experience easier for consumers and operators alike: "You had to believe that smartphones were going to become ubiquitous, and you had to believe that there was a broken system with restaurants that needed to get fixed. People sort of accepted that waiting in lines at restaurants is just a thing everybody did, but I saw it as an intolerable problem."

So what does Noah Glass's shrewd sense of future trends have to do with alternative channels to third-party platforms? Glass is the Founder and CEO of Olo, an interface between restaurants and the on-demand world. Because "Software-as-a-Service (SaaS)" companies are not consumer-facing, you may not have heard of Olo—but in the restaurant industry they are making big waves. "Olo provides a leading cloud-based, on-demand commerce platform for multi-location restaurant brands. We're primarily powering restaurants' direct-to-consumer channel, their app, their website with their own branding. But we're also syndicating menu content to third-party platforms that restaurant brand wants to work with," explains Glass. Frictionless experiences are essential for Olo. "I went from text message ordering to app order and to mobile web ordering as the less high-friction way of ordering. People don't like downloading apps and registering. You can just get right into the ordering experience on the mobile web and not even have to put in your credit card. It's already there."

Olo enables delivery orders through a restaurant's website, and their interface is winning plaudits across the industry. "We selected Olo because it was critical to choose a provider that not only offers a frictionless ordering experience, but also helps us navigate the rapidly evolving world of third-party marketplaces," explains Adam Fox, Director of Digital Experience and Media for Qdoba Mexican Eats, a fast casual restaurant chain.[12] Fox continues, "Our new platform allows guests to order what they want, when and how they want it. One example of this is future orders—our guests can now place orders not just for later the same day, but also for days in advance. This has been a huge convenience factor for those who want to place their lunch order the night before."

Olo integrates with over one hundred restaurant technology solutions, allowing restaurants to "pick and choose which ones they want to work with. That's appealing to brands that want to pick their own point of sale, pick their own front-end agency, pick their own loyalty partner, and pick the delivery partners that make sense market by market," Glass explains. Today, Olo is one of the leading providers enabling restaurants to create their own channel, but there are plenty to choose from based on the size of the restaurant business and the integration requirements with other systems. "While our focus has been on enterprise restaurants, during the pandemic, we [were] saying yes to a lot of smaller brands in an effort to help this industry." However, "Olo is not the simplest way of getting started with the digital world," he concedes. Smaller restaurant businesses that need simpler interfaces or, where the complexities of their business operations are less restrictive, may find a service such as ChowNow a better fit for their needs and budgets.

These direct-channel SaaS companies differ from the third-party marketplaces not only in their fixed pricing model, but also in their approach to the data they collect from consumers. This data is vital in understanding the impact of the profitability table introduced earlier. Why? "Because the relationship with the customer is so valuable," Glass explains. "The thing that gets a lot of focus is the profitability of two scenarios"—meaning the scenario where a customer goes directly to the brand's own channel versus through a third-party channel. Depending on which direct channel you select and after nominal set up fees, you will pay somewhere between $50 and $150 per month regardless of the volume of orders you receive.

Let's revisit our example from earlier, but now let's assume the restaurant operates for sixteen hours a day and sells twenty delivery plates on average per hour at $10 per plate for total off-premise revenue of $3,200. These twenty plates are within the labor capacity of the restaurant, so it needs no incremental labor to make these meals. Let's also assume the direct-channel subscription cost is $100 per month, or $3.33 a day.

	Off-premise (20 plates per hour)	Per day cash margin through third party	Per day cash margin through direct channel
Revenue		$3,200	$3,200
Food and Paper	35%	$1,120	$1,120
Labor	0%	$0	$0
Occupancy	0%	$0	$0
Marketing	10%	$320	$320
Third-Party Fee	30%	$960	
Direct-Channel Subscription			$3.33
Profit Margin		$800/ 25%	$1,756.67/ 55%

7.8 Comparing Third-Party Order to Direct Orders

The profit margin difference is startling, with direct-channel margins about thirty points higher than what a restaurant would receive through a third party. Once again, though, the representation skims over some nuance. The third-party platforms have acquired those customers that have bought 320 plates, but remember Fred Morgan's statistic of 50 percent of his customers being first-time guests? The challenge here for Morgan and other restaurateurs is to ensure that the returning 50 percent use the direct channel instead of going back through the third-party platforms.

	Off-premise	Per day through third-party (all first-time guests/ 50%)	Per day through direct channel (all returning guests/ 50%)	Total blended off-premise
Revenue		$1,600	$1,600	$3,200
Food and Paper	35%	$560	$560	$1,120
Labor	0%	$0	$0	
Occupancy	0%	$0	$0	
Marketing	10%	$160	$160	$320
Third-Party Fee	30%	$480		$480
Direct-Channel Subscription			$3.33	$3.33
Profit Margin		$400/ 25%	$1,757/ 55%	$1,277/ 40%

7.9 Comparing Third-Party to Direct—Blended Perspective (50/50 Mix)

If restaurant marketers can encourage their customer base to use their own channel instead of a third party, their foundations for digital success can be more secure. Here's the rub, though: third-party platforms place customer data under lock and key and restrict restaurant access to it because the threat to their own business model is all too clear.

Noah Glass believes the bigger obstacle to a blended solution for restaurants is consumer behavior. "Marketplaces [platforms] have trained consumers to go to their website and their app to look for the food that they want and then pick based on some attribute other than the brand." Glass compares it to Amazon's launch of the Amazon Basics range: a consumer wants Energizer batteries but sees the Basics range first on the listing at a better price than the brand they first desired. "The sum of all fears for brands is when they lose that direct relationship with the consumer, because the consumer has been retrained to order through marketplaces, and the marketplace is able through pricing and positioning to favor their own direct offering to the consumer and cut the restaurant brand out of the entire equation," he warns. "Really what the marketplace wants is not just 30 percent of the ticket. They want the ticket. They want the consumer ordering from them, and that's misaligned with the restaurant."

Looking to platforms in nations such as China, Glass sees his fears already manifesting. "It's a scary vision of the future from the perspective of a restaurant operator, where almost everybody I can think of has 80 percent of their digital sales coming through Meituan or Ele.me."

Let's take a look at what that would represent for a restaurant in the US. This time, let's add in the 15 percent labor charge to reflect the realistic scenario of a kitchen accommodating off-premise on top of a maxed-out kitchen capacity. The result is pretty damning: a 15.9 percent blended margin with only $509 to show for a day with 320 orders prepared.

	Off-premise	Per day through third party 80%	Per day through direct channel 20%	Blended off-premise margin
Revenue		$2,560	$640	$3,200
Food and Paper	35%	$896	$224	$1,120
Labor	15%	$384	$96	$480
Occupancy	0%	$0	$0	0
Marketing	10%	$256	$64	$320
Third-Party Fee	30%	$768		$768
Direct-Channel Subscription			$3.33	$3.33
Profit Margin		$256/ 10%	$252.67/ 39.5%	$508.67/ 15.9%

7.10 Comparing Third-Party to Direct—Blended Perspective (80 Percent Third-Party)

Many SaaS platforms like Olo are supporting restaurateurs to build their own direct-to-consumer presence to suppress a complete marketplace takeover. Restaurants benefit from having multiple channels of off-premise revenue to grow revenue, certainly—but also to provide more opportunities to gather consumer data from everywhere it exists. A key priority for restaurants, Glass believes, is to ensure loyal customers represent "a disproportionate sales volume—to come direct to them and not go on the third-party platforms." To achieve that, the direct channel needs to add value beyond interface and function. That starts with investing time and energy into developing a direct channel that customers will be willing to use more often than not when thinking of a particular cuisine or need state. By way of example, Glass suggests that he wants customers to think, "*I want to go to Wingstop*, not *I want chicken wings.*"

Not having a direct channel exposes a restaurant to this risk, which is essentially pertinent as off-premise channels continue to grow. Speaking in mid-2020, before the full impact of the COVID-19 pandemic was known, Boesch of 7shifts observed, "I think the pandemic is going to wipe out some of those folks that weren't operating efficiently and make way potentially for new folks that are going to come in and invest in a little bit of technology to help make this easier and more affordable. If you're not willing to evolve as the world changes, you're going to be left behind."

Chapter 8

GROWING BEYOND DINE-IN

"Happppy Birthhhhhdaaaaay toooooo yoooooou," the children sang on the final line of Jackson's birthday cake procession. Candles lit atop a Minecraft-themed birthday cake prompted Jackson's eyes to light up in bashful pride. Jackson's extended family and school friends watched on as he puffed each of his ten candles out.

The day had been a success so far—a happy, grateful boy whose presents had been exactly on point. Andrew stood in the doorway looking at the table in the garden and explaining to his younger brother, Nathan, himself a new father, the secrets to the day so far. "It's called "Birthday in a Box," he explained. "They took our order a week ago, brought all the food, the cake, the balloons, and even that drink from the margarita station you're enjoying."

"That's pretty cool," acknowledged Nathan. "Bet they don't do that where we live, though," he ruefully pondered. "It's not a company that specializes in birthday catering," revealed Andrew. "It's the Italian restaurant down the street that does it. We learned about it when they taped this leaflet to their pizza boxes," he explained, passing over the paper that helped keep the guests' bellies full and the parents' stress to a low level.

In 2019, the United States reached a new high in restaurant count. The combined forces of a strong economy, the press for convenience, and cheap debt created so many restaurants that the number of restaurants per US resident was the highest it had ever been. In 2017, pausing to reflect on the trend, *The New York Times* observed, "There are now more than 620,000 eating and drinking places in the United States, according to the Bureau of Labor Statistics, and the number of restaurants is growing at about twice the rate of the population."[1]

Although restaurant sales grew with restaurant count, they did not grow quite enough. Restaurant industry data analyst Black Box Intelligence, which tracks same-store sales performance across the industry—said, "There seems to be an oversaturation of restaurants and competition." Black Box Intelligence repeatedly reported flat to declining same-store guest counts and observed that when "price points lift comps, not additional customers, tempers optimism regarding the overall strength of restaurants, and spotlights industry-wide problems."[2] Victor Hernandez, Vice President of Insights and Knowledge for Black Box Intelligence, predicted, "Given the existing oversupply in the number of restaurant locations and the fact that, although growing at a slower pace than in recent years, chain restaurants continue adding to their net number of units, falling guest counts on a same-store basis will likely remain the norm in the near-term."[3]

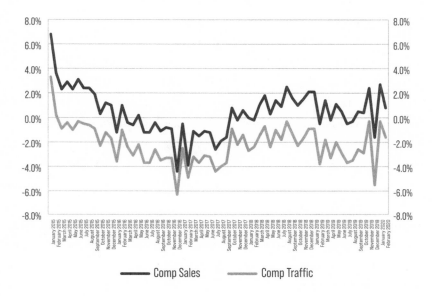

8.1 Restaurant Chain Same-Store Growth vs. Prior Year[4]

This stagnant state of affairs is not good for an industry that thrives on strong top-line sales. Further, the dependence on price increases to achieve growth is temporary at best and unhealthy at worst. At some point, the economy will not be as strong as it was in 2019, and further price increases will become impossible. While no one would have predicted that the long bull run would end with the COVID-19 pandemic, anyone would have said that at some point it would end, and a new way forward for restaurants would be required to win.

Into this unstable situation came the trends that shaped restaurant digital delivery: a lessening reliance on the nuclear family, a desire for customization, a growing awareness of health, and new technologies to increase frictionless access to menus. Restaurants that were starving for traffic growth saw off-premise—takeout, delivery, and catering—as a new avenue for sales. Black Box Intelligence described the landscape: "The trend of consumers shifting preferences toward off-premises dining does not appear to be going away. Restaurants looking to grow sales can find ways to strengthen to-go offerings to hold on to guests."[5]

At first, going after these new occasions may seem easy: just put the food in a box and watch it go out the door. After several years of innovation in convenience, it's becoming clear that winning in off-premise is more complicated than boxing up on-premise faire. The same attention that restaurants have paid to "sweating the asset" through product development and merchandising for dine-in sales now must be turned to off-premise. The off-premise innovation mindset requires a fundamental shift in perspective: from "what is my restaurant capable of?" to "what does my consumer need?"

The most obvious place to start, just as in a four-wall restaurant, is add-ons. The consumer is already purchasing from your restaurant. What else are they likely to buy? Most restaurants have mastered the upsell in a four-wall setting through beverages, desserts, sides, and combos. Menus are designed to create pairings at fine dining restaurants, while combos at Quick Service Restaurants (QSRs) serve a similar role. Full Service Restaurants (FSRs) might insert specials into their regular menu or rely on well-trained servers to recommend items that go well together and to offer an appetizer, drink, side, or dessert at every visit to the table. Even QSRs train order-takers at the front counter to ask (now infamously), "Do you want fries with that?" Drive-thru "stacks" (where the cars wait to order) are filled with large signs advertising everything but the main entree.

The biggest opportunity with digital ordering is that platforms typically result in higher checks when guests customize their items and order for groups. Customization and add-on fees can be a source of high-margin additional revenue that also results in a happier consumer. Many Fast Casual Restaurants (FCRs), for example, offer the option to "double the protein" for a fee. A consumer who creates their own salad often ends up paying more than one who orders a standard salad off the menu. When ordering digitally, consumers are apt to spend up to 25 percent more on their purchase as they take advantage of offers to make their meal the way they want it. Simple additions to the digital menu enabling consumers to customize will ensure that your restaurant can drive this incremental revenue (and consumer satisfaction).

The biggest challenge with digital ordering is that off-premise consumers typically forego beverages and desserts. Most consumers stock these items in their homes and offices and find that purchasing them in the grocery store is cheaper than buying them from a restaurant. Typically, beverages are one of the most profitable items in a restaurant, so systematically not selling them impacts the overall profitability of off-premise sales.

If consumers prefer to consume beverages from home when eating off-premise, how can a restaurant sell the full meal online? The tools are the same as for a four-walls scenario: menu design and merchandising. Creating combos and pairings that make sense for off-premise consumption, pricing beverages closer to the grocery competition, then programming the website to consistently offer the correct combos and delicious pairings is an identical exercise to that which restaurants implement in the brick-and-mortar world. The offers may need to be tweaked to appeal to a consumer who has beverage options at home or office, but the thought process is the same. First-party ordering (a consumer ordering through a restaurant's own website) makes these add-ons and upsells much easier. When a restaurant directly controls the consumer ordering experience, the restaurant can better determine what to offer when. Chipotle has done a brilliant job of this with their app, which offers chips and guac or a beverage just before checkout if the consumer has not already thought to purchase them.

The key to maximizing the off-premise check isn't just menu design and merchandising—it's also product. Consumer packaged goods (CPG) innovation executive Michael Connor has spent the last ten years pushing beverages toward the future at one of the world's largest beverage companies. To succeed in a delivery context, Connor thinks beverages need to be proprietary, safe, easy, and customized to the occasion.

"Going through Wendy's drive-thru, you can get a Dave's cherry cream soda, and you can't get that at home. As things shift toward delivery, you need to get a drink that's consistent with the branding, that you can't get anywhere else, that goes with your meal," says Connor. He continues, "I know a lot of people like the chunklet ice. You can't get that at home, so consumers get really fired up about the ice."[6] QSR players are typically out in front of the need to be proprietary or exclusive—think Chick-fil-A's lemonade or Taco Bell's Mountain Dew Baja Blast—because most of their transactions have long been consumed off-premise. About 70 percent of their sales go through the drive-thru, and drive-thru beverage attachment rates are lower than dine-in for all the same reasons that they are lower in delivery: many customers are going to eat their drive-thru purchase at home or in the office, where beverages are already on hand.

Sit-down restaurants are starting to apply the same logic. True Food Kitchen, for example, offers a lineup of beverages consistent with their anti-inflammatory nutrition philosophy. "We have a full bar with fresh-squeezed juices and cocktails," says True Food Kitchen CEO Christine Barone.[7] These beverages are so proprietary that the juice is squeezed fresh in-house, then blended with teas, spices, or alcohol, and bottled at each restaurant location. During the COVID-19 pandemic, when local restrictions on to-go alcohol were lifted, True Food Kitchen went after the opportunity not just with wine and beer, but with custom sangria and skinny margaritas. Their online menu features beverages that change with the season and the time of day (breakfast, lunch, or dinner service).

Because True Food Kitchen is bottling beverages in the restaurant, they are sealed and tamper-proof. Packaged beverages might be perceived by guests to be safer, "but the margins are lower. You're paying to ship water around," says Connor. "Fountain beverages are way better." This is a dichotomy many restaurants face—neater and safer versus higher margins. What True Food Kitchen has discovered is a way to get both. By bottling proprietary beverages in-house, they offer the consumer a better experience in a way that makes financial sense for their restaurant. "White Castle is moving to gallon jugs," says Connor, "so they could put a cap on it and seal it. Larger package sizes. Different vessels." Packaging in-house may very well be the answer. Boba tea places have been doing this for years by simply heat-sealing a cup. The heat-sealing approach will likely proliferate across the restaurant industry, enabling restaurants to sell high-margin fountain drinks that are sealed for safety.

At the most basic level, ordering beverages for delivery just needs to be easier. "Go look," says Connor. "On a lot of the platforms you type in your drink. That's not going to lead to good attachment rates. You need a beautiful image. McDonald's has done a good job putting meals together, including beverages, on the platforms." The restaurant industry understands merchandising and how combos drive basket size. Beverage upsells through menu design, server interaction, and merchandising are not new. Applying these same ideas in a digital format is new. "I think that is low-hanging fruit," says Connor.

Technology enables beverage recommendations to be more personalized, customizing beverages to the occasion. "The curation of drinks is massive," Connor notes. "If you're getting BBQ, are you more likely to get a tea-based beverage or a Powerade? It's way different. Using data intelligence to recommend the right product—when you recommend the right product, attachment goes up. That's where AI comes in. Those algorithms are dead simple. They already exist. That's easy to do." Even if your restaurant isn't quite ready for algorithms, your intuition as a restaurateur will guide you, just as it does with dine-in menu design. Observe your customers—what are they ordering when they order digitally? Are their items, timing, or party size different? What does that suggest about the beverages that will go best with the delivery occasion?

Desserts and sides follow the same logic. If you want consumers to buy them for delivery, they have to be proprietary, safe, easy to order, and customized to the occasion. For example, if your restaurant is famous for its ice cream sundae, selling it for delivery requires an assemble-at-home kit to ensure that the ice cream arrives frozen and the chocolate sauce hot, rather than one melted lukewarm, messy blob.

The consumer desire for food delivery will only grow, and we have seen that microfulfillment in other verticals is a huge challenge. Connor observes, "So many companies have a last-mile issue in getting to customers. And restaurants are everywhere, so maybe they have a role to play." During the COVID-19 pandemic, restaurants embraced this role and began to offer basic groceries, meal kits, and even toilet paper on their off-premise menus. Toilet paper on a restaurant menu is unlikely to be an enduring trend, but the idea of being able to add on a few basic items is. When we're choosing whether to cook or order dinner, a deciding factor is often other pantry items. A consumer who needs milk is much more likely to buy ingredients for dinner at the grocery store while picking up milk than one who doesn't. As long as they have to go to the grocery store anyway, they may as well cook. Grocery stores are starting to boost the opposite behavior—if a consumer has to stop and get milk, they may as well buy a prepared meal. Many grocery stores have added prepared foods sections at the front of the store. Texas retailer H-E-B has launched an entire line called "Meal Simple." In advertisements, H-E-B directly contrasts the line's health benefits with the nutritional downside of eating at restaurants.[8] Some, like Whole Foods, have even partnered with local restaurants or created their own restaurants to offer a store within a store. As grocery goes after the restaurant occasion, so restaurants must go after grocery occasions to remain competitive.

Many restaurants have extended this idea into meal kits—preseasoned, ready-to-cook items, and bulk foods that blur the lines between restaurant and grocery, prepared foods and ingredients. Pitfire Pizza, for example, offers a pizza-making kit that families can cook together at home. They also offer their meatballs unfinished in packs of six that customers can incorporate into another dish later. Pitfire completes the experience by offering cookie dough so consumers can enjoy freshly baked cookies directly from the oven after their meal.

All of these add-ons and upsells help to increase basket size and expand off-premise margin. While the direct benefit to a restaurant of a larger basket is clear, it also indirectly benefits the restaurant by helping the consumer and the driver. As basket size increases, the consumer's fixed delivery charges decline as a percentage of total spend. For the driver, a larger basket is likely to lead to a larger tip. The economic benefits to the consumer and the driver ultimately benefit the restaurant in a virtuous cycle: drivers perceive the restaurant pays them more, so drivers are more likely to pick up the order quickly, so consumers get faster, fresher food, so consumers order from the restaurant more often.

After add-ons and upsells, just as in a brick-and-mortar restaurant, the next product extension to consider is dayparts. According to the National Restaurant Association weekly survey of consumers, dinner is by far the most common off-premise daypart. During the COVID-19 pandemic, about 60 percent of adults said they used a restaurant for off-premise dinner occasions during the prior week. The number is about half that for breakfast and lunch.[9] Given this disparity, it makes sense for a restaurant to maximize its off-premise dinner performance before it gets too far into other dayparts. Assuming dinner is working well, the next most logical place to look is lunch. In the words of restaurant real estate legend Jim Kuykendall, "Fish where the fishin's good." Most consumers are online looking for food at dinner, followed by lunch—therefore, offer them dinner, followed by lunch.

But breakfast? Breakfast is hard. The single biggest cost to offering breakfast is the labor required to open at a time when the restaurant normally isn't. The second biggest cost is the waste and complexity of additional ingredients. Most restaurants struggle to get consumers to see them as a breakfast option, making it difficult to drive enough sales to pay for the labor and the waste. The exciting thing about a digital environment is that the restaurant can keep closed for dine-in breakfast customers and just support off-premise, thereby reducing or eliminating the need for front-of-house staff until later in the day. The restaurant can even operate online under a different brand name—one that makes more sense for breakfast.

Gourmet hot dog brand Dog Haus has done exactly that. Few Americans think of hot dogs as a breakfast food, but it turns out that many of the same ingredients that are on the Dog Haus dinner menu are ingredients that make sense to Americans in the morning—tater tots and sausages, for starters. Founder André Vener says they launched BadAss Breakfast Burritos by adding just a tortilla to their make-line.[10]

Digital delivery opens up new options in dayparting. Whereas in brick-and-mortar growing a daypart means getting a consumer to choose your restaurant twice—once for lunch and once another day for dinner—digital delivery can combine two occasions into one. Rather than driving visits through occasions, digital delivery can drive check. Smart online merchandising of sides, salads, and soups can drive consumers to buy dinner for tonight and add on another item for breakfast tomorrow. Offering extra-large portions or double meat for an upcharge is another way of extending one item into two meals. As we saw with add-ons, the increase in basket size has additional benefits in reducing delivery charges as a percentage for the consumer and increasing tips to the driver, thus making your restaurant more attractive for the delivery services to pick up from.

Digital ordering also opens up dynamic pricing opportunities. Offering an afternoon happy hour or early-bird dinner special is common in brick-and-mortar restaurants. Driving enough transactions to offset the deal offered usually requires an investment in marketing. Online, prices can be changed easily on the fly—on one item or across the board—to drive additional consumers to select your brand during slow times. Restaurants can change prices passively (without promotion) and test the price elasticity of their products at different times. Or restaurants can change prices actively and promote discounts, free delivery, or other benefits on the digital delivery platforms.

Kevin Rice, CMO of Hathway, believes variable pricing is commonplace in the travel industry and it's only a matter of time before it hits the restaurant industry. He says, "Being able to have yield management strategies around variable pricing based on individuals, time of day, all kinds of contextual data points, is super interesting. It could create a better experience for the consumer and drive better outcomes for the business." Why would this be of benefit? Rice believes it could be used to respond to excess inventory levels with risk of spoilage or even to "Drive people at times of day when you already have lower traffic . . . it's a win-win all around."[11]

Sweetgreen has pushed digital, off-premise service to its logical conclusion: subscription-based batch delivery of individualized meals to nearby offices. Called "Outposts," these offices have signed up to house shelves that Sweetgreen delivers salads and bowls to multiple times a day. Consumers can place a recurring order or order something different each day. Sweetgreen then prepares all the meals and delivers them at once. Employees benefit from how easy it is to get a healthy meal. Businesses benefit from keeping their employees onsite without a costly cafeteria program. Sweetgreen benefits from the consolidation of orders into one delivery—a benefit they share with customers by reducing the delivery fees. "Before COVID, we had over twelve hundred Outpost locations," says Jon Neman, Cofounder and CEO of Sweetgreen. Picture it: a restaurant company with just over one hundred restaurants expands each lunchtime to a chain ten times its size.[12]

"Outposting started as an experiment," Neman recalls. "There were lines out the door, and people were picking up off a shelf in the restaurant. So we thought, why not have a truck? And then we thought, why not just put a shelf anywhere? So we tried it and it went incredibly well."

"Restaurants are all about utilization of the asset. How do you sweat your box?" Neman asks rhetorically. Through Outpost, Sweetgreen has leveraged digital and off-premise to expand its footprint. Outpost is available at office buildings, residential buildings, and hospitals located close to Sweetgreen's restaurants. Neman believes many aspects of the company came together to make Outpost work. First, he says, "It wouldn't have worked without the brand. Employees wanted something they could eat every day." Second, Sweetgreen's online ordering and app capabilities translate all the way back into the restaurant. Successful digital-forward restaurants have to "integrate the digital into the physical. People think 'if you have a restaurant, just go build an app.' But it is way more complicated than that, because it is how you bring the technology into the restaurant." Third, Sweetgreen owns most of its own logistics network. Its 2019 purchase of Galley Foods gave Sweetgreen logistics technology, courier operations, and a new head of logistics. Neman believes internal logistics translate into better economics for Sweetgreen and better service for the consumer.[13]

For those restaurants that aren't in a position to make such significant investments in brand, technology, and logistics, catering mid-sized office meals offers many of the same benefits: utilization of shoulder-hour labor, large order sizes, and planned-ahead demand. Previously, an entire catering setup represented an expense that demanded one hundred plus attendees to make sense. A team of servers would show up at the office with hot trays and Sterno heating cans to set up a full buffet. Now, office managers can order a tray of sandwiches for a meeting of fifteen people or burritos for twenty-five.

Erle Dardick, Founder of Monkey Media, attacked this opportunity from a technology perspective, ultimately selling his company to ezCater, the largest catering-specific platform in the restaurant industry. He started much like any independent restaurateur—turning around a struggling deli. "Out the back door was an opportunity for us. I came from a B2B background, so I thought less like a retailer and more like a manufacturer," Dardick recalls. "Catering started to boom, but we ran into challenges because we were running it manually with QuickBooks and spreadsheets." To keep growing the business, he had to invest in technology. This was the late 1990s, long before any of the SaaS platforms were even dreamed of. "Then 9/11 happened, and that was the impetus for sharing my system with other restaurants. It was ERP [enterprise resource planning] for food manufacturing."[14]

ezCater has combined what they purchased from Monkey Media with their own ongoing innovation to create the largest catering platform in the United States. ezCater targets customers who order for gatherings, has a network of delivery drivers equipped to handle large orders, and charges a lower fee to restaurants compared to standard delivery due to the large average size of the orders. The hyper-growth start-up has attracted over $300 million in venture investment. Dardick predicts that "delivery platforms and catering platforms will replace workplace canteens. It's all going to merge." Dardick's words are starting to come true: Grubhub for Work, Uber for Business, and DoorDash Group Ordering have all been big avenues of growth for the delivery players. Meanwhile, start-up Fooda has tried to recreate Sweetgreen's Outpost product as a marketplace for multiple restaurants. Employees are no longer captive to their office's corporate dining, and this freedom creates opportunities for restaurants looking to grow their off-premise lunch business.

Home catering is also growing. Traditionally expensive with long lead times and therefore reserved for a special occasion, group meals are now popular with families for small gatherings and even nightly meals. For the restaurant, these meals are halfway between a typical consumer order and a full-on catering order. Home catering—much like delivery meals—tends to have the same peaks as dine-in dinner business. However, the average check size is much larger. Where it might not make sense to order four $20 entrees for a family, one $50 family meal does make sense. Like Kentucky Fried Chicken's original bucket of chicken with "all the fixins," restaurants targeting this occasion offer a preselected combo that feeds four. California chain Panini Kabob Grill is an excellent example of a menu formatted to drive home-catering sales. They offer a section on their menu called "Family Combos," which combine an entree and two sides for four to six people for the same price as ordering four individual entrees. It isn't just the online merchandising that highlights the product—the product itself is packaged family style. True Food Kitchen has also launched Family Meals since the start of the COVID-19 pandemic. Says CEO Christine Barone, "They allow guests to try different items that they might not have otherwise ordered because each meal contains multiple family-style entrees and an appetizer or salad for sharing."[15]

These approaches all grow revenue by increasing food sales while still keeping close to what restaurants already do. More adventurous restaurants who've mastered their digital add-ons and upsells might then turn to new avenues for growth: the real estate itself. Many restaurants are slow or completely closed midmorning and midafternoon. Starbucks made famous the "third place"—using their restaurant as a gathering place outside work and home. Starbucks was an early adopter of in-restaurant Wi-Fi and an environment that encouraged sit-and-stay. In reaction to Starbucks's innovation, the entire industry now offers Wi-Fi, charging stations, and improved ambience. Monetizing the front of house in the off-hours is the next logical step in the sharing economy. Restaurants could charge solo entrepreneurs to use the shared "office space" they've created through their investments in technology and furniture. It's not hard to foresee that some restaurants will also choose to monetize their back of house, renting it out to a catering company or a virtual brand during the dayparts they don't serve.

From meal combos to custom sangria, pizza kits to home-catered dinners, what all of these approaches have in common is the need to modernize the idea of revenue growth in restaurants. Consumers will no longer tolerate price increases without getting anything in return, but they have repeatedly demonstrated they are happy to pay for things they value. There is a world of innovation waiting to be explored by restaurants who are ready to meet their consumers where they are: online.

Chapter 9

GHOST KITCHENS (AREN'T THAT SCARY)

assimo Noja De Marco sat at his table, furiously checking his watch again. He looked over his shoulder at the crowd behind him milling around the hostess stand at Union Restaurant in Pasadena in greater Los Angeles. Already, he and his companion had been waiting thirty minutes for their dinner to arrive. Alongside him, his friend could sense his agitation as De Marco watched five drivers clustered around the hostess stand, disrupting guests with reservations trying to get seated. As a staff member moved the drivers off to the side, De Marco felt one of their bags scrape against the back of his neck. Five minutes later, another driver bumped into his chair as he tried to step out of the way of dine-in customers walking into the restaurant. Another driver reached over two guests eating at the bar to grab water from the barman. Seeing all of these things undermining the tranquil atmosphere Union Restaurant was known for, De Marco exclaimed, "This is crazy. There's got to be a better way."

De Marco emigrated from Italy in the 1980s. Born into seven generations of hospitality, his family had played host to many celebrities and prestigious families. De Marco was raised at his grandfather's knee, studying people from a street café and fine-tuning his eye to note their specific needs. On his fifth birthday, he was making cappuccinos for guests under his grandfather's tutelage. By the time he was twenty-four, he was in New York unveiling his own restaurant—and by age thirty-three, he was spearheading catering for the Oscars ceremony and its red-carpet stars.

De Marco's frustration with how delivery was impacting the restaurant experience fueled his initial outline for a shared kitchen model that specialized in delivery only—something that would later be labeled a "ghost kitchen." The more De Marco thought about a delivery-only kitchen, the more excited he became. This could be a way for restaurant brands to grow their off-premise offering without the expense of growing their restaurant footprint. Not only that, they could diversify with a relatively low capital outlay. As a restaurateur in New York and LA, De Marco had a lot of friends among celebrity chefs. They were always talking about opening chains that were more accessible than their high-end concepts, but none of them had time to do it. "What if a bunch of people joined forces, and they all paid the rent in one space, and they could all use different kitchens?" De Marco mused. The concept that would later become Kitchen United—one of California's first-ever ghost kitchens—was born.

Kitchen United's first ghost kitchen in Pasadena looked nothing like a restaurant. That's because it wasn't one. It was a former cooking school comprising various kitchens already built out in perfectly formed assembly lines. Kitchen United opened its doors in the spring of 2018 and shortly thereafter took an investment from Google Ventures.[1] That launch marked the beginning of a ghost kitchen deluge. Around the same time, former Uber CEO Travis Kalanick announced he was investing heavily in the ghost kitchen space with the acquisition of CloudKitchens.[2] Famed venture capitalist Andreessen Horowitz invested in Virtual Kitchen Company, now known as All Day Kitchens.[3] SoftBank-backed Reef Kitchens was born inside portfolio company ParkJockey.[4] Zuul and Colony quickly followed with openings of their own.[5] Uber Eats started experimenting with kitchens in France.[6] DoorDash built a kitchen in Redwood City, California.[7] Accor Hotels partnered with SBE Entertainment Group and Simon Property Group to start C3.[8] Hundreds of millions of dollars poured into the space.

The challenge in delivery is that most consumers want food in thirty minutes or less from when they order. With a recommended off-premise prep time of ten minutes, that leaves twenty minutes for transporting the food to its destination, assuming no queue in the kitchen slowing down prep. Remember, transport includes so much more than just getting from point A to point B. Parking at both ends, waiting for an order, and finding the recipient means most suburban drivers will go no further than five miles and will select short trips when they can. For most large chains, this timing works with their existing spread of restaurants. For full-service restaurant chains, however, their existing fleet can't cover the homes and offices of most consumers who want their food. For independent restaurants, the challenge is even greater—their one or two restaurants can't possibly cover the delivery radius needed to fulfill all potential demand for their food.

Ghost kitchen companies are solving several problems that restaurants cannot solve on their own, which is a perfect foundation for a new industry. Andrew Chen at Andreessen Horowitz, who invested in Virtual Kitchen Company through its a16z fund, says ghost kitchens—also known as cloud kitchens, shadow kitchens, or virtual kitchens—make it more affordable for a restaurant to get up and running and to quickly scale their customer base without worrying about many of the complexities of a front-of-house operation. Ghost kitchen operators handle the financing, the real estate, the technology, the digital marketing, the kitchen design, and much of the risk, leaving restaurant operators to focus on what they do best—producing great food.[9]

As CEO of Lifestyle Brands and Global Food & Beverage at Accor Hotels, as well as the JV investor in ghost kitchen company C3, Amir Nahai says that two simple factors are behind the major venture capital investment in ghost kitchens:

First, there is massive demand for delivery. People have less time but want higher quality food. They want food *now*, and they also want more variety. All of these factors drive growth in delivery. Second, there is massive room for improvement in the execution of delivery. For that improvement to materialize, you need investment in a new model. It's not sustainable to do a lot of delivery out of an existing restaurant. A ghost kitchen is better for the kitchen operations, but it's also better for the delivery itself.[10]

When David Kuo first learned of ghost kitchens, it was pouring down rain—an unusual event in Southern California in June 2019. Kuo remembers it because the delivery food from his restaurant Little Fatty was flying out the door that day—Californians do not like going out in the rain. But even on sunnier days, delivery in Los Angeles was growing in popularity, and Kuo realized his business would need to adapt to cope with the growing demand from all over the city. He noticed he was increasingly getting interest from customers on the outskirts of his available delivery radius.

Together with his wife, Kuo had opened Little Fatty to focus on Taiwanese comfort food from his own culture. The restaurant's name, Little Fatty, is an English translation of Kuo's childhood nickname— *xiao pang*. A former property manager, Kuo and his wife, Maki, scraped together the investment required to pursue their dream, raising the money to open a restaurant by flipping a house in Northern California.

Like many first-generation immigrants, Kuo missed his favorite dishes and wanted to share them with his new neighbors. The residents of Mar Vista on the Westside of Los Angeles soon became regulars and fans of his approach. Before long, David and Maki realized they had a problem of the best kind: the restaurant was doing so well they needed capital to expand. Historically, successful restaurateurs have faced a dilemma: Would they rather take on a lot of debt, franchise the concept, or bring on a partner with capital who would demand ownership? But David Kuo had a different idea.

"We couldn't make the food fast enough in our own kitchen, so we rented a commissary kitchen," he says. "I always wanted a commissary, so that whatever came along we could do." Also known as a shared-use kitchen, a commissary kitchen would enable Kuo to prep and store food off-site, expanding Little Fatty's capacity as well as enabling other ventures, such as CPG (consumer packaged goods). In this model, Little Fatty would make dumplings and other more stable products en masse. The products could then be distributed to Kuo's own restaurant, smaller ghost kitchens, other restaurants who wanted to serve his product, or even retail outlets.

The commissary had capacity to create food for several restaurants, so the next challenge was creating distribution points for the product. That was the point at which Kuo found Cloud Kitchens, Travis Kalanick's ghost kitchen venture. With Cloud Kitchens, Little Fatty would be able to serve its popular food all over Los Angeles without spending the money to build twenty restaurants.

Kuo was instantly drawn to the concept. Customers an hour's drive away in LA traffic could order Little Fatty food from the restaurant's own website or through third-party platforms, and it would appear promptly at their doorstep as if by magic. The customers would never know their meal was prepared anywhere other than the Little Fatty restaurant. And the only outlay Kuo had to make was the cost of a few pieces of used kitchen equipment.[11]

A traditional new restaurant location is expensive. Costs can range from a hundred thousand dollars for a light remodel and some new equipment to several million dollars for a completely new space. On top of the upfront build cost, signing a ten-year lease as a new business typically requires a significant deposit, a personal guarantee, or both. It is these kinds of financial pressures that cause high failure rates among restaurants. Beyond the relief ghost kitchens offer to dine-in customers tired of competing with drivers, De Marco believes ghost kitchens also help restaurateurs. They "don't have to spend three quarters of a million dollars to open. They're going in with six months deposit, let's say $5,000 a month. That's $30,000! They start a restaurant with $30,000."

Compare that figure to the traditional cost of expansion. Once a restaurateur proves their concept, they generally want to grow. Customers love it, they're making money—what could be stopping them from bringing this food to everyone? The trouble is, where one restaurant is expensive, many restaurants can be prohibitive. Assuming a build-out cost at the low end of the range—say $500,000 for a single location—a restaurateur who wanted to reach one hundred locations (the magic number for multi-unit success) would need $50 million in capital. The most successful restaurants pay back in about three years; that is, they generate as much income over three years as they cost to build out. A three-year payback is a fantastic investment, about triple what the stock market does on average. But restaurateurs who want to fund growth out of restaurant income can only double their unit count every three years or so. Without taking on outside capital, it would take a successful restaurant more than twenty years to reach one hundred units. By that time, someone with more money would have copied the idea and claimed the space—more pressingly, the idea may be well and truly stale.

Ghost kitchens eliminate the build-out requirement and spread the initial build-out cost into the rent. The most expensive parts of building a restaurant—engineering, mechanical equipment, refrigeration, permitting, utilities hookups, city fees—are all handled by the ghost kitchen provider. All ghost kitchen providers finance basic equipment: sinks, hoods, walk-ins, stainless packages. Many will purchase or give credits toward other equipment: cooktops, ovens, salad tables. There is no physical signage: instead, digital marketing drives traffic. Front-of-house decor is either entirely eliminated or shared by the ghost kitchen tenants, depending on the concept (we'll explain the various concepts further on in this chapter). The restaurant operator's primary costs are purely associated with hiring and training a team and loading in the initial inventory.

With lower upfront costs, operators can create near-infinite returns. Take-home profit might be a bit lower in dollar terms (because of lower revenue, higher monthly rent costs, or both), but without build-out costs to pay off, the profit is 100 percent available to the restaurant owner to take home.

The monthly costs (charged as rent or a service fee) can be surprisingly high in a ghost kitchen due to the amortization of build-out costs, shared labor, and ongoing maintenance. A 250–500 square foot kitchen can rent for nearly as much as the rent on a full restaurant space. Venture capital funds may subsidize lower initial monthly costs so that a ghost kitchen company can acquire restaurant tenants; some go as far as offering six months free rent to bring in new restaurants. Long-term economics will demand ghost kitchens to fundamentally change their capital outlay or raise prices. The savings a restaurant operator accumulates in a ghost kitchen scenario compared to a full restaurant show up in the build-out costs and the labor line, not the rent.

For many restaurateurs, high rent means high risk. However, ghost kitchens are not as risky as, say, a "build-to-suit" real estate deal. At least at this early point in the innovation cycle, ghost kitchen leases are relatively short term or month-to-month, deposits are minimal or waived, and personal guarantees are not required.

With lower upfront costs, short-term leases, and quick turnover from concept to concept, ghost kitchens also enable concept testing: launching a menu and brand, seeing how it does, then replicating it or shutting it down. Historically, launching a new concept took hundreds of thousands of dollars. Even big restaurant companies take write-offs when their new ideas fail in the brick-and-mortar world. Independent restaurants that fail might bring down the entire family's finances with them. Suddenly, ghost kitchens take the risk out of innovation.

For some restaurants, the reason to expand into ghost kitchens has nothing to do with financial risk. These restaurants have such high off-premise volume that their goal in operating from a ghost kitchen is to separate out their off-premise volume from their dine-in, walk-up, or drive-thru business. Much as we saw in Chapter 3 with the emergence of drive-thru, separating out order flow with different peaks, demands, and time requirements enables each channel to deliver on its promise to the consumer more effectively. For example, the Chick-fil-A ghost kitchen in the Chicago Kitchen United facility is only half a mile away from their Magnificent Mile location.

Other major chains are moving into ghost kitchens for similar reasons. Wingstop, Wendy's, Capriotti's, Greenleaf, The Halal Guys, and Panera Bread are all experimenting with how ghost kitchens can help optimize food preparation for delivery the way QSRs optimized for drive-thru. Engineering consultant Jane Gannaway notes that several major Chinese coffee brands each have hundreds of delivery-only locations throughout China, and she believes eventually the United States will follow. "As delivery sales grow, restaurants will be forced to service the demand more efficiently in order to be profitable. At the same time, to preserve their existing dine-in business, they need to separate it out. There is nothing worse than waiting in a cafe for the barista to make a drink for a mobile order ahead of your order when you are there and the mobile customer is not."[12]

From kitchen layout to adjacent parking for drivers, ghost kitchens optimize their entire system for delivery. They locate their facilities where delivery demand is highest. They incorporate technology like conveyor belts and smart cameras to reduce labor. They create unified order flows from many different sources, including their own multi-concept online ordering in some cases. They generate reporting on everything from sales mix to ingredient waste. They develop and refine branding and menus for digital presentation. They offer digital marketing services to help member restaurants drive online sales. Some providers even incorporate drive-thru lanes to speed delivery pickup. In the world of ghost kitchens, delivery optimization is the ultimate goal.

The ghost kitchen industry in the US is nascent. At the time of writing, consumer spend at restaurants with ghost kitchens is a tiny fraction of 1 percent of the total restaurant industry. The major competitors all emerged around 2017, and new players are still forming. Most ghost kitchen companies are in Series A or Series B financing (early-stage venture capital). None have developed runaway business models yet, generating so much cash that they can afford to redeploy it into additional sites at a rapid pace.

All Day Kitchens (formerly known as Virtual Kitchen Company) Cofounder and CEO Ken Chong compares the state of play to the emergence of QSRs. "Thirty years ago, QSRs were not the norm. That's where we are now in ghost kitchens." He has no doubt that the ghost revolution is coming, just as the digital revolution came for retail. "Everybody has to eat. And in the same way that retail saw this transition, people can see the potential fifteen years from how. The long term is so obvious."[13]

Ghost kitchens are still in the experimental phase of defining business models that make sense for the entire ecosystem. Four main models are starting to emerge, as shown in the graphic below. The models differ from one another in terms of which steps in the delivery value chain they participate in (horizontal axis) and which services they offer to their tenants (vertical axis).

	Real Estate	Ordering Interface	Brand	Food Preparation	Delivery Fulfillment
Technology	**Kitchen-as-a-Service**				
Marketing	e.g., Cloud Kitchens, Kitchen United, Zuul Kitchens				
Operations					
Supply Chain					
Technology					
Marketing	**Vertically Integrated Virtual Restaurant**				
Operations	e.g., Clustertruck				
Supply Chain					
Technology	**Forward Logistics Point**				
Marketing	e.g., Virtual Kitchen Company				
Operations					
Supply Chain					
Technology					
Marketing		**Virtual Brands in Existing Kitchens**			
Operations		e.g., Byte to Bite, C3			
Supply Chain					

9.1 Emerging Types of Ghost Kitchen Models

Model 1: Kitchen as a Service

Ghost kitchen companies like Kitchen United and Cloud Kitchens are essentially a modern build-to-suit landlord that offer fully enabled real estate to their restaurant tenants. As Kitchen United COO Joy Lai explains, "We provide restaurants with an outfitted kitchen and a shared labor component, but also a tech stack that includes demand generation." This ghost kitchen model is often compared to WeWork because the restaurant employees work in a fully kitted-out kitchen that they share with other restaurants. But unlike WeWork, which caters to mostly software and service companies that don't make anything tangible, "kitchen as a service" ghost kitchens cater to tenants that create output that is immediately delivered for consumption.

These ghost kitchens are mostly focused on providing "content" in the form of new cuisine choices to the online marketplaces. However, several of the ghost kitchens encourage their restaurants to offer first-party ordering. Further, Zuul and Kitchen United offer their own online marketplaces so that consumers can access the restaurants inside them. Kitchen United, for example, created an online ordering marketplace called Mix that is exclusively for its restaurant tenants. "Mix is our consumer-facing brand," says Lai. "On Mix, the consumer can order from one or multiple concepts on one ticket and have it all delivered together with one driver. This allows us to pass along the savings to the consumer."

Kitchen United is heavily consumer-facing. In addition to their consumer ordering interface, they also welcome consumers to come in and pick up. Their real estate selection reflects this bias toward consumers: Kitchen United locations tend to be in second-generation retail sites—spaces that have already been built out by a previous tenant—near neighborhoods, major thoroughfares, and offices.

Model 2: Forward Logistics Points

These ghost kitchen companies enable restaurants to expand their delivery radius by creating reheating and pickup points outside an existing restaurant's trade area. Ken Chong's All Day Kitchens is based on this model, which he describes as "instant expansion:"

> It's an instant way for restaurants to expand their geographical reach and serve more consumers: satellite kitchens or micro-fulfillment centers. It's a complement to their existing restaurant. We expand the footprint for pick'n'pack—shared services for labor, transport. We also help on the tech side with a set of internal tools as well as glue for the ecosystem. I plug into the distributed restaurant platform and instantly go from reaching thousands of customers to reaching millions.

Chong started All Day Kitchens with Cofounder Matt Sawchuk, whom he met when they both worked at Uber. "I personally was a power user of on-demand food platforms. They offered convenience, health, more options," Chong says. The restaurants, on the other hand, were struggling to make the most of the digital opportunities. "The one thing we kept hearing from restaurants was 'my business is changing. How do I adapt to this?' The core of our mission is to build a platform for restaurants to thrive in the delivery economy."

The two added Chef Andro Radonich as a cofounder. "We needed food and culinary to be part of the founding DNA," Chong explains. "Prior food-tech companies failed because they came at it from too tech an approach. Andro is CIA (Culinary Institute of America) trained with fifteen years in the industry and has built large commercial kitchens." Radonich's culinary credentials went a long way toward swaying restaurateurs to consider All Day Kitchens's services. "A lot of chefs and restaurant owners started out skeptical," Chong says, "but once they spent time with our culinary team, they got really excited."

Radonich adds, "All Day Kitchens looks at the partnership with the restaurant as if it's our name on it. We go through an intense R&D process to make sure we're aligned. Not everything works, and we aren't going to touch things that don't work."[14]

Model 3: Virtual Brands in Existing Kitchens

Ghost kitchen companies such as C3 and Byte to Bite are just like any other restaurant company, except they put multiple concepts into a kitchen and don't have a front of house. Essentially, these companies create brands then operate them in existing kitchens.

In the case of C3 (which stands for Creating Culinary Communities), the kitchens are located in hotels owned by Accor, one of their JV partners. "We have eleven thousand kitchens around the world," says Nahai. "The monthly rent on them could be two or three thousand dollars. That's $360 million of rental income. And many of them were sitting empty." C3's other JV partners also contribute concepts (partner SBE owns Katsuya and Umami Burger) and real estate (partner Simon Property Group is the largest mall owner in the US). In just over a year, C3 was able to open four virtual brands operating out of sixty different locations.[15]

In the case of Byte to Bite, the kitchens are rented second-generation restaurants or commissaries. Byte to Bite focuses on creating brands and menus that will resonate specifically with delivery customers. In less than a year, they have opened five locations operating thirty-one different brands. "We are geared to go from a standing start to running in twenty-one days," says Cofounder Christopher Petzel.[16]

"The real estate–only model is flawed in that it can't earn enough money to pay the CAPEX," Petzel believes. "Cloud Kitchens is selling a dream." Petzel and his cofounder, Alan Moore, believe that just as in brick-and-mortar kitchens, delivery-only kitchens require some vertical integration to make the math work.

Model 4: Vertically Integrated Virtual Restaurants

Vertically integrated virtual restaurants are ghost kitchen companies that participate in all aspects of the value chain from real estate and branding through to the order showing up at the consumer's door. This model is common internationally, but rare so far here in the US. ClusterTruck is the best example of complete vertical integration. Founder and CEO Chris Baggott says, "You can't build a new business model on an old business model."[17]

ClusterTruck deploys proprietary software to manage everything from menus to drivers, all of which are in-house. Baggott came from a software background. After starting and selling two companies, Baggott became a farmer. "We do regenerative agriculture and sell direct-to-consumer. It's a good business. It's fun and important work. We had a product imbalance of what was popular with consumers and what was left. So I had this bad idea to start a restaurant in Greenfield, Indiana."

"We started doing online orders with ChowNow, and my employees hated it. Two different POS systems and a lot of friction." Baggott saw other problems with the delivery platform model too: "As a deep data DNA guy, I would never give up my data to a third party. What's going to happen here is that five years from now, they will sell the data to the highest bidder. And guess what, when you type 'burger' in on Grubhub, McDonald's is the first thing that comes up." Finally, Baggott was concerned with the word he kept hearing: incremental. "To a small business, that word is magic. There's a belief that additional revenue will be easy. It's the Groupon story. You may get more customers, but they are lousy and low-margin and create a ton of friction."

Baggott is one of those people who is unable to sit still. His farm led him to a restaurant, which led him to software to support the restaurant, which led him to a completely vertically integrated ghost kitchen. "We started programming in 2015. First location in 2016." By 2020, ClusterTruck had six locations. Everything is branded ClusterTruck, but the menu includes a variety of cuisines—from Asian to Mexican.

ClusterTruck takes all of its orders through its own proprietary software—nothing goes through third-party marketplaces. Exclusively designed for off-premise consumption, ClusterTruck is able to offer great food at a great value with a great delivery experience. "We are five stars in every one of our markets. I don't think anyone else can do that," Baggott says about ClusterTruck's online reviews. "We are delivering between sixteen and twenty-six minutes across the fleet." Baggott sees speed as integral to their quality. "Our business is all about quality. We start with outstanding ingredients. We are scratch kitchens. If you order from us for delivery, it will never be older than seven minutes."

With so many reasons to embrace ghost kitchens, it's a little surprising they are not already everywhere. According to Vivek Sunder at Swiggy, India has five thousand ghost kitchen locations. Deliveroo has hundreds of "Editions" locations (its ghost kitchen offshoot) across Europe and Australia. Yet as with many things delivery, the US lags behind other countries in adopting ghost kitchens. Real estate is less available, building requirements are more expensive, restaurants are more tightly regulated— all of these factors contribute to longer build-out timelines and therefore longer test cycles for the emerging ghost kitchen niche.

Most mature restaurant chains spend more time and resources on growing the top line of existing restaurants ("same-store sales growth") than they do on adding restaurants ("unit growth"). In a country like India, where restaurants per capita is less than 1 percent of US penetration rate, the emerging restaurant industry can fit into ghost kitchens, rather than ghost kitchens having to accommodate existing brand specifications.

If delivered meals are to become equivalently priced or even less expensive for the consumer than dine-in meals, the single biggest change has to be in the occupancy costs and labor relative to the dine-in model. Americans are not going to tolerate lower food quality or smaller portion sizes in delivered meals. This is where ghost kitchens come into play, enabling cost reduction in the elements that don't affect food quality. Having been purpose-built for delivery, ghost kitchens redirect occupancy and labor costs. They also set the stage for volume-driven efficiencies in automation, sourcing, and utilities.

The COVID-19 pandemic that closed so many restaurants created an opportunity to fundamentally change the entire American restaurant industry infrastructure forever. Pandemic closures create an enormous inventory of kitchens that can be rethought and reimagined into something different. Some will be torn down and their land redeveloped into multi-family housing. Others will reopen as restaurants that operate in a very familiar way. Between those two extremes will be locations that don't make sense as a restaurant any longer but can't easily be redeveloped into another use. After seeing properties sitting empty, landlords will realize that these spaces can still make food but serve it in a different way than anyone ever expected: as a ghost kitchen via digital ordering and off-premise delivery.

Of the restaurants that were able to operate throughout the COVID-19 pandemic, all of them became ghost kitchens of sorts: cooking up food in the back of house with no customers waiting in the adjacent dining room. That is how David Kuo's Little Fatty stayed afloat and even thrived. Kuo quickly mastered online ordering, contactless takeout, and in-house delivery. Little Fatty was able to keep most of its employees, converting servers into delivery drivers as Kuo convinced customers to order direct through his website rather than a delivery platform. Kuo used the clouds of the pandemic to create his own rainbow: high enough off-premise volume that he could go it alone.

During the COVID-19 pandemic, Kuo says, "Everyone was just trying to survive. At Little Fatty, we are trying to make the future." Kuo believes that his background in house-flipping and property management has positioned him perfectly to create this new future. "I think going vertical is the right way. But everyone else who is trying to do it only knows one aspect—money, chef, real estate. We are in a unique situation because we can do all the parts."

Also tapping into his experiences of running a commissary kitchen, driving sales digitally during the COVID-19 pandemic, and working with Cloud Kitchens, Kuo has realized "the whole idea of Cloud Kitchens is that it is a low entry point. But there are so many restaurants available now." After the pandemic, there will be thousands of three thousand square feet restaurant spaces that will never again make sense as dine-in restaurants. It's an excellent time to be a restaurateur with the capacity to think and move outside the box.

Chapter 10

GIG WORKERS ARE THE NEW SERVERS

S am checked the clock on his car dashboard and grimaced as he saw the orange light flicker against his fuel gauge. If he could just find a parking spot outside the restaurant front door, maybe he could squeeze in a second order this hour. But now he would need gas too. It wasn't looking likely. Sam slapped the steering wheel in frustration. The evening had gotten off to a slow start with orders trickling in. Then he ran into red light after red light. To top things off, he got shouted at again at the Irish bar he took deliveries from pretty much every night. If this run of bad luck continued, making his bonus for achieving two hundred trips this month didn't seem likely.

Rideshare driving was more profitable per trip, but Sam preferred the silence of a food package. He also felt safer with food—some late-night bar pickups with intoxicated passengers were uncomfortable at best. Sam figured the tips food customers gave made up for the lower delivery fees, but still—it seemed like he was working longer hours to make the same kind of income that he achieved last year. These days he felt like he was spending most of his time climbing stairs in apartment buildings with bento boxes and carting salad bowls to office meeting rooms. *Maybe I should cancel my gym membership,* Sam thought. *It's not like I can afford it, or like I even have the time to get there.*

On the other side of town, Erica could feel her ankles swelling again. She had been on her feet for eleven hours now and was coming to the end of her shift serving customers at Pittsburgh's busiest Irish bar and restaurant. Her other full-time job—as a single mom of three kids—would kick in as soon as she got home. Mentally tallying her tips for that day's shift, she sighed. Her manager considered her one of the best on the team, her loyal customers asked to be served by her, and she often received outsized tips for stellar service. Erica prided herself on her craft and the hospitality lessons she'd been taught by her grandmother at a young age, but she resented the drivers coming in for food orders. She believed they were picking up tips from diners who could have been in the restaurant being served by her.

Earlier that same evening, Erica had to distract her guests from the driver shouting at her manager. Like many servers, she felt frustrated that drivers didn't have the same passion for food, customer service skills, or interest in the guests' experience. These scruffy drivers just cared about speed—and now they were getting the tips that once came to servers. The restaurant managers also grew frustrated as the drivers got in the way of guests. The drivers were impatient, too, frequently demanding where the food was—*probably the reason for that argument earlier,* Erica thought.

As a side hustle, the gig economy cannot be beat. Gig driving offers the ultimate flexibility, fitting around other jobs, kids' schedules, and school. It pays well per hour, as long as drivers opt to work only during busy times. More than 80 percent of drivers work less than twenty hours a week.[1] If benefits are already provided through a primary job, a spouse, or parents, gig working has many advantages.

As a primary job, though? Driving work can be tough. When Mostafa Maklad started as a gig driver, he was excited to hear stories of people who were "able to buy and pay off houses in the Bay Area, San Francisco."[2] That wasn't his reality. "They kept decreasing how much money they paid drivers, year after year," Maklad says. "Now, I have to live with six roommates in a two-bedroom apartment." Mostafa is an active spokesperson for Gig Workers Rising, which has coordinated protests outside many of the third-party platforms' headquarters. Gig working still suits Maklad's busy school schedule—he is studying cybersecurity—but his need to work twelve-hour days to make ends meet is slowing down his studies. Mostafa and the drivers he represents feel they are not adequately compensated for their fundamental role in the delivery ecosystem.

The restaurants don't make Mostafa's life any easier. He says, "Instead of having food ready when we arrive, most of the restaurants make the drivers wait for twenty, thirty minutes, and for like $5, it's not even worth it. The only thing we care about is how long restaurants will keep us waiting." Restaurants that consistently delay food preparation—waiting for the driver to be present before they prepare an order so it doesn't lose freshness—earn themselves a reputation for making drivers wait, leading drivers to cancel the order. But they can't afford to do that too often. The delivery platforms monitor each driver's cancellation rate and deactivate them from the platform if it gets too high.

Drivers also need to assess restaurants for ease of access and parking. Parking tickets like the $180 one Mostafa recently received "ruins your night's income right there—I didn't even make $180 that day."

Uber itself, the patriarch of the gig working economy, has faced intense scrutiny in recent years. Although Proposition 22 overturned it, California's AB5 bill foreshadows what's to come—gig-enabled companies are under pressure to treat drivers more like employees. Many of those companies dispute that this is the correct solution. Dara Khosrowshahi, Uber's CEO, wrote in *The New York Times* in August 2020 that "we need to do a better job acting on driver concerns"[3] and called upon gig-enabled businesses to form a collective benefits fund that provides more to drivers than just commissions and tips. The flexibility of the benefits a driver needs, he asserts, should be built into the fund's utilization. Such an approach would give drivers the freedom to choose between using their proportion of the fund to help with health plan coverage or for something else—like a paid vacation. Khosrowshahi says that had this been the law in all fifty states where they operate, it would have added $655 million to benefits paid out to Uber's drivers in 2019.

It's no surprise to see such alternative solutions offered by leaders like Khosrowshahi. If implemented, it would be a giant step in the right direction by gig economy businesses. In making such a suggestion, Khosrowshahi acknowledges the importance of the driver pool to the gig economy and food delivery, and the flaws that exist in the system as it stands.

When the restaurant, the consumer, and the delivery app are all dependent on a driver who is employed by no one directly, an array of frustrations show up in the consumer experience. Drivers struggling to find parking might lead to an order sitting and degrading. Restaurants refusing to start prep until a driver shows up might lead to an order taking over an hour to get to a customer who was promised the item in thirty minutes. Friction between the in-restaurant staff and the drivers might lead to order accuracy issues.

The restaurant business is built on pride and trust. Pride in sourcing, producing, plating, and serving its food. Trust from clients that they will meet the standards they have come to expect. When restaurants hand the food off to a third-party contractor, that pride and trust can easily come undone. We're seeing the system unravelling now—so what are the alternatives, and who is making them work?

First, let's take a look at how we got to this point in the delivery chain.

When the e-commerce gold rush began, online retailers like Webvan, Pets.com, and even Amazon found that physical distribution was hard to get right. Piles of venture capital cash couldn't build out a delivery infrastructure fast enough to keep up with consumer demand for goods purchased online. Amazon scraped by with years of red-colored financials supported by the long-term vision they were able to sell to the Street to keep funding them. Many e-commerce start-ups spent poorly and didn't survive. The gap persisted: How to connect the allure of online shopping with the realities of last-mile logistics?

Turns out the emerging e-commerce industry wasn't the one to solve this problem. Gig working arose more organically—through service providers and those in need of their services finding one another through the magic of the Internet.

Craig Newmark founded Craigslist in 1995. Newmark saw the potential of the emerging World Wide Web to do a job that previously was reserved for local newspaper classified ads. Craigslist started out by sharing information about events, roommate searches, and swaps of various items across 240 people in San Francisco. Within two years, Newmark had a million people visiting his website each month while newspaper revenues were dropping rapidly. A year later, when Newmark started charging job posters for ads on his platform, full-time jobs were advertised—but also one-off short transactional and informal "gig" jobs.

The gig phenomenon really snowballed when smartphones put workers and consumers directly in contact with each other. From there, platforms carved out their niches, allowing the gig economy to launch across numerous verticals: domestic errands and business tasks (think TaskRabbit and Upwork) and, of course, transportation of people (Uber).

As they were shaping Uber, Garrett Camp and Travis Kalanick realized a flexible workforce with a self-owned infrastructure could offer a more efficient alternative to the model that taxi firms had utilized for decades with an owned fleet of vehicles. To be effective, a platform connecting workers with jobs needs three things. First, consumers who need a service. Second, an existing way to get that service, with flaws that could be eliminated with technology. And third, a segment of the workforce that values short-term work.

No doubt the demand was there, and consumers were ready for an offering that was quicker, cheaper, and more flexible. Gradually, we got used to the notion of sleeping in a stranger's house, having a stranger assemble your Ikea shelves in your bedroom, letting a stranger bring you food, and riding in a stranger's car—even though at first they all seemed like things your mother would advise against.

Kalanick got early adopters used to the idea of Uber by only letting licensed black cars onto the first version of the platform. Once consumers began to value the convenience of the app interface, it was easy to get them into other types of cars with other types of drivers just by changing the price offered and enabling user reviews. More than that, the consumer was getting a deal: venture capital cash was subsidizing the services, making them not just easier and more convenient than other models, but cheaper too. Sound familiar? The food delivery business has followed a similar approach.

American workers seem willing too. There are now estimated to be around fifty-seven million freelance workers in the US alone, representing 35 percent of the country's entire workforce.[4] Many of them work for the primary food delivery platforms of DoorDash, Grubhub, and Uber Eats.

D'Shea Grant is one driver for whom gig work appeals far more than traditional employment. "The flexibility is enormous. I love it. I can literally get off the phone after talking with you, and go to work right now."[5] As a single mom of a special needs child, Grant needed to get out of the house more—and make more money. Driving for DoorDash suits her needs very well. Grant takes pride in being good at what she does. "In July I was ranked number one DoorDasher, and I just got another high ranking for the month of August." For her, delivering food feels like an act of service, not just a job. "When I bring someone their food, I'm helping someone out. There was a time I couldn't step out of the house as a parent of a special needs child. There were times I didn't feel like cooking dinner. I wish I had DoorDash back then."

For all the advantages of the new model, it's not perfect by any means. The Domino's employee wearing a branded uniform going from the restaurant to local houses carried a consistent item in a purpose-designed bag from the same place over and over again. Unlike the old-school pizza delivery system, the modern-day gig food delivery transaction's fragmented nature loosens accountability. If something goes wrong, does the fault lie where the consumer placed the order? Where the food was prepared? How the food got from the restaurant to the consumer? And regardless of where the problem occurred, whose job is it to resolve the issue?

Here's another glitch: platforms encourage tips to drivers but make it impossible to tip the restaurant. Two parties are involved in the level of service, but only one of them gets compensated for it. Worse still, consumers give tips before the order is in their hands, leaving them to expect whatever level of service they feel is justified by the tip amount they chose.

Trust between the parties involved is at a low ebb, and it's no wonder. In July 2019, a US Foods survey stated that 28 percent of all food delivery transactions are tampered with in some way by the driver (fancy the odd french fry, anyone?).[6] And the driver recruitment practices of the platforms don't do much to inspire confidence. As part of our industry research for this book, one of us (Carl) became a driver for DoorDash. After showing a driver's license and an insurance card, then agreeing to a basic background check, he was given a fifteen-minute briefing. That was it. Instead of any more substantial upfront screening and training, the platforms single out bad eggs based on data—cancellations and customer reviews. By its very nature, the gig economy doesn't allow for extensive training or feedback to the gig worker: if companies provided those things, the government would define the relationship as "employment."

The amazing thing about this state of affairs is that consumer usage of these platforms continues to grow. We might not trust the system, but we still want the value and convenience it provides. Those opposing forces make for a fantastic opportunity for restaurants to redefine how food travels from restaurant to consumer. Several models are emerging that radically redefine the driver's role, with the philosophy that happy drivers result in happy guests.

1. The Restaurant Co-Op Model

In Iowa City, Jon Sewell, CEO of LoCo, has created an online ordering co-op of 180 local restaurants supported by sixty independent contractor drivers. It's a model Sewell brought across from his former career in health care, where he developed co-ops and group ventures that would "allow hospitals to benefit from economies of scale without necessarily giving up their autonomy."[7] Unlikely though it may seem from the outside, he saw a parallel between hospitals and restaurants. "Hospitals tend to be very parochial," Sewell explains. "They're kind of like independent restaurant owners because they're used to being totally self-sufficient."

Sewell moved across to the restaurant business in 2013, becoming owner of D. P. Dough. He saw an opportunity for another kind of food delivery service: "I got about twenty restaurant owners together and pitched the concept of forming a cooperative or joint venture and creating our own delivery service. And that's what we did."[8]

For half of the LoCo drivers, this is a side hustle to supplement a full-time job, and many make over $25 an hour delivering food for the co-op—not bad when you consider the minimum wage in Iowa is just over $7 an hour. No wonder then, that Sewell expresses his pride in having over four hundred applications from people waiting to drive for his network. "I would prefer our system to have all employed drivers, but the problem is drivers don't want to be employed."

Restaurant groups from as far away as Dubai, UAE, are asking for his counsel on what he's built and why it works so well. Sewell explains that it starts by having a genuine relationship between the platform and the driver—beginning with an in-person interview. "You don't know the boss at Grubhub or DoorDash," he explains. "With LoCo, the drivers know who's doing the dispatch, and they know all the restaurants' general managers." The restaurants and the drivers are connected to one another more consistently than in a traditional gig model.

The restaurants benefit from his platform, too, as the whole co-op arrangement is designed to charge commissions that are "half of what DoorDash and Grubhub charge." How is LoCo able to do this? They spend less on customer acquisition than the national platforms do. "Those platforms have the students and the younger populations that are chasing free delivery. Our crowd appreciates we are locally owned and run our service the way a restaurant would run the service." Rather than spending money on advertising and subsidized food or delivery, LoCo acquires and retains customers through service—much as a well-operated restaurant would. Happy customers stay loyal to the platform and recommend the service to their friends, knowing they will get a high-quality delivery experience while helping the profitability of their favorite restaurants.

Sewell's philosophy has more in common with public service than with a profit motive, and he wants the entire restaurant industry to benefit. He plans to take the model outside of Iowa and spread the co-op logic across the United States and beyond.

2. The Driver as Server

Aaron Hoffman built DeliverThat in Canton, Ohio, for the sole purpose of supporting restaurants with catering order delivery. Catering, Hoffman suggests, is the "most underutilized piece of a restaurant."[9] Today, his company operates from coast to coast. Drivers have a different experience supporting Hoffman's service. He's proud to say, "DeliverThat is founded by drivers, and we are for drivers. Every single one of our employees has undertaken a delivery. Without drivers, our business is dead."

It's more than just words. His gig drivers enjoy better financial rewards, and tips are significantly greater too, as individual orders can be as high as $300 each.

With DeliverThat, the drivers perform services well beyond delivery. Many corporate clients request that the drivers set the table, present the food, and ready it for the audience, the same way an in-house catering manager or server would typically do. Hoffman believes drivers deserve this boost as they have a tough time out there representing the industry: "It's very easy for drivers to get blamed for restaurant's mistakes."

Unlike the leading platforms or Jon Sewell's co-op model, Hoffman sees his business not as a platform or a consumer interface, but a reimagining of delivery as a core part of the service. He points out, "You don't get mad if your food is fifteen or twenty minutes late when you're at home, but if catering goes into a boardroom and you're late, you're going to piss off a CEO." In catering, you don't get a second chance. As a result, DeliverThat maintains a maniacal focus on perfect logistics performance.

Investment in drivers makes DeliverThat's approach possible. "You have to set them up for success, you have to invest in education. I view them almost as customers because you have got to keep them happy at all times," Hoffman says. The drivers are applauded in the company's blog and championed through internal competitions. One result of this supportive culture is a much lower churn rate. Hoffman believes his cost to acquire a driver is just $20—some thirty times more efficient than the cost for the leading delivery players to replace a lost driver from their network.

3. The Driver as Customer

AllyNow CEO Roman Tsarovsky takes the "driver as customer" approach to an entirely new level. Drivers pay AllyNow—founded in LA in 2020— an upfront fee for access to its software subscription platform and then retain 100 percent of the earnings from their efforts. "I don't even think it's the fact they're making more money," Tsarovsky says.[10] "I think it's the fact that they understand that they're making *all* the money. If I know that no one is taking a piece of what I'm working for, and all of this is mine, I just need to make sure that I keep what's mine."

His service is complementary to most ordering interfaces that require a back-end delivery (like Olo or ChowNow). Tsarovsky's machine learning technology finely tunes the optimization of a delivery transaction, enabling drivers on average to undertake 3–3.5 deliveries per hour— some 30 percent more than the typical amount. His drivers benefit from supporting numerous verticals, including pharmaceutical deliveries and alcohol deliveries. Drivers can choose which verticals they want to support a few days in advance, giving them the flexibility to choose the type of delivery work they undertake. Where clients request it, drivers may also wear uniforms to add levels of branding and credibility to their service, allowing consumers to feel their order is in the best possible hands.

For restaurant chains and independents alike, the AllyNow platform solves many of the challenges that restaurants and drivers face. With drivers as customers, Tsarovsky explains, "We're trying to solve the problem of commissions while optimizing earning potential, so that drivers can be motivated to perform. We make them feel like they are fighting for something, so that their quality of life is increasing."

Improved compensation and greater control for drivers has a flow-on benefit for the consumer. Happier drivers are incentivized to take more care with the service they offer. As Tsarovsky says, "Our main goal is not even to empower the businesses and merchants—it's really to save money for the end consumer." If his claims of savings of 8–20 percent prove consistent and accurate, then maybe everyone stands to benefit in the long run.

4. The Restaurant Employee Driver

If a restaurant wants to take the reins on the delivery experience, you could reason, they need to employ their own drivers. And some restaurants believe that is the right path for them.

Back in 2015, Panera Bread's executive team invested early into their delivery driver infrastructure. In the years that followed, they built a driver force over thirteen thousand drivers strong who supported delivery from over two-thirds of the 2,100 Panera Bread locations.[11] In 2019, Panera Bread's Chief Growth Officer, Dan Weigel, stated, "We initially landed on our [in-house delivery] model because it allowed us the fastest geographic reach and seamless experience that matches Panera quality. The most important consideration for Panera is owning the guest experience—and making sure it's a great one."[12] By owning the entire chain from order to delivery, Panera can ensure consistency while maintaining control of their customer data. Marcus Higgins, former Chief Operating Officer of Eat Street, responsible for delivery services in over 250 US markets, thinks the same and chose to use all W2 workers. He says, "The retention rates on drivers were less than ninety days. You can never make this business work unless you improve driver retention. And the best way we found to do that was bringing them on, giving them real wages, giving them the opportunity to earn benefits."[13]

Having an employed workforce adds control and increased training and performance management into the restaurant's system. The flip side is that many restaurants using their employees for delivery "don't have a lean business model," according to DeliverThat's Hoffman. He acknowledges those with consistently high delivery volume, catering offers, and a premium brand worthy of protection particularly can benefit—like Panera. With eight drivers per store on average, Panera locations can manage local demand peaks and troughs—but that's still eight extra employees to hire and manage.

Even so, the Panera operation points back to the fundamental principles of hospitality and service. To the degree a restaurant can afford it, they can effectively extend the dining experience through their own employee drivers. Where restaurants can afford it, where they can optimize its enablement, and perhaps where they can't trust anyone else to do it better, a restaurant may be better off employing its drivers.

If drivers are the servers of the digital economy, their happiness can make all the difference to the restaurant experience. We know that happy workers are as much as 13 percent more productive, according to research by the University of Oxford.[14] How drivers are treated and how they are made to feel when they are doing their work will reflect in the way they carry out their deliveries, in the same way a server who is treated with respect will respond by leveling up her hospitality and service. Here's the question, though: How can restaurants create a culture of care for drivers they do not employ or even know?

Maybe room service is the answer.

Lloyd Wentzell, a former VP of Food Service, has lived and breathed hospitality and service throughout his career, having worked at the Waldorf Astoria in New York and Caesars Palace in Las Vegas. He's overseen an operation with fifteen hundred staff producing five thousand meals a day, serving world leaders like Ronald Reagan and Gandhi and celebrities like Frank Sinatra. He suggests that room service for 1,650 rooms represents a challenge on a similar scale to that of the driver food delivery system. Just as with restaurant delivery, you're not placing the order with the server—instead, the server is "reliant on the dispatcher to get the order right,"[15] Wentzell explains. "If something's missing from the order sheet, it's the dispatcher's fault."

Room service staff and drivers share other challenges. "Imagine a restaurant with one hundred tables compared to 1,650 rooms—that's like 1,650 tables," Wentzell says. Here's the difference: "If a restaurant is full, you have people queuing up. In room service, the guest can't see what's going on or that there are fifty to sixty orders in front of them." That can make for one annoyed guest. Or a hundred of them.

When room service personnel create an excellent experience for the guests they service, their tips increase. At the JW Marriott Hotel in Vegas, where Wentzell concluded his career, his room service staff offered a fresh pepper mill across a dish or made handcrafted cocktails in the room in front of the guest. He acknowledges that drivers can't provide the same incremental touches that he asked of his team but suggests they can still "kill them with kindness." Courtesy goes a long way.

This is especially important when something goes wrong. In the delivery system as it stands, drivers are not empowered to address issues of service effectively. Restaurants are not doing enough to make things right in their food packages when they already know they'll end up at a customer's door late. Wentzell says that when a room service delivery was late, they'd send the guest an apology note with a chocolate-dipped strawberry with their meal. In food delivery, however, service corrections remain a glaring opportunity missed for turning a bad experience into a good one. Drivers are in the best place to achieve that, if they are taught how to do so and incentivized appropriately. And there's no one better placed than restaurateurs to help them.

Wentzell tried to smooth out the wrinkles by having condiments located on each floor to assist in the room service runner's efficiency when something like a condiment was missing or where an extra napkin or cutlery set was requested. Unlike servers, drivers often have to self-train, learn how to optimize their time, and be the tzars of customer service—even though they interact with faceless apps and restaurant teams too busy to talk to them. They may not have a Lloyd Wentzell helping them figure it out, but there are popular YouTube channels where the most successful drivers share their advice. Services such as DeliverThat and AllyNow demonstrate that drivers will focus on great service if supported by a system that helps them communicate with guests proactively, transparently, and honestly.

We as customers have a part to play here too. Consumers need to appreciate that when things go wrong, not every factor is in the driver's control. And when a driver offers excellent service and communication, consumers should be prepared to recognize them, in the same way they would one of Wentzell's team members at Caesars Palace. Whether it's a tip or a simple acknowledgment, these acts of connection and gratitude are increasingly important. Just like servers, drivers work hard, long hours, and they act as the engine of hospitality in our business. And just as much as servers, drivers deserve respect and gratitude for their efforts to make our meal experience the best it possibly can be.

If restaurants start to think of drivers as servers, taking food to a table two miles away from the kitchen, they can enable them to give the best possible experience for their guests. Drivers are clear about what they want: more deliveries per hour worked, because that equates to a better income for them. Anything a restaurant does to help drivers achieve this goal will be appreciated and make the restaurant a favorite with drivers. A good reputation with drivers will translate into immediate acceptance of orders, low cancellations, and better customer service to the end consumer. As Aaron Hoffman of DeliverThat says, "Treat the delivery drivers like they are part of your team. They are either going to take that food, provide a great experience, and get you a recurring sale, or they're going to treat your customer like crap because that's how they were treated." And if the tech-focused platforms that connect the restaurants to their drivers can learn a thing or two from the innovators highlighted in this chapter and recognize that hospitality and service are vitally important to any food experience, maybe restaurants will have half a chance to help the drivers become the new servers they so clearly need.

Chapter 11

OPERATING IN A VIRTUAL WORLD

"Come on, come on, come on," Andrew muttered with rising tension. He checked his phone for the fourth time in sixty seconds, wondering whether he had processed the order correctly. The food should have left the restaurant about fifteen minutes ago, but the app said it was still being prepared. "Of all nights," he grumbled under his breath. Andrew had become accustomed to the orders not always being on time, but tonight he needed to be somewhere else in precisely fifty-four minutes, and Jessica was running late getting home from work.

At that exact moment, Sean—the driver delivering their dinner—was typing a message to Andrew. "Food coming up soon. Kitchen backed up with orders. Apologies for the delay." Sean had arrived at the restaurant about fifteen minutes earlier at the designated time for pickup, only to be left waiting in the reception area while the flustered front-of-house attendant dashed between seating guests, handing off other delivery orders, and placating frustrated takeaway customers.

It was nothing new to Sean—it happened all too often. Sean reflected that this restaurant had many of the same excellent staff serving the same fantastic food they did a few years earlier. Still, they hadn't adjusted how their operation functioned to service delivery orders. He glared across the road at the drivers pulling up outside the fast food restaurant where Arbel, the general manager, was overseeing another evening of sophisticated, seamless operations.

Arbel manages one of the largest QSRs in Columbus. He is responsible for $2 million in sales a year, thirty-five employees, and six hundred customer orders each day. Arbel is aided by computer algorithms that help him manage his inventory, schedule his team, and prep food to match expected consumer peaks each day.

Much of the inventory that enters his store is at least partially prepped. At the extreme are completely cooked items that just need to be reheated and served. Even the items needing additional care, such as salad vegetables, are already washed and cut. The prepped ingredients are placed into stainless steel pans on "the line"—a manufacturing term borrowed to describe how food is made. Arbel's team can combine just a few ingredients in different ways to create hundreds of items. The cooks rarely move from their position on the line and instead hand food from one station to the other for different phases of building out their final dish, much like Henry Ford's moving assembly line.

This automation helps Arbel focus on the numbers he is responsible for driving, which are measured weekly: order-to-delivery times, item accuracy, customer satisfaction, sales, inventory efficiency, labor deployment, and employee turnover. At Arbel's restaurant, drivers wait for less than a minute when they arrive—hardly enough time to look at their watch—unlike Sean and Andrew, who both were looking at theirs with increasing levels of annoyance.

For most who choose the restaurant industry as a profession, it's all about serving people—face to face. The joy on guests' faces after trying a new dish gives many restaurant owners far more satisfaction than any other metric. Of course, restaurant owners aren't in the business solely because of their ability to make great tasting food. Many are as excited by creating a welcoming environment where the atmosphere and every detail of a customer's interaction with their restaurant is purposeful. The art of restaurateuring is celebrated through Michelin stars and celebrity chefs.

While the art of hospitality will always be a big part of the restaurant business, the science of operating has become increasingly important in the last few years. It becomes even more important in an off-premise context. If all a consumer knows about a restaurant is what arrives at their door in a little box, then the result of operations (for better or worse) is all a consumer will see. Setting up an off-premise offering is not as simple as throwing the current menu online and handling the extra volume. The different demands, rhythms, and contexts of off-premise consumption require applying science.

Restaurant veterans are hard workers. Owners, chefs, line workers, and servers alike show up day after day, often working long hours and multiple jobs or never taking a vacation. The natural tendency in restaurant industry problem-solving is to just work harder.

However, a wonderful thing has happened as a result of the digitization of restaurants: data is everywhere. The trick to being a restaurant operator in this new digital context is not working harder. It is mastering the acquisition, management, and insights of data. It can be challenging to wrangle data, but industry forerunners are systematizing it and learning from it.

While data can improve all restaurant operations—off-premise or on—it is an essential element of what separates the best from the rest in fulfilling digital consumer demand. It's far easier for smaller restaurants to see, hear, and react to the data that's occurring in the moment, right there in their dining room. It's not so easy to see and react to something that's occurring fifteen minutes away from your kitchen as the customer unwraps their food and sees that what they ordered is not what they've received.

When Off-Premise Operations Go Wrong

!	*Delivery is incorrect in terms of quantity or the wrong item being delivered;*
🔧	*Adjustments are not correctly made;*
🕐	*Food is delivered outside the expected delivery window (e.g., late);*
∿	*Food has lost its intended state of integrity during transit (e.g., the package has fallen over); or*
🌡	*Food has lost temperature or quality because of the time that has passed since it was produced.*

11. 1 When Off-Premise Operations Go Wrong

Customers expect three basic staples of an excellent food service delivery experience:

1. Accuracy—the restaurant delivers precisely what was ordered.
2. Speed—the restaurant delivers the order within the expected window of time.
3. Quality—the restaurant delivers the meal as advertised, tasting and looking great.

Fail in one of these areas, and the customer may never use the restaurant again for a delivery order and may even stop coming for dine-in occasions. Unless it's consciously managed, delivery immediately poses a risk to accuracy, speed, and quality because kitchen and consumer are separated by a car ride. Further, because of the added distance between the end user and the provider, issue resolution takes longer, costs more, and could be less satisfying to both parties.

The easiest and cheapest way to fix issues? Avoid them in the first place.

Avoiding issues requires excellent operations. And excellent operations, consistently delivered, cannot be achieved by just working harder. When asked to do more, an already hardworking team is bound to make mistakes. Worse, people call in sick, have bad days, and deal with unexpected challenges all the time—such as a run on a menu item or the unavailability of a key ingredient. These variables have to be accounted for in the design of the operating system.

Great off-premise operators use three tools to drive their operating system and increase quality, accuracy, and speed:

1. Design to purpose
2. Lean manufacturing
3. Closed-loop communication

Let's take a look at those three tools in detail.

1. Design to Purpose

Compared to dining in, the digital ordering interface all but guarantees a poor experience. We can browse a restaurant menu on a small smartphone screen, but we often then make decisions with less information compared to ordering in-restaurant. We may not click through to the detailed description. We don't get to ask a member of the restaurant team a question about the food. We might be able to request some changes to an item, but our ability to customize will likely be limited by the ordering platform. A menu designed for a different ordering context simply cannot function well on a tiny screen with no human interaction.

"Adapt your menu for delivery" is the advice of Henry Roberts, owner of Two Hands restaurant in New York City.[1] He believes that having a deliberate off-premise menu strategy is the first step to improved accuracy and reduced errors in the cooking process. Roberts suggests the best lens for menu adaptation is "dishes that travel better. Simple—let's make everything more simple." Along the same lines, Ordermark's Alex Canter suggests the best adaptations for delivery are "very limited menus; we're not trying to overcomplicate this or make it really challenging for a restaurant to get it right."[2]

Simplicity reduces variability, which reduces the potential for error within the kitchen. Pulling from a smaller pool of ingredients reduces complexity in both the preparation of items and the ease in which they are made. Too many restaurants offer their exact dine-in menu online, thrown into the exact same takeout box they use for leftovers, then wonder why their online and in-platform reviews aren't great. Essentially, the filters a restaurant would use to choose its dine-in menu are the same ones to use for off-premise—it's just that different menu items will make it through the filter. Does the consumer want it? Can the restaurant sell it profitably? Can they execute it consistently? The easiest way to decide which items will be successful and which need some work is to make them, package them as if they are going out for delivery, and then taste them twenty minutes later.

Incorporating the reality of when and where the food will be eaten into the design of the food means quality is measured upon arrival, not departure. Andrew McClellan, an industrial engineer specializing in restaurants, believes the best way for any restaurant to determine the quality of their current menu is "personal mystery shopping. Order your own food." That means cooking each item, placing it in your designated packaging, taking it for a drive for twenty minutes, and then assessing the temperature, product integrity, presentation, and general texture, taste, and consistency—while eating it with any provided condiments or cutlery. Trying this during peak and off-peak periods to test the consistency of your back-of-house teams during busier and quieter times is also essential.

No matter which items are chosen for the off-premise menu, the quality of the food must be as excellent when it arrives at the consumer's door as it is when it arrives at your guest's table in the restaurant. Even the best-tasting menu items might not be suited for a long journey in a car. Evaluating how you prepare items for delivery helps address this. For example, french fries are inferior after twenty to thirty minutes in transit. But customers will still want french fries delivered. Air frying and ingredient innovation can improve the crispness of fries at destination. Suppliers like Simplot are now creating fries with a special coating to improve quality in off-premise situations.[3] For other menu items, some restaurants are modifying their cooking practices so that items are slightly undercooked, knowing that their internal temperature will continue to cook the food during transit, ensuring that it arrives in perfect condition.

Presentation, too, affects both the look and the taste of delivered food. Saving a few cents on cheaper packaging may cost you far more in lost business. Consumers eat first with their eyes, and a poorly packaged item looks unappetizing. Recent packaging innovations designed specifically for delivery also improve how food travels, with vents that allow the steam to escape, nonstick paper sleeves or pizza tents to retain item integrity, and thicker packaging to ensure the item isn't crushed.

Some QSR and pizza chains have perfected packaging over the years, because most of their food has always been consumed outside the restaurant. McClellan observes that fast food chains excel in packaging because "they have packaging engineers. They work directly with the supplier and do lots of testing."[4] Thankfully, as off-premise consumption becomes the norm, packaging companies are innovating for everyone, including those without specialist engineers.

2. Lean Manufacturing

Manufacturing may seem like the wrong word to describe an art that satisfies the soul through food, hospitality, and atmosphere. Stephen Crowley disagrees. Crowley is an expert in operational efficiencies and cofounder of Service Physics, a company dedicated to helping restaurants identify opportunities through lean manufacturing principles. He says,

"Lean as a philosophy has been really refined and a lot of expertise built around it for the manufacturing sector—how the factory is designed, how it is operated, and the management systems of those factories. If you think of a retail or restaurant location as a mini factory, all of these principles can be applied."[5]

For all the advantages, the lean approach hasn't taken off in the restaurant industry. Crowley can count on one hand the number of restaurant chains who have fully embraced lean. "The largest example is Chick-fil-A," he says. "There's a huge opportunity, and perhaps one of the problems lies in the name," Crowley says. "'Lean' has a connotation of less, and no one in hospitality wants to do more with less."

The tools of a lean coach are straightforward, Crowley says: "Knowledge, perspective, and pressure." Knowledge is information that we bring from similar situations. Perspective is just that: "If you are in the system, you can't see the system and improve the system." Pressure moves the process forward. "How quickly can we do an experiment to see if we make it better?"

First, though, you need to feed the lean machine with data. In the e-commerce world, there is data everywhere to validate or invalidate hypotheses. "In the operations world," Crowley says, "we have to create it." Once again, simple is the best approach: flaws in the system can be illuminated with tally sheets to keep track of occurrences like stock-outs. Spaghetti diagrams show where employees go to accomplish a task and where there may be wasted motion. Spaghetti diagrams are created by simply tracing a team member's movement over five minutes without lifting your pen from the paper. Crowley does this exercise regularly with restaurant general managers. "Within thirty seconds, the GM will ask, 'Why is she going over there?' I can guarantee you she's going over there because there is something over there she needs." Those seconds add up significantly when repeated and result in unnecessary motion. This translates into slower production processes, which makes hitting a targeted time for delivered food all the more difficult to achieve.

Shaving time in this way is a detailed-oriented and painstakingly challenging method, but it's utilized by the very biggest restaurant chains when refining their operational practices. The chains use it because they see the potential that is not limited by the number of tables serving dine-in customers. Takeout and delivery customers can be unlimited in number, so pushing the kitchen's output is critical for off-premise.

The lean methodology is ruthless when dealing with waste of all kinds. Waste is the relationship of resources to the end customer—inventory, processing time, and defects.[6] One source of waste is waiting times—not for the customer, but inside the kitchen itself through bottlenecks in the food production process. Bottlenecks are those spots in your kitchen where semi-prepared items start to build up and wait because of something slower or less efficient, precluding it from moving to the next stage of its production.

Andrew McClellan's career in industrial engineering has focused on the minutiae of operational excellence, where refined tweaks to processes can save seconds on critical tasks, and in large chains those seconds can amount to millions of dollars. To eliminate bottlenecks, McClellan says, "have the slowest station first, the quickest last. Always design for the pull method so that the next person is waiting. You can't push a rope; you can only pull one." This means you've always got someone ready and waiting for the next item on the assembly line.

Crowley shares that view, putting it this way: "If you start the slow machine first and embed the quick machine in the slow machine's machine-time, then you reduce the total cycle time of that order." The same is true of any food production task in any kitchen. Exploring how to reposition tasks in the production line so that they sit ahead of bottlenecks will save valuable seconds that, in a delivery context, push your restaurant to the top of the digital delivery platform homepage, and therefore consumer awareness.

Fast casual chain Eatsa was an excellent example of what's possible when the entire process is created to remove bottlenecks. A quinoa-bowl concept best known for its forward-thinking data-based process refinements and ambition to address food waste, Eatsa's takeout system was wholly optimized for quality, speed, and accuracy. Cofounder Scott Drummond says that their time for food preparation would have been "under a minute."[7] This was true even for dishes that consumers had customized during the ordering process.

Eatsa used technology like kiosks well ahead of the rest of the restaurant industry. It meant that customers did not have to "interact arbitrarily with order-takers and all this extraneous process," Drummond says. Eatsa had identified the engagement between guest and server as a bottleneck in many restaurants, so they designed it out of their process. For order fulfillment, Eatsa used small cabinets where customers could see their name, collect their order, and depart without any interaction with the restaurant team members. "There's this magic to the experience where all the friction is gone," Drummond enthuses.

Eatsa was able to tackle the challenge of accuracy by removing a point of potential error, but speed was their primary focus. They mined every facet of technology to make the process utterly seamless. "It really boiled down to the back-of-house system and the customer user interface, the alert system, and the ongoing engagement with order status—both from a handheld device, and then ultimately inside the food space, working in concert and being tightly synced," Drummond explains. "Knowing when the customer orders, knowing where they are—we were experimenting with geolocation to ensure that the handoff happened at the exact right moment. Food production times were so tightly calibrated that we had the ability to do massive throughput. We did a ton of user experience testing around how to manage customers' expectations: If they arrive early, what do you do? If they arrive late, how can you build it into the algorithm?" Their goal, Drummond says, was "the ability to deal with those scenarios in a way where the food is at its highest quality and the expectations of the customer are perfectly met."

Sadly, Eatsa's vision of the future was ahead of its time. In 2019, all of their restaurants closed. The company has repurposed itself as a technology company. While the company's automat theme wasn't completely novel, their technology to create customized dishes speedily and accurately certainly was. Drummond points out that "a lot of people believe that the hardware was the magic. It's not. It's all the things that happened around the hardware. We were never really concerned about the intellectual property with respect to the little magic boxes. The box is not the solution. What Eatsa did was demonstrate these themes [data, process engineering, technology] in a new way."

Brian Reece, Cofounder (alongside Stephen Crowley) of Service Physics, believes:

> We're still at the very beginning of our understanding of how to integrate digital orders into existing operations. This is one place where we're finding a lot of opportunity in the industry. It's not just about building a super sexy digital experience for the guests. You also have to make sure that the back-end systems and tools work, for the operation to be able to act on those orders in a consistent and high-quality way.[8]

Reece says the addition of the digital delivery channel has confused restaurant operations by adding yet another layer of complexity—first dine-in, then drive-thru, and now delivery. "I have not seen a lot of direction on how to integrate new channels into the existing operations. Now you have a third channel [delivery] coming in, and there isn't really a playbook for how to integrate that. All this industry knowledge has been built around a drive-thru as a second channel. But it hasn't been done on digital."

3. Closed-Loop Communication

A more straightforward menu designed for delivery, a suite of efficient processes, and a robust technology system will go a long way to improve quality, accuracy, and speed of a restaurant. However, the restaurant industry is a people business, and people make mistakes. Even the best-operated restaurants maintain a level of risk in the handover of a dish from the kitchen to the table. In dine-in settings, this "handover risk" is why a server approaching your table with plates in hand is not simply asking which dish you chose; they're checking to ensure you ordered the plate they intend to serve you. Both the server and the guest confirm that the order is correct. It's a classic example of closed-loop communication, a technique that reduces the risk of errors arising from misunderstandings or false assumptions.

For the digital delivery consumer, there is no such opportunity for customer verification, so the restaurant team has to double down on communication. Service Physics Cofounder Reece says, "Most human endeavors fail due to problems with communications. For an operation to get from A to Z, information needs to flow, and materials need to flow. In our experience, 90 percent of the problems are information flow problems." Communication is critical, and an operating system is only as good as the communication that binds it together.

Seamless technology integration helps. When the consumer's intention is translated directly to the line cook, the opportunity for human error goes down. Alex Canter's Ordermark system tries to achieve precisely that. Orders from all sources go through a single receipt printer so that a kitchen can aptly manage the orders that arrive at the kitchen, regardless of which channel they come from. Canter says, "When we built the single device where restaurants can receive all their online orders, we realized it was equally important to give restaurants a single dashboard so they can manage their whole delivery business from one command center. When a restaurant runs out of a specific item and needs to pause service across all of their delivery [channels], they can do that from the Ordermark tablet with a click of a button."

Even with great technology in place, the best restaurant operators institute multiple checkpoints to ensure the quality and accuracy of each order. For example, in the drive-thru line, brands like Taco Bell still "triple check" each order—even though consumers verify their order on an order confirmation board as the employee enters it into the POS. The line cook checks for completion. The expediter checks for accuracy. And the window employee reads the order back to the guest as they hand the items to the car. Other restaurants use a "call it out" system that is similar to the system used in hospital operating rooms, where surgeons say what they are doing out loud and support staff repeats it back to confirm process steps.

And the ultimate in closed-loop communication? Feedback.

It costs much more to acquire a new guest than to retain an existing one. In the restaurant industry, this puts the pressure on meeting or exceeding guest expectations every single time. Fail at quality, accuracy, or speed, and the damage can also far exceed one lost customer. If guest expectations are not met or a guest doesn't feel heard, it doesn't take long for the issue to be broadcast. Negative reviews of a guest's experience go public on Yelp, Google, Facebook, Instagram, and more.

Off-premise consumption makes failure even more keenly felt: a consumer's lousy experience intensifies when a faceless digital delivery app and a third-party driver are the only possible recourse. The consumer might not be able to pinpoint the cause of a problem, but they will be quick to point out the results of poor operations. "Trial by social media" has become the bane of all public-facing industries. As Amir Nahai of Accor Hotels puts it, "Fifteen years ago, if your restaurant sucked for two weeks, no one would ever know. Today, if your restaurant sucks for two weeks, you drop forty spots in TripAdvisor."[9]

As complaints shift from in-person to online, the responsibility for guest satisfaction is slowly moving from the restaurant itself to off-site management—or even worse, not being looked at by anyone. As Aaron Newton, Chief Product Officer of Thanx (a guest engagement engine for restaurants) says, "In a ten-location business, when a customer drops a plate, the manager is there to sort it out and deal with the situation. It doesn't even become known to anyone in upper management."[10] The same is not true in digital delivery occasions, Newton argues. When something goes wrong off-premise in that same ten-location business, emails fly, but "there's no one on hand to resolve the situation in a timely manner. Customer resolution takes real-time." Not only is this a failure for the individual customer, Newton has seen how it fuels any unease the restaurant staff may feel with off-premise consumption. "The person who is tasked to resolve the problem has the feeling 'we never had this type of issue when we weren't online,' and their distaste for off-premise continues."

Alex Beltrani is the CEO and Founder of Tattle, a guest feedback engine designed to streamline this exact process. Beltrani saw how his parents' Long Island restaurant benefited from utilizing the same feedback-card approach that Denny's introduced in the 1980s. Eight key categories (such as menu knowledge, service, food quality, and speed of service) were judged by customers and then tabulated so the Beltranis could understand and respond to the over- and underperforming areas of their business. This kind of customer feedback data can prioritize efforts, identify statistically relevant opportunities for focus, and improve operational effectiveness in a way that directly ties back to what guests have said.

Tattle connects the off-premise customer and restaurant through a similar but more digitally oriented approach than paper feedback cards. Tattle channels customers (both happy and angry) away from reporting dissatisfaction on the public forums by providing a private forum for constructive and specific feedback. Each restaurant on their platform is provided a specific operational area to focus on, determined through an algorithm that denotes the area which has the greatest impact on the guest experience. The feedback is reserved for restaurant management. Beltrani explains, "Much like Uber sends you a survey to rate your driver after you get to your destination, we now 'uberize' feedback for restaurants. We ensure all the data we're collecting is served up to be super actionable for all these really busy restaurant owners."[11]

Beltrani designed the platform for general managers or district managers as the primary audience, rather than C-suites. The data provides actionable insights through causation-based surveys, which include questions designed to elicit specific feedback. These kinds of surveys can help managers learn, for example, that customers are confused by pizza descriptions because what they receive has uneven topping distributions. "It's that level of actionability that appeals to the general manager whose job it is to ensure the even distribution of toppings on a pizza. It's not the CEO's job—so when we built Tattle out, we thought about how we can galvanize the people on the front lines."

Feedback, of course, is only valuable if restaurants act on the data they receive. Beltrani believes, "If the data is real-time and it's synthesized in a way where someone at the location level can act, that makes a world of difference, so that whatever has gone awry is not persisting throughout the rest of the day."

Tattle is further evidence of the growing capability within a restaurant operator's digital toolkit. It is a toolkit that no longer belongs exclusively to large chains and their heavily resourced technology departments—now restaurant operators of all sizes can seize opportunities that were once beyond their grasp. Technology aside, restaurant operators must seek to capture every shred of available data and synthesize it into a usable control system by changing and improving their operational execution for a more straightforward, leaner, faster delivery.

Chapter 12

ATTRACTING CUSTOMERS WHO "GET" YOU

> *People don't buy what you do; they buy why you do it. And what you do simply proves what you believe.*
> —SIMON SINEK[1]

Tressie Lieberman has had a front-row seat in the restaurant digitization journey over the course of her career. Recruited out of the University of Texas at Austin to Ogilvy One—the digital sub-firm within agency powerhouse Ogilvy & Mather—she went directly into digital advertising out of school. "There was no social at the time. It was display banners. It wasn't that exciting, but looking back it was the best thing that ever happened to me."

Lieberman now sits on the board of the Mobile Marketing Association, having digitized beloved historic brands like Pizza Hut. She is now responsible for digital marketing and off-premise at Chipotle Mexican Grill, one of the leading restaurant chains when it comes to digital marketing, digital ordering, and digital fulfillment.

Besides her background at Ogilvy One, Lieberman did a stint at Slingshot, an agency exclusively focused on digital. The restaurant industry was calling her, though, so she moved across to a traditional product manager role working on the WingStreet concept inside of Pizza Hut. In 2006, the entire digital marketing team—all two of them—left and Lieberman's boss asked her, "You know digital, right? You should go try."

"During the time I was at Pizza Hut, the iPhone launched, Facebook went from a private college network to open, and Domino's created the pizza tracker," Lieberman recalls. "Well ahead of the founding of Uber and an app telling consumers where their driver was, a pizza company was telling consumers where their pizza was." 2006–2009 were innovative years, and a restaurant company was right there with the now tech giants creating new consumer expectations. "There was so much innovation and opportunity," Lieberman says. "Disrupt before you are disrupted." But how? "It was all completely unknown. When I said, 'Hey, we need an app in the app store,' no one knew why." By the time Lieberman left Pizza Hut for Taco Bell, she had created a billion-dollar e-commerce business.[2]

This is how many of the best digital marketing stories begin: experimentation. Either a start-up trying to break through on a shoestring or a large brand trying to figure out the upcoming consumer cohort puts a little money behind someone with big ideas, and a new way of doing things is born.

Transactions make or break a restaurant. If enough guests are coming in the door, the restaurant has a good chance of making it. If guests aren't coming, no amount of lovely ambiance, perfect food, great operations, or cost reductions will keep it in business. Restaurateurs know this—it shows up in industry sayings like "sales hide all sins" and industry behavior embracing anything that purports to drive the top line. It also explains why the restaurant industry spends billions on traditional advertising every year.

The fixed costs associated with operating a restaurant—rent and labor chief among them—mean that revenue leverage does more to determine profitability than almost anything a restaurateur can spend time on. Rising revenue against fixed costs expands margins. In a competitive industry where labor is tight and consumers expect 30 percent of their dollar back in food, there are very few other line items that can deliver profit the way revenue does.

As a result, restaurant marketing is a big business. Restaurants are the fifth-largest TV advertiser in America. Most franchise agreements factor in a required 5 percent spend on marketing, which suggests that in total, the restaurant industry is spending about $50 billion a year on various forms of advertising. McDonald's alone spent $1.5 billion in the US in 2018, according to Ad Age.[3]

From the door hanger left at your house to the sponsorship you see during the NBA Finals, restaurant marketing is clearly considered critical to any restaurant's success. But old-fashioned marketing is rapidly losing favor with the advent of digital marketing. "Traditional marketing when done well can have massive impact," Lieberman says. "There is huge power in reach. But digital marketing can be faster and cheaper. With the speed that the culture is moving right now, you can't have that old-school mindset."

The restaurant industry has taken note. Restaurant industry marketing spend has shifted over the last ten years. "When I started at Taco Bell in 2012, we spent nothing on digital advertising, and that was pretty typical," Lieberman says. Now, media investment company GroupM estimates that digital ad spending across all industries has matched that of traditional— fully half of all advertising spending. The restaurant industry is a little behind other industries, primarily because it is not as easy to fulfill your purchase intent online—unlike, say, being able to contact a car dealer or an insurance company online to find out more. "Restaurant industry-wide, that number is getting close—perhaps now a third of its marketing budget is spent on digital," says Lieberman.

Digital marketing has come far in the past decade. "You can go to the Wayback Machine [online archive] and see the very first version of the Pizza Hut website," Lieberman says. "Early days was taking the same thing you were doing in the physical world and doing it in a digital world—explaining why consumers should order online instead of using the phone without giving them a uniquely digital experience. Or asking them to follow a brand on Facebook using display banners and landing pages with no real benefit to the consumer for doing so."

Many restaurants still do digital the same way today. They know they need a website, a Facebook page, an Instagram account. They ask consumers to follow and like them. They may even give the occasional discount for doing so. But most of the activity online is simply a digitized version of a postcard the brand might have sent in the mail twenty years ago. "Most good innovation comes from solving a problem," Lieberman points out. "Some businesses struggle because they are doing digital for the sake of doing digital. Consumers don't think about digital. They think about how their lives can be easier."

While being present in the place where consumers spend their time is an important step in awareness-building, it's just the first step of an overarching digital ecosystem that drives not just awareness of a brand, but the start of an ongoing engagement.

Even that first step of catching attention is more of a challenge than it sounds. "You have one second to grab attention," Lieberman says. "The average attention span of a person is now less than a goldfish. People are very busy and very distracted. Everyone is multitasking." You have to put yourself in your consumer's head and ask "Why would I care? Why would I share?" A great offer, a great product, or a great message might do the trick, but getting attention depends on the medium. The consumer is sitting in front of the TV while looking at TikTok and messaging their friends. As Lieberman puts it, "You can't just take one piece of content and peanut butter spread it across all mediums. TikTok is very musically driven, so sound and music are really important. In Facebook, the consumer likely doesn't have sound on, so the first lines are really important. Instagram requires stand-out images. Everything has to be customized for where it is going to be seen."

The amount of work required to create content for each platform is a daunting task. The largest brands have entire departments or outside agencies engaged in generating different versions of the same message. They plan campaigns months in advance to give teams time to fine-tune the content for up to ten different platforms and do a final "wall-walk" to make sure it all feels connected. Lieberman says, "As long as you know who you are and what you stand for, then you can give trust to the individuals leading different aspects of the campaigns."

Amy Kavanaugh Mason has spent her career helping companies define who they are and what they stand for. First as a Global Relationship Manager at Edelman supporting Starbucks with Howard Schultz during their turnaround in 2008, then at Taco Bell with Greg Creed during their turnaround in 2012, Mason applied what is now called "social listening" to take the brands back to their roots and connect them with their consumers.

In the years leading up to 2008, "Starbucks was focused on growth over the experience." Rather than letting the growth be a result of the experience, Starbucks was prioritizing unit growth and monetizing "every square inch" of the restaurant, Mason recalls. "We did a consumer brand study that told us that customers were coming to Starbucks not based on want or need, but based on convenience. They told us they were coming because they had to. They wanted a fresh-brewed cup of coffee, and we were not delivering on that. As Howard says in [his book] *Onward*, 'We had lost our way.'"[4]

Mason saw an opportunity to champion public engagement as a growth strategy for the company. By her definition, public engagement is the intersection of who your brand is and what it stands for, with the needs of the target consumer. "We gave consumers an opportunity to have a say, and we went back to what made us great to begin with. They were walking into this barrage of things and all they really wanted was Pike Place Roast with thirty minute or less hold times," she says, referring to their commitment to brew smaller batches of coffee so it was as fresh as it could be.

It's true that large consumer brand studies can cost hundreds of thousands of dollars, and sophisticated social listening tools that monitor millions of consumer utterances across platforms can be even more expensive, yet the beauty of social media is that a single restaurant can engage in listening to its own customers without spending a dime.

"The mindset I would instill regardless of size is to be passionately curious," says Lieberman. "For a big business, that might be a team analyzing data. For an independent restaurant, that might be reading your Yelp reviews. Get close to the consumer to understand what you should be focused on. Be customer-led." An astounding number of small businesses never read their Yelp and Google reviews, much less act on the feedback they receive, yet the information is right there for the taking. Listening with curiosity and leaving defensiveness behind can be eye-opening.

In 2011, Taco Bell was not listening. The class-action law firm Beasley Allen filed suit claiming that Taco Bell's beef did not contain enough beef to be called beef.[5] "I was brokenhearted about their response to the accusations that they did not have beef in their beef," Mason recalls—even though at that point she was not employed by Taco Bell.

> I met the Chief Marketing Officer of Taco Bell at a Selena Gomez concert [where they had both taken their daughters to hear the star perform]. I told him, "You're ruining my favorite brand." There were all these things being said about them, and instead the brand was responding with price promotions on thirty-second spots that had nothing to do with the consumers' questions or desire to know the brand. If you think you can scream over what people are saying or create an incentive to come, it won't work.

When she went to work for her favorite brand the following year, Mason saw that Taco Bell had two jobs to do in order to get the love back with their customers. Job number one—just like at Starbucks—was to remember what the core of the brand was about. The company needed to reclaim its purpose—or as Mason says, its "why." Early in her career, Mason worked in the PR department at Apple, another of her favorite brands. "And that's how I learned about the why. 'Why' enrolls people in your cause."

The why at Taco Bell became their current tagline "Live Mas," a consumer-friendly Spanglish version of the brand statement Mason wrote:

"We feed people's lives with mas."[6] *Mas* in Spanish means "more," and it was the perfect word for a brand that had introduced Mexican food to much of America, redefined what a consumer could get by offering a consistent "value" menu, and introduced the refillable drink station on the front-of-house side of the order counter. It was also a guiding star for ongoing innovation: Would this product, channel, messaging, or team experience offer more value? More flavor? More heart?

Even smaller restaurants can take a leaf from Taco Bell's playbook. "For independent restaurants," Mason says, "the exercise is not that different. Why did you start the restaurant in the first place? What were you trying to bring to your community that was lacking before you opened your doors? The clarity in knowing your purpose will help you decide where to spend your time and effort, and how to make sure that everything you do ladders back up to your brand's distinctive why."

Job number two for Taco Bell was to remember who their customers were and what they wanted from the brand. About half the US population eats at Taco Bell each month, making it seem like everyone is a customer.[7] Indeed, Taco Bell customers come from all demographic profiles and geographies. But half the US population does not eat at Taco Bell each month, so if all demographic profiles and geographies are represented among customers, which half is which? What is different about them? And for those who are coming, are they all seeking the same things, or do they use the brand for different reasons at different times? For each group, what do they want from the brand?

"What we found was a glimmer of hope. We had a rabid fan base. And they all wanted the same thing from us: they wanted us to love the food as much as they did," explains Mason. If the why was the brand's purpose, then delivering on what consumers want was the brand's promise, and it required Taco Bell to demonstrate their love of the food. The insights consumers offered freely to the brand through social media led to clean-label ingredients, the creation of the vegetarian menu, the launch of Cantina Bell, and a commitment to excellence for every single crunchy taco that went out the door.[8]

Once these foundational elements are in place—a firm understanding of who you are as a brand and a firm understanding of who your customers are and what they want from you—sharing your message across channels becomes much easier. "I've seen brands use all the channels, but it's disjointed," Mason says. "They've lost the plot on what they are trying to communicate. If you know your purpose and your promise, you can deliver on them. That consistency generates trust. As media gets more fragmented, and our attention gets more fragmented, you can't necessarily tell an entire story with one headline, picture, or six-second video. Instead, you tell aspects of the story through each channel. Certain content makes more sense on certain channels. They might be different, but they have to add up to something. The bite-sized pieces have to ladder up to a larger story."

Unless they are incredibly digital forward or have a digitally savvy employee hiding among the hourlies, a small brand may not have the bandwidth to engage in this kind of multi-front war. It is most likely not even practical to try. Better to start small—with the channel where your consumers mostly live—then branch out as your restaurant achieves success in marketing or its revenue growth generates a larger marketing budget.

For most independent restaurants, mastering the digital delivery platforms is the first step in marketing their restaurant digitally. But mastering them takes more than just flipping them on. "This all takes money," Lieberman says. "The easiest thing to do is default to the marketplace [platform]." A digital delivery platform can get a restaurant started on its journey without spending a fortune. The beauty of the platforms is their ease in making any restaurant with any capabilities immediately available online. Going full digital requires hiring a team; using a platform does not. Lieberman continues, "Hiring a digital marketing manager is as expensive as hiring a brand manager. That's expensive for a small company."

Jenn Parker, Founding Chief Operating Officer for virtual restaurant company Nextbite, has spent the last three years honing digital marketing for restaurants, especially getting the most out of the delivery platforms. Parker's restaurants were not national brands. Instead, they were very small brands that existed only on the Internet. Without a brick-and-mortar presence or a big marketing budget to drive brand awareness and that first purchase, Parker did exactly what Lieberman recommended: she defaulted to the marketplace, but in a way that served the interests of her brands, not just of the platforms.

Parker's main goal for a restaurant? Use the third-party delivery platform algorithms to your advantage. To do that, she says there are three must-dos for restaurants on the digital delivery platforms. You could think of all three as the equivalent of search engine optimization (SEO).

First, Parker says, "I always recommend running promotions super heavy for the first ninety days." The platforms have carousels on their sites and apps that highlight specific restaurants to users. "One of the carousels is the order again or the favorites. By running a promotion, you're essentially buying new customers, and then for those customers, you're always going to show up in that carousel, which is usually a top carousel on the delivery platform homepage."[9]

Which promotions to use? Parker says her favorite is the new customer promo, which, depending on the platform and the restaurant's choices, offers customers new to that brand a discount off the food, free or reduced delivery costs, or even a free item with purchase. Typically, the new customer promos offer a higher discount than others. "It probably costs the restaurant another 20 percent. So if the third-party delivery companies are already charging you 30 percent, and the discount costs another 20 percent, it's going to cost you 50 percent of your ticket price."

Parker recognizes that sounds steep. "Most restaurants ask, 'Why would I do that?' But there's always a cost to acquiring a customer," she points out. "This option is immediate, it's quick, and it's short term—you aren't going to offer these promos forever. Do it for ninety days, get your new customers, provide good service, and then turn the promos off."

Switching your mindset about tracking costs is critical here. Restaurants who view the 30 percent of ticket delivery platform fee and a 20 percent discount to the food as food and paper costs are always going to resent the delivery platforms and find the fee too high. Restaurants who view the 50 percent of ticket fee as a marketing fee to acquire a specific customer will find it one of the best deals in the industry.

Acquiring new customers is hard. And expensive. A restaurant is either going to spend money on traditional media (like ads and flyers), digital media (like Instagram influencers and paid search results), or platforms. In light of the importance of revenue to restaurant survival, and compared to the options, the platforms offer a great way to introduce consumers to your food.

The second must-do, Parker says, is to be smart about how you label your menu items. "You need to create categories, and then you need to label each of your items with keywords. For example, if you're a salad concept, rather than calling it something like 'The Meredith,' it would be 'The Meredith Salad.' You need to put in as many keywords as possible in the item name." Parker always recommends some brief description to the food items that include some key ingredients as well.

> Consumers won't always search by your restaurant name or your specific item name. Again, if "The Meredith Salad" was a farro-based superfood salad with roasted vegetables, people might find you searching your restaurant name or the item name if they already know you—but if they don't, they are more likely to discover you searching for a "farro salad bowl" or "kale roasted vegetable salad." The more you can include in your description, the better. Put yourself in the mind of the consumer, and imagine what they would be looking for that would lead them to each of your products.

The third and final must-do is to choose the lowest possible prep time in your settings. That makes sense for operational reasons—as we saw in the previous chapter—but it matters for marketing purposes too. Parker recommends, "Keep your prep time at ten minutes or below. Once the third-party delivery platforms add their time on, it's going to be another twenty minutes for delivery at best. So right then, you're at thirty minutes. Being in that thirty-minute time frame is going to put you into the fast delivery carousel." Once again this highlights your restaurant right on the homepage of the delivery platform.

Even if your restaurant isn't fast enough to make it on to the fast delivery carousel, the delivery time still matters. People don't generally think ahead to when they will be hungry. They place orders when they are already hungry. So, Parker reasons, customers are looking for short delivery times. "When you start seeing hour-long delivery times, it's because the restaurant is probably setting a twenty- to twenty-five-minute prep time. Unless you have very strong brand equity or some really fantastic, differentiated product, you're going to get passed over."

Parker has one bonus tip to go with her three must-dos. "Photos are an incredible investment," she counsels. "You need something that looks a bit better than what you can do on your own. All of the online ordering services offer to do the photography for you, but you can hire a food stylist and professional photographer for about $2,000 a day. One hundred percent it's important, and restaurants should not skimp on the photos." Parker says the platforms don't (yet!) use the photos in their search algorithms the way Google does, "but they are super important for the consumer. Even if you are a mom and pop, you have to remember that you are competing with the big brands that employ full-time food stylists and ad agencies."

Once you have put all of these strategies into action, Parker recommends continuing to experiment with the various promotions that the platforms make easy to run. "Each platform has different ones. Of course, my favorite is the new customer promo, but there are lots of interesting things you can do. For instance, setting happy hour times if you're really slow in the middle of the day or if you are trying to drive late-night delivery." The key is trying, measuring, and pivoting. "I like to try a bunch of different ones," says Parker. "You can turn them on and off so easily. I like to try them for a week and see where you're getting an ROI."

This kind of test and learn is a critical part of marketing digitally. The platforms make it easy to tweak and trial. If a restaurant finds something that works, they can do more of it. And if they find that something doesn't pay off, they can stop it. "The back-end user experience on the platforms is getting a lot better," Parker says. "They're incorporating a lot of graphs and statistics and spell it out for you. There is literally a button that says, 'see how your promo did' and you can compare it to other promos. Just try a bunch of different things and see what works. If you have multiple restaurant locations, let the GMs do it and see what works at the location level." Such local experimentation, of course, demands that each contributor to the experiment knows the brand. What is in bounds? What is out of bounds? What is the brand voice? What is its look?

You can't go wrong if you apply Mason's two principles: remember what the core of your brand is about and remember who your customers are and what they want from the brand. Purpose and promise—that's how your restaurant will attract the customers who really "get" you.

Now all you need to do is keep them coming back for more.

Chapter 13

ENGAGING AND DELIGHTING YOUR CUSTOMERS

essica's Tuesday was full of back-to-back meetings. The late-morning pang of hunger shuddered through her as she remembered another day without breakfast. Today's lunch would need to fit between the finance meeting at 11:00 a.m., her team's project meeting at midday, and the creative director's outline of the rebranding work for one of their main clients.

She checked her phone as she was running late. A banner popped down from the top as she headed toward the meeting room. "Feeling guilty about yesterday's steak sandwich?" it asked. *Well, I do now*, she thought to herself, inadvertently selecting the banner that stretched across the screen: "Try the new Cajun Chicken Salad—it's less than five hundred calories and will get your week back on track." She didn't have long, but within a few clicks, the order was processed and would be delivered an hour later at the time she chose. One less thing to worry about as she entered the room to greet her colleagues in finance.

Once a consumer has discovered your restaurant brand, your number one job is to engage them as a repeat customer. But here's where the discord really gets loud between the restaurant operators and the digital delivery platforms. The digital delivery company sees the customer as theirs—they acquired them, they serviced them, and they own the data. The fact that your restaurant fulfilled the order is, to them, irrelevant.

Zach Goldstein is a true believer that third-party (digital delivery platform) to first-party (direct/owned channels) conversion is a must-have. He built his company, Thanx, on the idea that all restaurants—not just the largest enterprise-level brands—needed to focus on the lifetime value (LTV) of their customers. Through digital customer engagement, Thanx helps restaurants and other brick-and-mortar businesses reach new customers and broaden relationships with existing ones.

Goldstein puts it this way: "You and the third party have completely different incentives for the next time that customer orders food. Imagine you are a salad restaurant, and a consumer orders a salad from you. You are incentivized to make the best salad possible to keep that customer coming back to order more salads. The digital delivery aggregators are incentivized to drive frequency to the marketplace—and variety drives frequency."[1] So rather than promote your salad restaurant to that same consumer again, the digital delivery platform will also put other choices in front of the customer.

When he founded Thanx in 2011, Goldstein says, restaurants were focused on customer acquisition—but those newly acquired customers were simply leaking out of the bucket. Restaurants spent more to acquire more but never created value through the customers they already had.

Goldstein has long voiced concerns about the negative impact digital delivery platforms might have on the restaurant industry. In 2019, he wrote an article comparing the rise of digital delivery platforms to online travel agencies (OTAs).[2] Goldstein argued that the platforms not only charge high fees, but also take the opportunity away from restaurants to drive loyalty to their brand. When OTAs executed the same playbook in the travel industry, they were able to shift large portions of revenue and profit from the operators to themselves. The travel platforms as of this writing are worth more than the brands themselves—Booking Holdings (the largest publicly held travel platform) is valued at $70 billion, and Marriott (the largest public hotel company) is valued at $32 billion.

Goldstein shares his views like an economics professor giving a lecture—and an economics professor would agree with him. Industries "with greater supplier fragmentation," he writes, "experience more severe disaggregation" (*disaggregation* being the technical term for a third party stepping between the brand and the customer). Goldstein again makes a comparison with the travel industry: hotels were more fragmented than airlines, and it was in the hotel sector that OTAs took a greater share of the bookings. In the restaurant industry, the situation is even more extreme. "Restaurants are orders of magnitude more fragmented," Goldstein points out. "If you exclude the top handful of restaurants, it's incredibly fragmented. The restaurants can't fight back."

Converting a customer from a third-party order to a first-party order drives significant benefits to a restaurant. The first we covered in Chapter 7: better profits. The digital delivery platforms can charge up to 30 percent of revenue for an order placed on its app. When the order comes instead through the restaurant's own website, there is no fee. The delivery still must be fulfilled, and there's a cost to that, but it is a fraction of the 30 percent total fee a platform charges for bringing the customer to the restaurant.

The second benefit is less obvious: the consumer relationship and the data that relationship generates. When a consumer places an order directly with the restaurant fulfilling that order (first-party), the restaurant has the opportunity to engage that consumer in ongoing dialogue about customer satisfaction, promotional offers, and loyalty rewards. When a consumer places an order through a digital delivery platform (third-party), the fulfilling restaurant will never know who ordered the item, whether they liked it, if they will come back, or what the restaurant could do to influence the consumer to order again.

Assuming a restaurant has succeeded in executing a great menu flawlessly all the way through to the receiving consumer, a window opens to convert a happy customer to a first-party ordering customer. The consumer should never be confused about where the food came from. If the answer to "Where did you order from?" is something along the lines of "Oh, some pizza place"—that's a bad outcome for the operator. Worse, the consumer might remember which delivery platform they used to place the order but not which restaurant fulfilled it. Without the brick-and-mortar restaurant—with its signage, design, experience, and other tangible "brand moments"—restaurants must use what they have in the delivery bag to drive brand awareness. Packaging at the very least should be stickered or stamped with branded images, if not customized. Napkins, bags, and thank you cards are all additional opportunities to leave an impression.

Taiwanese dumpling restaurant brand Din Thai Fung excels on this front. No customer receiving a delivery of their white cardstock packaging printed with bold red and black Taiwanese characters would ever say vaguely the next day that they ordered from "some Chinese place." The goal, though, is not to indiscriminately spread branding at every opportunity. The goal is to selectively use packaging materials to convey the brand and make the recipient feel a connection with the restaurant.

In many ways, this is similar to the beautiful packaging phenomenon that was first innovated by Apple, proliferated across technology, and is now emulated by omnichannel and direct-to-consumer brands.[3] The idea is simple: if a consumer's first experience of your brand is opening a box rather than coming to your store, make that box tell a story that is aligned with your brand. The "unboxing" video review trend takes this a step further: if consumers are likely to reveal their new products via Internet video, design your packaging so that it looks beautiful and your brand stands out in that video.

For restaurants, if a consumer is no longer experiencing your brand through your brick-and-mortar location and its in-person customer service, you must find relevant ways to share the brand. Delivery consumers run the risk of experiencing the restaurant as simply a fulfillment partner of DoorDash or Uber Eats. It is, after all, the driver who is handing off the food, usually from a DoorDash or Uber Eats branded bag. Even if the food is in plain brown craft paper without the delivery platform brand on it, the consumer will quickly forget the restaurant and remember only the delivery partner.

Los Angeles sushi restaurant Sugarfish offers a standout dinner unboxing experience. The restaurant hired Zaudhaus design firm to develop its branding, including its delivery/takeout packaging.[4] Each box is a pleasure to open, and rumors are that the box itself costs more than $5—an incredible expense for a "Trust Me" prix fixe meal that starts at $27. Items are separated by dividers, ensuring that nigiri does not touch edamame. Sauces are individually labeled, and the meal comes with instructions about which sauce to apply to which item. Yelp reviewers rave about the packaging. And, sure enough, there are unboxing videos of Sugarfish meals available on YouTube.

The next step after delivering excellent food in a branded experience is inviting the consumer to order directly with the brand. If the restaurant has nailed the prior two steps of execution and branding, consumers are much more likely to follow through. Consistent reminders of the availability of online ordering—on the receipt, a thank you card, or even the packaging itself—are table stakes. Instructions on how to order directly, or even a reward for ordering directly, can push an indifferent consumer to take the extra effort to order on the restaurant's own website.

Especially during the COVID-19 pandemic, many consumers were swayed by pleas to order directly from restaurants to help them stay afloat. DoorDash, Uber Eats, and Grubhub all temporarily reduced or eliminated fees during the 2020 shutdown. But as the economy started to revive, fees returned to normal, and restaurants started to actively market direct ordering.[5] However, most consumers, even the most community-minded, aren't willing to consistently put in extra effort to order directly. This is where creating a "frictionless experience" becomes the most important factor in influencing consumer behavior toward first-party ordering.

Tressie Lieberman of Chipotle says frictionless means "your experience is delightful. You can't feel the pain points." No images of the food, the app not working on a phone, having to go through a log-in process—these all rate as pain points. She's quick to point out that no consumer would describe anything as frictionless, "but they know when things are." As a point of comparison, Lieberman says, "Amazon is my favorite app because it is super, super easy. They have been relentlessly focused on solving for any tiny pain point." She thinks the same can apply to restaurants.[6]

Lieberman points to the launch of Chipotle's "Lifestyle Bowls"—a range of offerings for people who follow specific dietary regimes such as keto, Whole30, and paleo—as an example of frictionless commerce. "When I joined Chipotle, being the passionately curious person that I am, I started listening. People were trying to figure out which Chipotle ingredients could go into Whole30. With the Whole30 Lifestyle Bowl, the team member doesn't have to know. The consumer doesn't have to know. All they have to do is push a button and shortcut the experience." Chipotle could see in its online ordering data that the lifestyles its consumers were accessing most were Whole30 and keto. "The Lifestyle Bowls solved a problem. It's hard to eat Whole30. Being able to make it easy for consumers is a great way to drive sales, but also to demonstrate that you get the community."

That kind of ease flows through the entire online experience. It helps to consider a restaurant's website as their "virtual front of house," suggests Caroline Sizer, an investor with RSE Ventures, whose restaurant investments include &pizza, Bluestone Lane, Milk Bar, Momofuku, and Fuku. Whatever functions the brick-and-mortar front of house served, the website has to do digitally: make it easy to order, share the brand story, create a connection, and enable a feedback loop. "To serve the function of a brick-and-mortar front of house, the website has to create human interaction and a human relationship." Sizer believes firmly that "food is an experience; it is not a commodity. You can't just put your menu online. You have to create a digital experience."[7]

Kevin Rice, Cofounder and Chief Marketing Officer at Hathway, a digital experience developer with top digital restaurant clients among its roster, could not agree more. "Convenience is king right now," he affirms. "Our data across our clients shows us that about 75 percent of restaurant website visitors are there to transact. So if ordering isn't front and center, you are making consumers jump through a lot of hoops. Most restaurant websites are bifurcated: a CMS-powered [content management system] website about the brand, then their white-labeled ordering interface. If you go through the flow the consumers do—home page, menu, menu product, white-labeled transaction cart—it ends up being a fifteen-step process." A lot of restaurants don't think about user journeys, Rice says: "They think about their needs—limited-time offers, loyalty program, corporate social responsibility. These things are important, but they don't belong on their homepage."[8]

It's the same evolution that retail went through about ten years ago, Rice points out. "If you want to see what's going to happen, just look at where retail was. Most retailers had a CMS-powered website that clicked you over to shop.nordstrom.com." It took time to get to placing e-commerce first and then story second. "Ultimately, that's where the restaurant industry is going to go," he predicts. "True Food Kitchen is a great example of the future. There is a story not just behind the brand, but behind each individual menu item."

One of the greatest consumer wins that platforms deliver is the ease of price comparison, but it can be a two-edged sword. Many restaurants experiment with differential pricing to get and keep customers on first-party channels. It is common for restaurant owners to tell us, "I just price my menu up on the delivery platforms to account for the 30 percent fee they are taking." However, as a customer acquisition tool, a menu priced 40 percent higher puts itself at a major disadvantage when set against the other restaurants on the platform. Most consumers have some degree of price sensitivity, and when comparing similar items at different prices, they will choose the lower-priced items. This means increasing prices prevents most consumers from ever trying your brand and keeps your restaurant from impressing them and bringing them back. Worse, many consumers will not assume the price has been increased to account for platform fees—they will just assume your brand is expensive. This may in turn affect not only their willingness to try your brand for delivery, but their overall perception of your brand's value. What may have started as a strategy to even the margins between channels may end up turning customers off from your brand entirely—even in a brick-and-mortar setting.

The travel industry faced a similar dilemma. Airlines and hotels quickly found that increasing prices to offset OTA (online travel agency) fees ended up hurting their ability to attract guests. This led to the now-familiar fees that travel companies tack on to the base price quoted by the OTAs—fees for baggage, seat selection, standby flights, room types, resort services, checkout times, and more. OTAs combated these tacked-on fees by showing fees broken out separately, or including "fee assistant" filters among their options. Restaurants already have similar fees in the form of a delivery fee, which restaurants can set on each platform's back end. Likely more fees are coming—as we saw internationally, it is possible to charge a fee to guarantee delivery time. Already in e-commerce it is common practice to charge different shipping fees for different shipping times. Most restaurant consumers are willing to pay for the convenience of delivery. Better yet, and just as travel companies found, the creation of fees enables the practice of eliminating them as a benefit to the best customers. Restaurants can remove or reduce fees to first-party consumers, customers who have opted in to receive marketing from a restaurant, and frequent diners.

Once a consumer has opted in to a restaurant's system instead of a third-party platform, the digital marketing possibilities expand. Effective digital marketing that drives a strong ROI requires knowledge of the individual customers that buy from a particular restaurant. Email addresses, phone numbers, and purchase behavior enable targeted digital marketing that is much more likely to drive sales than blanket digital messaging all over Facebook or Google.

But creating benefits for your best customers requires knowing who they are. Customer relationship management (CRM) is a blanket term for all the strategies and technologies a company uses to interact with their customers, both past and future, and analyze those interactions. In a restaurant context, CRM enables restaurants to track who customers are, how to contact them, and what their purchase behavior is. Sophisticated restaurants can combine their in-house information with external sources such as demographic data or online behavioral tracking.

Even the most basic CRM can help restaurants scale hospitality. Remember Massimo Noja De Marco, Founder of Kitchen United? Before his ghost kitchen ventures, De Marco was first and foremost a restaurateur who knew his customers intimately. He knew their names, their birthdates, and their favorite items. And he used this knowledge to make each guest feel welcome, special, and valued. Ideally, every restaurant would have a De Marco working every shift, but that kind of consistency isn't possible. Technology makes it so. Human hosts, servers, and bartenders don't need to remember, out of the thousands of people they see each year, who spent the most on what and how often. Computers do the remembering for them and increasingly recommend offers that are suited exactly to guests based on their historical relationship with the restaurant. "Phase 1.0 of this evolution was everyone thought they needed a loyalty program and an app, but they didn't drive much value," says Thanx Founder Goldstein. "Phase 2.0 embraces the fact that there is more data: the use of marketing automation and being able to segment your customers to deliver them the right messages at the right time. The next frontier will be real data science and machine learning."

Platforms like Thanx make it easy for restaurants to develop relationships with their guests—who they are, what they like, how to you make them happy, and how to do it easily. "We run the front-end experience [websites and apps] of first-party online ordering. We combine that with CRM that groups consumers into cohorts. We then give robust tools to close the loop on marketing," says Goldstein. "It appeals to high-value customers who will not tolerate friction. With our platform, customers automatically get recognized and automatically get loyalty rewards. Brands that join our platform see a 30–75 percent increase in data capture."

Stacie Colburn Hayes, the CMO of Oath Pizza, is an avid user of the Thanx platform—and a digital marketing convert, having started her restaurant career in field marketing at Chipotle. She recalls the old days of traditional marketing: "You had a local team that marketed the restaurant to local neighborhoods. Building relationships. Sampling. With field marketing, you know it works over time, but with digital, you can see immediately what is happening. Higher ROI. More targeted."[9]

Digital marketing enables brand-building, customer acquisition, and remarketing (serving ads to people who have already visited your website) that doesn't feel like marketing. And as Colburn Hayes points out, "Gen Z doesn't want to be marketed to. If they feel like they are being marketed to, they won't eat with you." Loyalty programs work well, both as a way to help build the customer database that enables marketing and to drive frequency among the best guests. They don't have to be complicated, and in fact, Colburn Hayes thinks the simpler the better:

> Ease of use is really important. With platforms like Thanx, consumers just sign up their credit card and any time they use it, they get loyalty points. Rewards pop up; the consumer doesn't have to remember. At Oath we keep it very simple: $5 off for $55 spent. It's more fun for marketers to come up with programs than it is for consumers to use them, so that often creates really complex loyalty programs. It is confusing for consumers to understand what they get out of it.

The best programs also "make users feel special with surprise offers or perks," Colburn Hayes says. "It's really important to keep loyal customers engaged and happy."

Thanking your customers through a well-designed loyalty program is one thing, but reaching the right customer with the right message at the right time is quite another. This approach, called "one-to-one marketing" (often written 1:1 marketing), customizes messages to consumers based on their behaviors. "One-to-many" marketing (traditional broadcast or published marketing) serves the same message about pepperoni pizza to everyone watching the NBA playoffs, whether they have a history of buying pepperoni pizza or not. Through 1:1 marketing, a brand can offer the right kind of pizza to each prospective customer based on their order history.

These types of customized offers can increase frequency and check size among existing customers. Like the well-trained server offering a favorite dish or something new to try at just the right time, 1:1 marketing offers consumers customized offers—but at scale.

Adam Brotman is CEO of Brightloom, which creates behavioral segmentation and actionable marketing programs. His company takes the position that "a consumer, a human being, who has a relationship with a brand, deserves to be engaged with in a way that's relevant. You deserve to be engaged with by a brand in a way that *knows* you. It makes you feel like your love for the brand is being reciprocated." By way of example, he says, "If you're vegetarian, you shouldn't get steak offers."[10]

Now considered a leader in the digitization of the restaurant space. Way back in 2009, Brotman was the Chief Digital Officer at Starbucks. At that time, Brotman's strategies that took Starbucks into apps, online ordering, order-ahead pickup, and loyalty were somewhat shocking to the rest of the restaurant industry—and with good reason. Up to that point, he says wryly, "You couldn't download a burrito."

Only large, national brands could even afford the anonymized credit card data and data science required to prove out the business case of these new strategies. But those same brands were likely to be publicly held companies and have pressures on their metrics from Wall Street. For a small company with no data scientists, it was impossible.

Brightloom now makes this intelligence available to all restaurants, not just the megabrands who can afford to build custom apps and have extensive in-house developer teams. "We use data science to create our segments. We use a predictive customer LTV [lifetime value] model and a predictive recommendation model, and some others." These predictive models churn out what each customer should be recommended and offered. "We have built-in control groups. You can automatically measure the incremental lifts."

"Every CEO of a restaurant company today has to think of themselves as a Chief Digital Officer," says Brotman.

> If 50 percent of your revenue went through a single store, think of how good that store would be. So if 50 percent of your revenue is running through your digital channels, you have to be proficient in that. You can't fight what's going to happen. The consumer's mindset has shifted, but they are still human. The same basic principles still apply. The emotional connection hasn't changed. That's still your North Star. The experience, the relationship. Consumers just expect to have that interaction digitally now.

If all of this sounds overwhelming, the good news is that companies like Thanx and Brightloom are making technology accessible. SaaS (software as a service) companies can build for independent restaurants and small chains the kinds of software tools that previously only national brands could afford. "If you want to get an app, loyalty, order ahead, and even connect them all—you can do it tomorrow. Any number of services can get your digital ecosystem going. It won't be super high fidelity, but it will be fine. Even great," says Brotman. Once your brand has that digital ecosystem in place, you can use the data it generates to drive incremental sales. "The most powerful thing you can do is personalize your communications to a customer."

Sebastien Pavy, partner with consulting firm Bain & Company, describes the technology behind the Brightloom and Thanx approach. It sounds like science fiction, but is already happening today. "Starbucks and Domino's totally get it," Pavy says. "As a result they get better frequency [of visits from returning guests] and higher check. Sending the same offer to everybody is insane. Send different messaging and offers to different segments."[11]

The most advanced companies, like Starbucks and Domino's, are sending out offers perfectly optimized and perfectly timed to drive action by the recipient. They do this by analyzing individual consumer purchase history data and offer response data. Segmentation and A/B testing is the most basic version of this approach, but restaurants are now starting to emulate tech companies in their use of multi-armed bandit (MAB) algorithms to match the perfect offer to each consumer. These algorithms use machine learning to improve the offers in near real-time. "A/B testing is now like the Middle Ages," says Pavy. "It's very manual. It takes too long. It can take years to scale. Machine learning makes you learn as you go."

Nevertheless, Pavy says, starting small is better than not starting at all. "Step zero. Start with five segments. Activate them with different messages." Just the refinement of targeting specific offers to specific types of consumers will increase the likelihood of a guest engaging with the message. Which then begs the question, "What is the library of offers you are sending to your customers? They shouldn't all be discounts. Someone who is ordering $25 of pizza on a Friday night maybe isn't looking for a discount. Talk about the products. Talk about LTOs [limited-time offers]. Talk about returning."

These tools all sound fantastic for deepening commercial relationships with existing consumers—increasing frequency and basket size once a consumer has affiliated with your brand. But growth also requires expanding brand awareness and generating brand trials among nonaffiliated consumers. Goldstein says, "Your highest value customers are a great source of future customers. When prompted to do so, they will refer. Our platform leans on that pretty heavily. That is a direct way to acquire." Colburn Hayes agrees: "Refer-a-friend offers are really important—both for the referring customer and the receiving customer."

Indirectly, the algorithms that drive the Internet can also lead similar (or "lookalike") customers to discover your brand. "The more sophisticated evolution is to find more people who look like your VIPs," says Goldstein. "Use our segmentation, which is updated in real-time, and run digital ads with lookalike audiences. It's a DTC (direct-to-consumer) digitally native approach that has been used for ten years . . . and it's now available to restaurants."

Colburn Hayes says, "It doesn't have to be complex. Some restaurant companies with one location will have literal physical signups and an intern that puts it into a spreadsheet, and that's the beginning. You can integrate into a more premium platform later." In the meantime, even that spreadsheet of names and contact information is incredibly valuable. "Many services that exist today help you identify a group of new people that look like your existing customers. For example, you can take your list of email addresses, upload it to Facebook, and then say, 'I want to market to people who are exactly like these.'" This approach, called "lookalike audience targeting," has become the standard in digital marketing. Using a "seed audience" (known guests) of as few as a thousand people can help platforms like Facebook find customers who are likely to be interested in your restaurant.

All of this is not to say that digital delivery platforms don't have a place in building relationships with customers, both current and future. Even the most digitally forward restaurant brands, who have mastered first-party ordering, digital marketing, CRMs, and 1:1 marketing, continue to use digital delivery platforms. Chipotle, Chick-fil-A, and Wingstop can all be found on the DoorDash app. Why? Because customers can be found on the platforms. And where customers are searching for options, the wise will make themselves an option—then convert those customers to first-party fans.

Chapter 14

VIRTUAL RESTAURANTS

F
or Alex Canter, his family's restaurant was always his playground. First, when he was a child hardly tall enough to see over the tables, and later entrepreneurially, as an adult overseeing innovation and e-commerce for the family business.

Alex was born into the fourth generation of a famous Jewish delicatessen, Canter's Deli, started by his great-grandfather in 1931. Located in the heart of Los Angeles's Fairfax district, it rivals New York's best. "My dad started working there as a teenager and hasn't taken a day off since," Alex explains. His own entrée to the business happened even earlier. "When I was four years old, they used to push me around on a busboy cart, which earned me the name of 'Mini Patron.' At thirteen, I started waiting tables."[1]

Not long after, Alex started taking on larger projects: running the bar, setting up a vegetarian menu, developing a catering service. The question in his mind, he says, was always, "How do I take this and make it relevant to what's coming next?"

His childhood hobby? "I used to collect restaurant menus as a kid; I was fascinated with the menu creation process and pricing." It wasn't long before Alex's childhood love of restaurant menus intersected with the new world of digital delivery. Alex developed a virtual brand operating within

Canter's and named it Grilled Cheese Heaven. Utilizing the deli's kitchen, it began delivering a separate in-demand menu for the LA market. There is no outdoor sign, and there are no plans for brick-and-mortar locations. Alex's nascent brand exists only online.

There is no guessing about their signature product. That's by design. Millennials and Gen Z are less loyal to brands than the Gen Xers and Boomers before them.[2] Instead of thinking brand first, menu second, item last, they search for the exact food they want and settle on the source from there. If you're a hungry twenty-one-year-old taking a video game break, Grilled Cheese Heaven is a match made in . . . Well, you get the idea.

"When online ordering started to pop up, we [Canter's] were one of the first restaurants to be on a lot of these platforms," Alex says, referring to apps like Postmates, DoorDash, and Uber Eats. "Postmates tell me Canter's is one of their top-selling restaurants." Alex is also now Founder and CEO of Ordermark—an online ordering platform for restaurants—and the virtual restaurant creator Nextbite.

Digitally native restaurant brands are starting to experiment with new models that may well change the restaurant industry entirely. These brands have been born in the digital world to fulfill a virtual restaurant strategy. From brand discovery through to promotions, ordering, and fulfillment, they exist entirely online without the need for a brick-and-mortar location. This may sound counterintuitive to those who have based their career on building a local favorite brand or developing a brick-and-mortar empire with identical unit expansion of the same brand. But restaurants struggling with the growing challenges of operating a brick-and-mortar location profitably, the increasing demand for online food ordering, and the post–COVID-19 pandemic new normal of social distancing have good reason to embrace a virtual restaurant strategy.

As consumer interactions become increasingly digital, the rules of the game change. No longer is the brand primarily about a restaurant's location, its ambience, or its servers. Instead, the brand is now about a restaurant's authentic voice online, its frictionless ease of use, and its ability to target, serve, and retain relevant customer segments.

A word of caution here: some restaurateurs say, "We're already there!" believing that possessing a website or an app makes them a virtual restaurant. Nothing could be further from the truth. A brand may offer online ordering and delivery fulfillment but still be a far cry from being a virtual brand. Being digitally native requires designing everything—from consumer experience to operating model—based on digital interaction being the only interaction a consumer has with your restaurant. Think of it this way: If a guest never walked through your door—if you had no door to walk through—what would they experience, feel about, know about your brand?

Virtual restaurants are coming, and fast. Some will be an additive "sales layer" to an existing restaurant, while others will emerge as new restaurants in their own right. Traditional brick-and-mortar brands will need to disrupt themselves to avoid being disrupted by these innovative and capital-light new concepts. How will they do that? Well, there are several tactics available to pivoting restaurateurs. The Canter family's willingness to risk cannibalizing their existing restaurant in order to launch a brand from within that carried many of the same items was one way of protecting the business from disruption from the outside. Alex Canter's insight put Canter's well ahead of the market.

Four distinctive models of virtual restaurants operate today: the owned model, the licensed model, the franchised model, and the completely virtual restaurant. All four represent business strategies that can operate inside existing restaurants, as a collection of restaurants, or inside of a ghost kitchen.

1. The Owned Model

By conceiving a digitally native companion—Grilled Cheese Heaven— Canter's created an owned model of virtual restaurant. The owned model is attractive because it keeps the restaurateur in control. After all, who knows your kitchen's capabilities better than you?

It's true that kitchen capabilities were a key consideration in Alex's menu design for Grilled Cheese Heaven. The items on the menu are similar to, but not the same as, Canter's core menu. They share ingredients, require minimal additional preparation, and have comparable cooking approaches—requiring no new equipment and only a small amount of incremental training for their line cooks.

Anticipating the virtual world that was then on their doorstep, Alex asked his dad one day, "If you could sell more of anything on the menu, what would it be?"

"Grilled cheese sandwiches," his dad shot back immediately.

It made sense to Alex. "Our food costs are low. They are easy to make. So as an experiment, we spun up this brand of several different grilled cheese sandwiches with different sauces and fillings. As soon as we uploaded this brand in 2018, we started getting twenty to thirty orders per day." When the menu was launched on various digital delivery platforms—Uber Eats, Postmates, DoorDash, and Grubhub—the Canters saw that brand in the virtual world was entirely different to its brick-and-mortar equivalent. "We learned in the Grilled Cheese Heaven model that GCH is not a brand that people know or care about or have seen before. Grilled Cheese Heaven doesn't even have a website or a direct ordering channel. Simply by existing on these platforms we're generating order volume—and that goes to show that branding helps for sure, but it's not even necessary in this format."

Grilled Cheese Heaven immediately added an entire sales layer to the underlying Canter's business. Several hundred thousand dollars of incremental orders coming through various delivery platforms generated tens of thousands of incremental profit dollars—all without spending capital on a new location, hiring additional cooks, or carrying additional inventory. The brand simply enables Alex's family business to market more effectively through hyper-focus on a different segment of consumers that cares more about cheese than pastrami—without compromising the guests that Canter's traditionally caters to. Ultimately, Grilled Cheese Heaven served a different consumer for a different occasion. "We added about $250,000 per year in gross sales with no additional overhead," says Alex.

The downside of the owned model is that few restaurateurs are good at everything. Some are stronger at operations, others at culinary, others at branding, and still others at marketing. And few in these first innings of digital adoption are excellent at digital marketing and delivery logistics. Canter's Deli is unique in its ability to leverage Alex's early understanding of the potential of online ordering and digital marketing for the restaurant industry. Alex is also unique in his combination of passion for the family business and willingness to experiment.

For many restaurateurs, there's a quicker path to replicating what Alex did for Canter's. If this is you, there are other ways to participate in the virtual restaurant game.

2. The Licensed Model

With a licensed model, any restaurant can overlay predesigned digitally native brands on top of their existing operations. Restaurateurs pay a fee—calculated in an array of ways—to use a brand that another entity has created. Here, the onus is on the restaurateur to ensure that the added virtual brand is compatible with the kitchen operations of the base concept.

The first company to help existing restaurants add delivery-only menus was Uber Eats in 2017.[3] It makes sense: after all, no company better knows local demand than a leader in delivery services. Elyse Propis led the virtual restaurant team. "I spoke with a lot of restaurants early on to understand what they liked and what they didn't [about the Uber Eats platform]. Pretty consistently, we heard that they liked incremental demand and logistics infrastructure that would have been very difficult for them to build on their own," Propis says.[4] "Virtual restaurants were created as one of several ways to help restaurants drive incremental revenue. Our priorities were to increase revenue for restaurant partners and increase selection for consumers."

"We first came up with the idea when we saw an uptick in searches for poke in Chicago. This was early 2017. At the time, poke was popular in

New York and California. But the slow brick-and-mortar rollout pace meant although consumers were searching for it, a customer could not find it on the platform," Propis recalls. So they approached high-performing sushi restaurants on the platform and provided them a virtual restaurant with minimal upfront costs and minimal risks. "We used data from the platform to design the menu and pricing and to estimate the revenue a restaurant could expect to earn. It was manual in the beginning, but once we saw that we were increasing revenue for restaurant partners, we could invest in the data science models to predict cuisine gaps at scale."

At Uber Eats, the focus is hyper-local. They know what consumers are ordering at the neighborhood level. More importantly, they know what consumers wish they could order—because they see what consumers search for and cannot find. Restaurants can partner directly with Uber Eats to bring a concept to the local market based on the demand that delivery platforms know is there. This minimizes the risk for any operator experimenting with new concepts through their kitchen.

These brands are "Uber exclusive." Lucky Cat Vegan, Ha! Poke, Hot Lips Fried Chicken[5]—none of them have their own websites. The only way consumers can find them is on Uber Eats's own platform.

Especially tempting, too, is the fact that restaurants already offering delivery through Uber Eats can add a brand without paying the delivery company beyond the normal Uber Eats percentage delivery fee. So what's in it for Uber Eats? Variety. Creating these brands for restaurants increases the variety on their app, which in turn generates frequency of use. Consumers get more choice while Uber increases its share of the ever-expanding food delivery market. Uber Eats's US market share was nearly 30 percent of meal delivery sales in Q1 2020, meaning one in three consumers who is ready to place an order is exposed to the brands that are most relevant to them.[6] And because the Uber Eats algorithms determine the brands that users get to see, the company can teach these fledgling offerings how to benefit from the algorithms.

Alex Canter expanded his Grilled Cheese Heaven idea into the company Nextbite creator of several different virtual brands. Similar to Uber Eats,

Nextbite also launches and licenses brands to restaurants that have capacity to serve more food and are looking for an off-the-shelf brand. Chief Growth Officer Geoff Madding sees Nextbite's key benefit to restaurants as "making this almost entirely painless to get up and running. We are building virtual chains that are being fulfilled by a number of restaurants across the country. We're designing concepts that are scalable and delivery-friendly. We're allowing any restaurant that has extra kitchen capacity to sign up this preloaded experience where they can follow these instructions, carry certain ingredients, and start turning on additional revenue through the same Ordermark device that's already in their kitchen," he says, referring to the service that combines orders from the different online ordering platforms.[7]

Like Uber Eats, Nextbite succeeds by leveraging big data analytics to predict what concepts will thrive in a hyper-local market. Unlike Uber Eats, Nextbite's brands have more reach than just one platform. They are all "national"—with the combined advertising dollars, consumer-facing websites, quick replicability, and scale to negotiate with the delivery platforms that benefit national chains.

Nextbite combines "the best of a national brand with the best of a hyper-local digitally native concept," says former Chief Operating Officer Jenn Parker. "It's a numbers game when you're dealing with the big delivery companies. Nextbite created five to ten brands and then launched them across the country to become a big player. Without any kind of brand equity, Nextbite can get five hundred locations on Uber Eats and become a strategic partner."[8]

The upside for an independent restaurant can be enormous. With all the fixed costs already in place, the incremental revenue from a virtual restaurant is mouthwateringly high, even with the licensing and delivery fees. "We have a restaurant in Indiana that turned on five of the Nextbite concepts," says Alex Canter, "and they started generating $75,000 a month in incremental sales—which for a single restaurant is a huge amount of extra money. We're generating all the traffic for them, and all they need to do is put their heads down and make food—which is what they do best."

The numbers tell the story: the table below offers a straight comparison between costs in a traditional restaurant versus a virtual restaurant. "If a restaurant turns on three brands doing $10,000 each a month, and they are keeping 30 percent of that as profit, that small business owner just added $10,000 a month in their pocket," says Parker.

Operating Cost	Traditional Restaurant (line item as % of revenue)	Virtual Restaurant (line item as % of revenue)
F&P (food and packaging)	30%	35%
Labor	30%	0% (no incremental labor, assumes all items can be produced by labor already in the restaurant)
Other (occupancy, insurance, marketing, royalties, etc.)	30%	5% (royalties only, assumes all other costs have been paid by the base business)
Delivery Fees	0%	30% (also the main marketing spend)
Profit	10%	30%

14.1 Profit and Loss Statement with a Virtual Brand

A third option for licensing a virtual brand is to add the product of a unique, successful, and digital-first brick-and-mortar restaurant to your own line. Licensees don't serve these menu items in their dine-in restaurant; rather, the kitchen produces the items for digital orders. This is the approach Wow Bao has taken. From its first days in 2003, it quickly became popular for its healthy, delicious Asian street food featuring bao (stuffed buns) and bowls. Six years later, the ownership group was ready to find new ways to expand that didn't require a lease or tablecloths. Geoff Alexander was brought in to lead the new concept.

"The world was different in 2009," Geoff Alexander reminisces as he tells the story of the organization he now leads. "Back then the iPhone was still the original iPhone. I remember the CEO of Lettuce Entertain You restaurant group [owners of Wow Bao] saying to me, 'You have to do online ordering.'" Smiling, Geoff recalls his response: "Why do I need online ordering? My food takes fifty-six seconds from the time you order to picking it up. That's ridiculous."[9] But later that year, Alexander was one of the first to enable desktop ordering of food delivered via bicycle to customers across Chicago.

Fast forward a decade, and Alexander is seen as one of the country's leading experts in scaling digital food brands. In 2017, Valor Equity Partners took a majority share in the company. Recognizing that their new investors owned other restaurants around the country, Alexander proposed, "Why can't this other group [of restaurants] just do what we're doing? It was an aha moment."

Wow Bao has made available a third of their menu—the delivery-optimized menu items that can be prepared in their centralized commissary—for restaurants of all cuisine types to adopt as an incremental brand served out of their existing kitchen. They deliver frozen food items that are simply heated by steaming. As Geoff says, they can do it with "no additional labor, no recipe, no training, no waste. It's all done for you." His team provides six weeks of digital marketing support and audits every location remotely to determine where support is needed to tweak and improve the unit's sales.

Compared to the Uber Eats and Nextbite approaches, the Wow Bao virtual brand does require novel ingredients and dedicated equipment. But because the footprint is small, no incremental mechanical air-handling is needed (proper ventilation is a major cost consideration when adding new equipment and processes to a restaurant kitchen). And because the product is easy to make, most existing kitchens can handle the additions. The licensing "fee" to use the Wow Bao brand and their product is included as restaurants place orders for the product after a small upfront charge.

It doesn't stop with the over two hundred locations that Wow Bao has open across the country today. "I have a goal of one thousand Wow Baos in twenty-four months, but if we do seven hundred and fifty, I won't think we've failed," Alexander says. "I'll think we did something pretty outrageous. It's never been done before—we can be the fastest-growing restaurant company *ever*." Wow Bao's goals are not as crazy as they may appear. With low startup costs, increasing demand for additional revenue channels, a compelling support infrastructure, and an easy means to enter the virtual restaurant arena, Alexander may be the one calling any doubters crazy for not joining his brand's journey to digital success.

3. The Franchised Model

The franchised model offers a bit more support than the licensed model. Much like franchising in the brick-and-mortar world, in this model the operator (the franchisee) pays the brand (the franchisor) fees and royalties to use their menu, branding, supply chain, and operating systems. The most innovative franchisors are offering franchisees an array of virtual brands to layer in with their core offering.

André Vener is a cofounder of one of the most forward-thinking restaurant brands in the US and an early leader in franchising digital brands. Founded as a traditional brick-and-mortar restaurant in Pasadena, Greater Los Angeles, California, Dog Haus serves artisanal, clean-label hot dogs, bratwurst, sausages, chicken sandwiches, and burgers. It quickly became a popular spot locally, leading the founding group to consider how best to expand to serve more consumers. They chose the traditional franchising path and grew to twenty locations. However, the hardest part of building out a new brand is getting the capital to build out all the restaurants—whether the franchisor is seeking the capital or their franchisees are. The Dog Haus founders began to experiment with ghost kitchens to grow their base with minimal capital investment.

Once they were operating inside a ghost kitchen, reaching consumers in far-flung cities through digital channels, Vener realized that in these new markets, where consumers didn't have a brick-and-mortar restaurant to refer to, Dog Haus *was* a virtual brand. Their only channel to reach consumers—to teach them about the brand, give them a reason to try the product, and keep them coming back through a seamless delivery experience—was via digital tools.

One of their challenges was getting their brand to show up when a consumer searched for "burger" or "chicken sandwich." Although Dog Haus offered popular menu items beyond hot dogs, its brand name was leading the search algorithms to skip over Dog Haus in non–hot dog searches.

Their solution? Launch additional brands—produced in the same kitchen, on the same line, by the same cooks, using the same ingredients—that were focused on the other aspects of their menu. "We looked at our current menu: dogs, sausages, burgers, chicken, plant-based," says Vener. "So we started Bad Mother Clucker. The sides are all the same. The chicken sandwich is the one we already have but with additional sauces. Then if you type in *burger*, we come up as FreiBurger. If you are looking for plant-based, we come up as Plant B."[10] Every order was delivered in the same kind of white bag, stamped with the specific logo of the brand ordered.

It is the equivalent of shelf space in the physical retail world. There, consumer product brands take up prime real estate with multiple product permutations, catching the consumer's eye as they walk up and down the aisles. You see it in the candy section of your local convenience store: Mars draws you in with their array of M&M's, Snickers, Bounty, Milky Way, and Twix, while Hershey's tempts you with their shelves of PayDay, Almond Joy, Krackel, Mounds, and their namesake Hershey's. In the digital world, the additional Dog Haus brands served to fill up search results—the equivalent of shelf space—with Dog Haus product.

The focus of Dog Haus's culinary efforts is entirely around driving the top line through additional discovery—that "shelf space" factor—while minimizing operating complexity and cost. Franchisees buying into the Dog Haus system are therefore buying into five different brands operating out of one kitchen, with digital marketing expertise supporting each one. And as Dog Haus launches more brands, Dog Haus franchisees have the option to expand their sales layers further.

The growth rates this model opens up are phenomenal. Franchisers typically expand by selling large market developer agreements, negotiating incentives to grow, or convincing existing franchisees to reinvest capital into the brand and build more locations. Dog Haus can simply release new brands to existing locations. "We could have three hundred points of distribution by the end of this year . . . without actually having to build a store," says Vener. Further accelerating growth, the additional sales layers improve unit economics for franchisees, making them more likely to reinvest in additional locations.

The umbrella organization for Dog Haus's brands, The Absolute Brands, was originally slated for a 2021 launch. The COVID-19 pandemic caused Dog Haus to accelerate its strategy in 2020. "We said, 'Let's go,'" Vener said. "Originally, we thought we would offer the virtual brands only to ghost kitchen locations. Instead, we launched in all thirty-five locations. No, everything wasn't perfect, but that's what's making our sales at 105 percent of last year, even with our stores being closed [by safer at home orders] right now."

4. Completely Virtual Brand Model

What if you don't have an existing restaurant to host a virtual restaurant? Buying or building a brick-and-mortar restaurant would be too expensive just to launch a single virtual restaurant. But launching a series of virtual restaurants in a ghost kitchen right-sizes the economics.

The team over at virtual restaurant group Salted is making it look easy, pumping out six concepts from one single four hundred square foot kitchen. All six concepts only exist online. And because they don't have a brick-and-mortar storefront, Salted can be open whenever they like. If pizza sells better on Fridays than Tuesdays, they don't open the pizza concept on Tuesday. If salads sell better at lunch than at dinner, they operate the salad concept only at lunchtime.

Entrepreneur and Salted CEO Jeff Appelbaum came to virtual restaurants through his personal passion for food and his professional skills in digital customer acquisition. Formerly VP of Growth and Innovation at e-commerce company BeachMint, Appelbaum wanted the kind of exponential growth that is out of reach for brick-and-mortar restaurants. "We create experiences that can spread nonlinearly," he says. "There's an opportunity for exponential growth [online], whereas a restaurant is limited to its radius."[11]

Salted's original iteration was an online cooking school. Jeff recalls those early days: "We sent film crews around the country; we filmed with a couple hundred well-known chefs. It was a great and profitable business, but it was not scaling to be a giant business. So we spent a lot of time thinking about expanding the brand to make an exponential impact."

It was not enough to just go bigger, in Jeff's view. He wanted nothing less than to improve the food that the typical American eats regularly. "More and more people are interested in the quality of the supply chain and the ingredients going into their bodies," he says. People describing themselves as "plant-based" has gone from "1 percent to 3 percent in the last two to three years. Everything we make is food that we are proud of. Everything is gluten-free and clean label. Everything is made from scratch."

From a business perspective, this approach is borrowed directly from the e-commerce world: identifying niches that enable microtargeting in digital marketing, which in turn drives more efficient ad spend. Digital ordering enables Appelbaum and his team to go after specific niches that larger, more traditional players can't manage. The scale that a national brand operates at requires, by definition, a broad appeal. If half of all Americans are going to walk through your doors each month, half of all Americans need to like the product—resulting in lowest common denominator product design choices.

A virtual brand, on the other hand, does *better* the tighter its customer segment. A niche product, while perhaps never large, can drive excellent economics. Customers are easier to target and acquire, and they are much more loyal once acquired—assuming the brand delivers on its promise. "It's better to go after an audience that is more eager for their problem to be solved," Appelbaum says. "Our food is focused on solving dietary needs: better for you but also highly craveable. Food and an experience that is so good that you tell your friends about it. Start with passionate fans and build out, rather than be all things to all people."

Salted puts its effort into two things: designing food they are proud of and scaling the brand-consumer relationship through the Internet. "B2C [the business-to-consumer model] is short-sighted in thinking that hospitality and trust only exist when you have one thousand plus square feet and a front door," says Appelbaum, who believes the opposite. Salted exists on the theory that a digital brand-consumer relationship can actually be stronger than an in-person one. How? Digital interactions can cover all customers, be completely customized, completely automated, and completely consistent. Unlike the restaurant general manager or server knowing the best customers, a computer can know all customers. Unlike a direct mail piece that shares the same message with everyone, a computer can say the right message to the right person at the right time. Unlike your best server sharing an upsell message that your worst server forgets, a computer remembers every time. What's more, the steady drip and consistent messaging of these contacts builds trust with the consumer. The brand shows up reliably and continually, following through on what it says.

All of the consumer benefits drive the top line, but the model also contributes to the bottom line, as Appelbaum explains. "The biggest shift is the amount of capital needed at the front end. We can launch extremely cost effectively and in extremely short time horizons. If you are less worried about the physical infrastructure, you can put more focus on the customer. This is an opportunity to double down on communication with consumers."

Appelbaum describes the predecessors that have proven the model in other sectors:

> A lot of the playbook for what's possible has already been outlined in other categories where there has been a lot of disruption—retail, beauty, mattresses. Upstarts have said you don't need this legacy infrastructure to build deep relationships with customers. Warby Parker, Everlane, Bonobos—they have baked deep into their culture values that apply [to the restaurant industry too]. Transparency of supply chain. Customer support. Beautiful packaging. And content.

Being late to the digitally native brand party behind retail and CPG gives the restaurant industry one key advantage: they can follow the trailblazers from other industries and learn from them. Restaurateurs, investors, and those starting a purely digital play don't have to make a leap of faith—pioneers have created a repeatable formula that is applicable to restaurants as easily as to any other consumer-facing business.

Chapter 15

MENUS BECOME OBSOLETE

Jackson tapped the skin on top of his wrist—he was still getting used to not wearing a watch. The Apple Wrist X was his girlfriend's present to him for his thirty-fifth birthday. Delicately implanted underneath the skin, the Wrist X chip now interacted constantly with the receptor near his ear. He remembered the day he got his first smartphone as a child and how excited he was. This was another game-changing technology. His newly retired parents thought it was absolutely crazy and had no intention to follow their son's footsteps. Even Jackson found it a little unsettling at first, but the convenience of it was truly astounding.

As he stepped into an autonomous vehicle and settled into the back seat, he simply thought "Home," and the car pulled away into the mix of other vehicles, systematically falling into the lane alongside other travelers. He had only needed his driver's license for five years; now with automation and shared vehicles across the city, his driving and car ownership days were over. It allowed him to focus on other more important things—like "what's for dinner?"

The thought prompted a list to appear on his smart glasses.

- ○ Doctor Parsons reminds you that your blood pressure this week was still high
- ○ You're twenty-six minutes behind your required cardio goal of 145 bpm exercise this week
- ○ Avoiding salty foods, red meat, and excessive alcohol is important to counterbalance your current nutritional profile. You are currently over your daily allocation of sodium
- ○ Here are your recommendations for tonight's meal . . .

The list that appeared included items designated from Jackson's dietary profile that he had established online through his nutritional therapist's guidance—and, of course, based on the ratings that Jackson had recorded on all the previous interactions with his delivered food in recent months. It was like having his own personal chef, he thought. After selecting his food, he remembered to add toothpaste to his basket before processing his order through the integrated digital wallet.

Instantly, the order was being processed. His garden salad and chicken order was automatically entered into an online bidding system across sixteen nearby food vendors. An established Italian restaurant, a few home chefs, three food trucks, and several virtual brands out of the nearby ghost kitchen locations all were autonomously scanning inventory levels, production availability, customer loyalty profiles, and capability to deliver the dish as desired to Jackson. Within a matter of seconds, the successful vendor saw the order appear in their kitchen display. A robotic arm swung into action, grabbing the necessary ingredients from the prep line in front of it. Sixty seconds later, the salad was ready and plated. A single cook finished the breast of chicken on the skillet within six minutes, packaged the dressing on the side as requested, and placed it in the dispatch chute for loading onto the delivery drone.

Some eleven minutes later, as the autonomous car was turning the corner to arrive at Jackson's condo, the car's roof began to open to the right of his seat. Jackson didn't look up—he knew what it was. The drone flying above him delicately landed on the moving vehicle and from within its center emerged a package including tonight's dinner and a tube of toothpaste. Within seconds, the drone had disappeared. Jackson stepped out of the vehicle, which pulled out of his driveway to start another customer journey.

Dinner in hand, Jackson walked inside to what used to be called a garage but is now known as an immersion room. Sitting down in his favorite seat, he unpacked his dinner, unsheathed his cutlery, and placed a headset on his head. *Tonight, let's go to Italy*, he thought. As he dug into his food, Jackson took in the sun setting across the Isle of Capri as if his meal had been made on the Jewel of Southern Italy itself.

The restaurant industry, the restaurateur's business model, and the consumer who engages with food made outside their home are changing at a pace that is hard to fathom and therefore react to. But the changes are not a fad. Having arrived at the final chapter of this book, you can see why this is happening, who is navigating through those struggles, and how restaurateurs across the country need to adapt.

For many, the present day is challenging enough, especially in the wake of the COVID-19 pandemic, but the United States is still in the early innings of change. There is more to come. The innovative thinkers who shared their thoughts for this book also talked about how they saw the future evolving. Combined with examples from other countries and other industries and observing the flow of funds in venture capital, four consistent themes emerge:

- The future of dine-in
- The rise of personalization
- The sustainable supply chain
- The augmented business model

1. The Future of Dine-In

Dine-in will ultimately be reduced to 25–50 percent. Eating inside will be a risk, and there's an opportunity for it to be a hot commodity.
—ANDREW MCCLELLAN, FORMER PROCESS ENGINEER, TACO BELL[1]

A lot of restaurants in China are downscaling their physical location. Their entire business is focused on delivery, but when that happens, the restaurant experience kind of dies with it.
—ABEY LIN, FILM STUDENT[2]

I could see down the road you don't even get a server; you get a tablet on your table. And then when you're all said and done, you place your order and the first time you see a server, he's bringing your drinks. So it's going to get much, much more efficient that way.
—LLOYD WENTZELL, RETIRED VP HOSPITALITY FOR WALDORF ASTORIA[3]

It'll go back to what it was. There'll be fine dining, there'll be sit-down restaurants, people going out and celebrating. The [COVID-19 after-effect] will last three to five years. So we build things that can sustain us through this time right now.
—DAVID KUO, OWNER OF LITTLE FATTY IN LOS ANGELES[4]

Even if you cook as much as I do in my house—and I cook every day—that is nothing like going into a restaurant and really being served, just sitting down, having a glass of wine and . . . being pampered.
—LORENA GARCIA, CELEBRITY CHEF, *TOP CHEF MASTERS*[5]

The central question of 2020 was: When can we go back to normal? Everyone who asked the question had a different idea in their head about what normal they longed to go back to, but for restaurateurs, the question was specific: When will diners return to my once-bustling restaurant?

The problem is, "normal" has been forever changed by the COVID-19 pandemic.

Digital delivery was not caused by the pandemic. It was created by changing American eating habits and the application of technology to restaurants. The pandemic merely accelerated adoption of off-premise consumption. As we saw in Chapter 6, digital delivery (excluding pizza and Chinese) represented less than 10 percent of total restaurant sales pre-pandemic. During the pandemic, that number more than doubled—but internationally, that number is 30–70 percent. These benchmarks suggest that, above and beyond the pandemic surge, digital delivery in the United States will likely grow further before reaching its steady state.

A permanent 30 percent reduction in dine-in sales represents a massive economic shift in the restaurant industry, but it doesn't mean dine-in will go away. Rather, dine-in experiences will improve. Those restaurants with a clear definition of "value" in the broadest sense will succeed. For a fine dining restaurant, it may be the best service. For a salad concept, it may be the freshest organic ingredients. For a fast casual, it may be best catering to children. Those with a clear identity are well placed to survive the aftereffects of the COVID-19 pandemic. There are few better places than restaurants to provide the social interaction that people long for.

Thriving dine-in restaurants are likely to give customers a reason to eat on-premise. Neurogastronomy and augmented reality, for example, can be combined to create immersive dining experiences that cannot be replicated at home. Visionary chef Heston Blumenthal and Oxford University psychologist Charles Spence created "The Sound of the Sea" to this end. The signature dish at Blumenthal's famed Fat Duck restaurant was first developed to evoke more sensorial activation, with sea spray misting over the dinner table, ocean waves crashing through audio headsets, and a wooden treasure box filled with what looks like sand but is in fact a mixture of tapioca, breadcrumbs, fried baby eels, and cod liver oil. The seafood is exquisitely arranged, and the juices from the shellfish foam to represent the ocean's edge. "It's all about nudging," Blumenthal explains, "so you can lose yourself in a memory that's triggered by food."[6]

Dine-in capacity may also be permanently altered. The average guest's willingness to share their meals on communal tables or be crowded together in a sea of two-tops is not likely to survive government mandates to socially distance. Expect more spaced-out dining rooms and an increase in outdoor dining, even in colder climates with the use of blankets and heaters.

Because of the reduced capacity, each opportunity to serve a dine-in customer will be both more costly to serve and more cherished. Expect to see online reservation systems with nonrefundable deposits to become more prevalent. The Tock platform has introduced a version in Chicago:

15.1 Tock Reservation Example[7]

Consumers will be willing to pay such fees because eating out will be a rarer and more treasured occasion. Expect restaurateurs to carry this to its logical conclusion: enabling diners to pay more for a particular table (as with seats on an airplane) or for a particular service (as with business versus economy class).

Just as they did during the pandemic, guests will continue to seek out venues where they feel safer. This might include clear communications around air filtration and sanitization protocols, the addition of air quality to local health department checks, or continued availability of hand sanitizer. Our desire for safety will benefit digitally enabled restaurants. Even when dining in, guests will prefer no-contact ordering, using their own smartphone to order and pay.

2. The Rise of Personalization 3.0

There's a cool opportunity for marketplaces to do even more around things like dietary choices and allergens and pull out for you across a big set of available menus: here are the things that we really recommend for you. We know you like these things. We know you eat this way, or we know you're allergic to this thing.
—NOAH GLASS, CEO, OLO[8]

The potential of dynamic personalization doesn't just apply from a food selection perspective. It also occurs from a geographical location perspective. I think geofencing will play a much bigger role in the delivery experience, learning the car is three minutes away to fire the food.
—ALEX CANTER, CEO, ORDERMARK[9]

What will become table stakes tomorrow will be personalized content before a guest orders, even while they are dining in. Really personal content. The relationships that consumers have with brands will be stronger than they have ever been.
—ADAM BROTMAN, CEO, BRIGHTLOOM[10]

In ten years, more options. More healthy options. More options to pick from, for what consumers want to eat and how they want to eat.
—D'SHEA GRANT, DOORDASH DRIVER[11]

The beauty of the Internet is that each consumer can find the specific thing that makes sense for them—a group of like-minded friends, a community of people with similar backgrounds, education about nutrition relating to their personal circumstance, access to food that fits their nutritional requirements. Imagine a doctor creating a diet for a rare disease, then giving a TED Talk on the diet. Imagine a person with the rare disease seeing that TED Talk, then using the Internet to find ingredients and supplements online that aren't available in their small town.

The browser "cookies" and search and advertising algorithms that make this magic happen help advertisers reach the consumers they're trying to target and help consumers find what they are interested in. But they also have a dark side. Somewhere in our imaginary patient's behavioral history reside records of foods and products they have previously ordered, websites they have previously viewed, and data entwining our patient with their social network—their family, friends, coworkers, and even doctors. This means that the more an individual likes, engages with, or purchases something, the more of that something they will get. In the case of our imaginary patient, one can easily see that if the recommended diet were keto and the behavioral history included a lot of pastries, the patient would have a hard time retraining the algorithms to stop showing baked goods in favor of meat, cheese, and vegetables.

The best possible application of algorithms scale hospitality. No longer dependent on one great server who can immediately intuit how a guest is feeling that day or the perfect host who keeps detailed records of the restaurant's best customers, restaurants can use technology to enable *every* interaction with *every* guest to feel as if they were being served personally by the head chef of the flagship restaurant. Like Amazon's ability to recommend products based on each user's browsing history and purchase history, restaurants, too, will be able to serve guests the right offer at the right time in the right place.

Geofencing enables advertisers to reach consumers *where* they are with an offer relevant to that location. Because geofencing is ultimately about reaching the consumer, future technologies—like Jackson's embedded watch—will connect more directly with the consumer. In the interim, devices act as proxies: most notably the smartphone, but also computers, smart watches, and connected cars. GPS technology and near-field communications like Bluetooth enabled strategically placed beacons trigger messages on nearby devices, like connected cars. If a consumer orders the pop-up offer, the meal could be timed to arrive at the same time as the consumer gets home.

Contextual advertising enables companies to reach consumers *when* the timing is right. Impulse and indulgence will always remain as key drivers to consumer choices, but data enables advertisers to reach consumers just before they are ready to choose. As companies collect data on consumer routines, they can connect with consumers prior to custom eating windows, to hit hunger before hunger hits the consumer. Jon Steinlauf, Chief US Advertising Sales Director for Discovery family of networks, said at the National Association of Television Program Executives event in 2019, "The advertisers that I talk to, they're interested in taking a big leap into data, which means we're not buying eighteen to forty-nine, we're not selling twenty-five to fifty-four year olds—we're buying consumers who have shown the proclivity to be heavy purchasers of frozen entrees to a company like Conagra [packaged foods]."[12] Contextual advertising can become so specific and so localized that watching a streaming Italian cooking show will trigger an offer from an Italian restaurant close to your home.

Dynamic menus have the power to better target *what* consumers are offered. Much like each Prime member's Amazon homepage is different from another and the content your best friend sees on Facebook is different from the content you see, no two people will ever see the same menu again. The technology to customize menus based on order history is already here and already in use in other industries. Companies like Starbucks are starting to use it already. In the future, consumers will utilize a combination of software, their personal genome profile, their recent bloodwork, and nutritionists' recommendations to guide their food choices. Think of dynamic menus being like Dr. James Lind in the 1700s recommending citrus to sailors to prevent scurvy. Dr. Jeffrey Blumberg, a professor at Tufts University, is also on the advisory board for a company called InsideTracker, which provides services to improve consumers' knowledge of their nutritional status. "Personalized nutrition," as he calls it, can "tell your blood level of critical nutrients and biomarkers, so you know exactly where you are. People don't know how effectively they're exercising or eating until they see those results."[13] This type of recommendation system is already in use in South Africa through health insurance company Discovery Insure. Their Vitality Health dining program integrates with Uber Eats to reward their five million customers for making healthy eating decisions.

Today, leading restaurant, delivery, and grocery companies are in a race to develop the best customer relationship management (CRM) software to collect and analyze the data that makes personalization possible. The loyalty programs that offer great deals to consumers are simultaneously creating the data history that enable companies to speak to each consumer individually rather than as a member of a segment of similar customers. Thus, the battle between restaurants and delivery platforms is not just about the fee associated with a specific order—it's about the data collected on each order.

Ultimately, consumers will have the most control when they own their own data. Imagine utilizing an integrated profile that addresses all of your nutritional, behavioral, and geographic data. As a consumer takes her profile from one restaurant to another, the right food items will be highlighted wherever she goes.

3. The Sustainable Supply Chain

I'm very optimistic that we're moving in a very positive direction to give people more selection, more control, and more convenience. And just greater transparency to their food.
—KEN CHONG, COFOUNDER, ALL DAY KITCHENS[14]

We also want to make room for more human communication beyond the food order. Restaurants can talk more about sourcing.
—NABEEL ALAMGIR, LUNCHBOX.IO[15]

Procurement of food will be considered in a more ethical manner. I see a lot of people moving off meat. A lot of us today would not buy a diamond if we thought it had been bought from conflict. There's no reason why we should put so much food waste and plastic into the waste system.
—VIVEK SUNDER, SWIGGY[16]

Food in NY and in LA should probably be different, and different at different times of year. The idea that a Big Mac should taste the same all around the world . . . that's not how it comes out of the ground.
—JONATHAN NEMAN, COFOUNDER AND CEO, SWEETGREEN[17]

I'm super excited in the food-growing space and how we're creating alternative ways to weave the growing of food into the places we live. Think about the entire supply chain, and it being closer to where we live.
—SCOTT DRUMMOND, FOUNDER, EATSA[18]

I think that the origin of ingredients are going to be paramount. Organic versus non-organic. Processed versus non-processed. Where the ingredients are coming from. How sustainable they are. How the climate is affecting production. This new generation pays such attention to the environment. If Millennials are paying so much attention to the environment, imagine their kids.
—LORENA GARCIA, CELEBRITY CHEF, *TOP CHEF MASTERS*[19]

As we explored in Chapter 2, younger generations have greater knowledge about how food affects not only their own bodies, but also the wider ecosystem of the world. Awareness of environmental impact will lead to more plant-based menus and even more farm-to-table stories than we see today. The multi-billion-dollar start-ups Impossible Foods, Beyond Meat, and Sweetgreen are not outliers; they are harbingers of things to come.

Favoring plant-based ingredients is but one avenue to improve health and environmental outcomes. Favoring locally produced food is the other main road. Proximity of food production to food consumption will shrink in the years ahead. The number of urban farms will increase, reducing transportation and water waste. As food production moves closer to consumers, food will retain nutritional value otherwise lost in transport. Although it is unlikely that indoor farming could replace the billions of outdoor acres under production around the world, the local philosophy and extreme efficiency offered by technology will help improve yields, environmental impact, and nutrition for everyone.

Waste and environmental impact are closely related to cost-savings potential. In America's past, we have frequently seen environmental care as being at odds with profits. Today's technologies can align these interests. For example, US Foods, one of America's leading food suppliers, sees the opportunity in ghost kitchens to create efficiency in the supply chain. Delivering to one ghost kitchen servicing many restaurant partners is both more environmentally sound and cheaper than delivering to each restaurant's individual locations.[20]

Similar alignment is possible in the world of packaging. What the dabbawala system figured out in India hundreds of years ago is the opportunity for the Western world now: how to reuse delivery packaging. Today's off-premise industry largely serves its customers through one-time use packaging. Already leading restaurants are using compostable or recyclable packaging, and many consumers consider their environmental impact when choosing a restaurant. Other emerging businesses are looking to reuse packaging. LoopStore, part of TerraCycle, provides reusable totes so that no packaging is ever wasted as landfill. In Portland, Oregon, GoBox is another emerging company. They produce reusable packaging deployed at over one hundred restaurants then collected via bikes across the city. Consumers use the company's app, present a code to the restaurant to "check out" the packaging, and then scan the used package upon return at one of the many drop points across the city via a QR code.

Americans currently throw out 120 billion disposable cups each year.[21] Eliminating this kind of waste is better for the environment *and* cheaper for the restaurant. Within the next ten years, integrated reusable food packaging from restaurants will likely become the norm for off-premise transactions. Clearly, some responsibility lies with the consumer as well as restaurants, but companies like GoBox and LoopStore will eventually become integrated into delivery platforms as more and more consumers demand this as a feature of their delivery experience. Imagine your delivery driver bringing tonight's meal to you while collecting the used packaging from the evening before and placing credits into your account for helping the environment. Deliveroo has already launched one such partnership in Australia with Returnr, a start-up focused on reusing delivery food packaging.[22]

4. The Augmented Business Model

Long term, if restaurants rely on delivery to no longer be 25 percent but 65–70 percent of their revenue, something's got to give. I don't think restaurants can survive. I don't think restaurants will bother having to pay rent or design a nice store front, they'll just have a ghost kitchen.
—HENRY ROBERTS, INDEPENDENT RESTAURATEUR, TWO HANDS NYC[23]

The restaurant industry has been disrupting things for years. This is a job that is never going to be done. We will always be thinking about how to improve the lives of our guests. I think it is super fun.
—TRESSIE LIEBERMAN, VP, DIGITAL AND OFF PREMISE, CHIPOTLE[24]

We could truly be in the George Jetson age—just pushing a button on our wall and magically food appears.
—CHARLIE MORRISON, CEO, WINGSTOP[25]

My hope is that we see a completely different way of thinking about what it means to be a restaurant that puts [restaurants] in the race at the speed that DoorDash is innovating, as opposed to just getting completely run over by that innovation.
—ZACH GOLDSTEIN, CEO, THANX[26]

I would love my sushi to get delivered by drone. I would love to see those little robot cars everywhere too.
—JENN PARKER, FORMER COO, NEXTBITE[27]

You'll have your drive-thru and walk-thru (like a click and collect). There will always be an ability to sit down, but it won't be big. It's more going to be 80 percent walk-thru/drive-thru and about 20 percent for sit down.
—FORMER DELIVEROO EXECUTIVE[28]

Joelle Parenteau, owner/operator of Ottawa's Wolf Down restaurant, caused a stir with her article "Why Restaurants Are Not F****d."[29] She believes the void left behind from the inevitable restaurant closures during the COVID-19 pandemic will allow others to rise up and serve the same demand from guests but across a smaller base of restaurants. Even during the economic boom times, the restaurant industry was oversaturated. The COVID-19 pandemic clearly demonstrated that those restaurants ready for a digital world had a better chance to succeed, and the changes weren't going away anytime soon. For those that can ride the digitization of the industry, how does the restaurant business model need to change?

As we explored in Chapter 8, multiple revenue streams will become the norm. The platforms are pursuing a similar strategy to address their own economic challenges: combining food delivery with other retail, drugs, and pet food, like the more mature platforms Ele.me and Meituan in China.[30]

In doing so, third-party delivery companies have the potential to make delivery cheaper—especially for independents without the scale and clout to demand reduced fees.

Restaurants that reshape their business models to put off-premise first in their thinking and no longer a by-product of their dine-in business will likely find the shift easier to navigate. Future restaurants will have reduced square footage, clear flows for delivery drivers, and space to pack large catering orders. Some restaurants may find that off-premise meal preparation belongs in a ghost kitchen, dispensing with the front of house altogether. In a world where many will use hired cars—autonomous or with a driver—restaurants may rethink how they use the parking lot. Most suburban restaurants have about three times the amount of space dedicated to parking than to the actual restaurant. Temporary outdoor dining set up during the COVID-19 pandemic may become permanent. Curbside pickup and passenger drop-off zones will likely use up more of the parcel than parking.

15.2 Restaurant of the Future[31]

Restaurant operations will change too. The largest cost in a restaurant, comparable only to the food itself, is labor. As wages and consumer demand for quality food increases, the use of labor in restaurants has to go down. Cooking may become fully automated—more like the large-scale factories that produce packaged foods—or chefs more augmented by technology. In 2020, *Newsweek* ran an article on which jobs may no longer exist in fifty years: farmers, servers, and fast food workers were high on their list.[32] If dining rooms are shrinking, then the number of servers will go down too. Fast casual concepts proved that consumers would rather their money go to better food than to the ordering, payment, and distribution of food. Guests are willing to do the work themselves rather than pay for a server.

Even in the kitchen, cooks are warily looking over their shoulder at the advances being made in cooking automation. The first generation of cooking robots were large and required major changes to kitchen layout to accommodate their size. Automation is likely to creep into the kitchen more incrementally through devices such as programmable convection ovens, timed air fryers, and rotating woks that increase output per cook rather than replace workers outright.

The capital required to reformat restaurants, change out kitchen equipment, and build ghost kitchens seems daunting. Without alternative business models—like ghost kitchens built by developers and rented out fully equipped or kitchen innovation leased by the month—many smaller restaurants would be left behind. In this regard, the venture capitalists pouring money into all parts of the food supply chain are helping to shape the future for everyone, without one particular brand or restaurant having to shoulder the entire burden.

The last piece of the puzzle is the cost of delivery. Removing the cost of a driver takes a substantial chunk of cost out of the supply chain. Since 2012, $300 million has been invested into drone technology. Some think the drone market will grow four times to $43 billion worldwide by 2024.[33] Google's parent company, Alphabet, is behind Wing, a commercial drone delivery service that is partnering with Walgreens, FedEx, and retailers local to Christiansburg, Virginia, where they've attained Federal Aviation Administration approval to test delivery to people's homes.[34] Of course, many other companies are also trying to perfect the model, with services such as UPS's Flight Forward and Amazon's Prime Air—the latter of which has been trialing drone delivery to customers in Cambridge, England.[35] Each of these models of delivery sees a drone hover above a yard or a driveway before delicately placing a package to the ground.

In Milton Keynes, in suburban England, Starship Technologies has delivered over five hundred thousand grocery deliveries on the ground via contactless interface robots.[36] Former cofounders of Skype are behind this emerging technology leader, whose robots travel along streets used by pedestrians, delivering daily essentials. Amazon is not far behind, beginning trials with similar robots in Atlanta, Georgia, and Franklin, Tennessee, adding to services in Snohomish County, Washington, and Irvine, California. Founded by two former Google engineers, Nuro recently raised $1 billion to support their service. Nuro's robots can travel on the road at speeds up to 35 mph, whereas sidewalk robots must remain at a safe pedestrian speed.[37]

Drones may enable delivery more cost-effectively outside of densely urban areas, whereas ground-based robots may be more suited for shorter suburban microfulfillment journeys. Imagine the potential if robots can evolve to support the integrity of each dish's temperature and consistency or even finish the cooking.

Once this last mile is solved, attention will turn to the last twelve steps. Instead of customers collecting the delivery outside of their home, perhaps the home itself will change to receive deliveries. Does it make sense for a drone to drop the food package on a cold doorstep? Perhaps in time there will be an interface directly to people's homes, where the food package is funneled directly toward the dining table. A huge "chef's kitchen" with high-end appliances will also make less and less sense. Already in countries like Australia, home design is being impacted by the shift to delivery with smaller kitchens.[38] The space that once would be allocated to a double oven is now more likely to be allocated to a home office. Further changes are coming in the next decade—drone landing pads paired with heated, cooled, and room-temp boxes that can be accessed from both inside and outside the home.

The future for restaurant business owners is not as bleak as it may sometimes feel. It's filled with incredible potential for those willing to navigate the changing tide. For some, that may mean consolidation with a more established operator armed with the tools and skills to succeed in digital environments. For others, those that see the potential of the future, this book can act as a means of tapping into the greatest minds and innovators shaping the restaurant industry's future.

And perhaps that comes full circle as to why this book was written. The love for the small, independent restaurant is something intrinsic to each of us and features in the special moments from our lives. Those restaurateurs deserve a chance to make it through these transformative times. Many don't want to change, but change has already arrived. It's now or never to determine whether they'll be part of the excitement that lies ahead.

ACKNOWLEDGMENTS

Writing a book is no small undertaking. There's no denying that while two names sit on the front cover, there's an entire team of people integral to the book's creation. We'd first like to thank our families—for their support, encouragement, and willingness to sacrifice time we'd usually spend with them to this project. Next, a huge thank you to the one hundred plus interviewees that took time out of their busy schedules to speak with us and gave generously with their insights, perspectives, and excitement around their views on the changes affecting the restaurant industry. So much is changing so quickly in the restaurant industry that truly the best way to understand what's happening is through the eyes of those driving the changes. Interviewees' encouragement and connection with the themes of the book motivated us to be mindful of the incredible restaurant industry and its people throughout.

Thank you to Jacqueline, our wonderful editor, Nicole Hall, our diligent and resourceful project manager, Caitlin Smith, our artistic wizard, and Sky Wilson, our marketing guru at Amplify Publishing. Their support, counsel, and methodical attention to detail ensured we have a well-designed, solidly bound book to share. Thank you to Paula West for her patience and willingness to edit and reedit our book cover to convey the entirety of a book in one picture. And finally, to Sally Collings, whose wisdom and experience ensured our words were conveyed clearly and whose deep appreciation of grammar jokes make her one of the best editorial coaches around.

Finally, we are deeply grateful to our subscribers at (www.learn.delivery) and the veterans and new entrants to the industry willing to share their ideas, successes, and struggles with us. Restaurateurs have inspired all of us throughout the years; this book is ultimately for the unnamed restaurant owner striving to use the new digital tools to thrive. We met countless amazing entrepreneurs over the last four years, not all of whom are reflected on these pages. Thank you to the restaurateurs who inspire us from an industry that never ceases to innovate.

READY TO CONTINUE YOUR JOURNEY
INTO THE DIGITAL FUTURE?

LEARN.
DELIVERY

WWW.LEARN.DELIVERY/DIAGNOSTIC

ENDNOTES

Introduction

1   National Restaurant Association, "100,000 Restaurants Closed Six Months into
     Pandemic," September 14, 2020, https://restaurant.org/news/pressroom/press-
     releases/100000-restaurants-closed-six-months-into-pandemic.

Chapter 1

1   Wendy Wang and Paul Taylor, "For Millennials, Parenthood Trumps Marriage," Pew
     Research Center, March 9, 2011, https://www.pewsocialtrends.org/2011/03/09/for-
     millennials-parenthood-trumps-marriage/#fn-7199-1.

2   Stephanie Hanes, "Singles Nation: Why So Many Americans Are Unmarried," *Christian
     Science Monitor*, June 14, 2015, https://www.csmonitor.com/USA/Society/2015/0614/
     Singles-nation-Why-so-many-Americans-are-unmarried.

3   Gretchen Livingston, "Is U.S. Fertility at an All-Time Low? Two of Three Measures
     Point to Yes," Pew Research Center, May 22, 2019, https://www.pewresearch.org/
     fact-tank/2019/05/22/u-s-fertility-rate-explained/.

4   Joyce A. Martin, Brady E. Hamilton, and Michelle J. K. Osterman, "Births in the United States, 2019," NCHS Data Brief No. 387, October 2020, https://www.cdc.gov/nchs/products/databriefs/db387.htm.

5   Kim Painter, "As Births Decline in Young Women, They Keep Rising in 40-Somethings. Here's Why," *USA Today*, May 21, 2018, https://www.usatoday.com/story/news/2018/05/19/childbearing-why-women-40-s-having-more-babies/624028002/.

6   "For the 1st Time in 4 Years, Life Expectancy Rises, but Only a Little," PBS, January 30, 2020, https://www.pbs.org/newshour/health/for-1st-time-in-4-years-u-s-life-expectancy-rises-but-only-a-little.

7   Bella DePaulo, "America Is No Longer a Nation of Nuclear Families," *Quartz*, June 30, 2015, https://qz.com/440167/america-is-no-longer-a-nation-of-nuclear-families/.

8   David Brooks, "The Nuclear Family Was a Mistake," *The Atlantic*, March 2020, https://www.theatlantic.com/magazine/archive/2020/03/the-nuclear-family-was-a-mistake/605536/.

9   Ilana E. Strauss, "The Hot New Millennial Housing Trend Is a Repeat of the Middle Ages," *The Atlantic*, September 26, 2016, https://www.theatlantic.com/business/archive/2016/09/millennial-housing-communal-living-middle-ages/501467/.

10   Kevin Dickinson, "Millennial Income 20% Less than Boomers at Same Stage in Life," *Big Think*, November 23, 2019, https://bigthink.com/politics-current-affairs/millennial-income?rebelltitem=2#rebelltitem2.

11   Ashlee Kieler, "Groceries & Millennials: They're Buying Less, Shopping Online," *Consumerist*, October 31, 2016, https://consumerist.com/2016/10/27/groceries-millennials-theyre-buying-less-shopping-online/.

12   Gretchen Livingston, "It's No Longer a Leave It to Beaver World for American Families but It Wasn't Back Then Either," Pew Research Center, December 30, 2015, https://www.pewresearch.org/fact-tank/2015/12/30/its-no-longer-a-leave-it-to-beaver-world-for-american-families-but-it-wasnt-back-then-either.

13   Rachel Siegel, "Women Outnumber Men in the Workforce for Only the Second Time," *The Washington Post*, January 10, 2020, https://www.washingtonpost.com/business/2020/01/10/january-2020-jobs-report/.

14   Jacob Goldstein, "Young, Single & Childless: Women Who Earn More than Men," *NPR*, September 1, 2010, https://www.npr.org/sections/money/2010/09/01/129581758/.

15   "American Time Use Survey," US Bureau of Labor Statistics, December 20, 2016, https://www.bls.gov/tus/charts/household.htm.

16   Esteban Ortiz-Ospina, "How Do People Across the World Spend Their Time and What Does That Tell Us about Living Conditions?" Our World in Data, December 8, 2020, Retrieved from https://ourworldindata.org/time-use-living-conditions; Data referenced "OECD Based on National Time Use Surveys," http://www.oecd.org/gender/data/balancingpaidworkunpaidworkandleisure.htm.

17   Ibid.

18   Ariane Hegewisch and Valerie Lacarte, "Gender Inequality, Work Hours, and the Future of Work," Institute for Women's Policy Research, November 14, 2019, https://iwpr.org/iwpr-issues/employment-and-earnings/gender-inequality-work-hours-and-the-future-of-work/.

19   Esteban Ortiz-Ospina, "How Do People Across the World Spend Their Time and What Does That Tell Us about Living Conditions?" Our World in Data, December 8, 2020, https://ourworldindata.org/time-use-living-conditions; Data referenced "OECD Based on National Time Use Surveys," http://www.oecd.org/gender/data/balancingpaidworkunpaidworkandleisure.htm.

20   Christopher Ingraham, "Nine Days on the Road. Average Commute Time Reached New Record Last Year," *The Washington Post*, October 7, 2019, https://www.washingtonpost.com/business/2019/10/07/nine-days-road-average-commute-time-reached-new-record-last-year/.

21   Esteban Ortiz-Ospina, "How Do People Across the World Spend Their Time and What Does That Tell Us about Living Conditions?" Our World in Data, December 8, 2020, Retrieved from https://ourworldindata.org/time-use-living-conditions; Data referenced "OECD Based on National Time Use Surveys," http://www.oecd.org/gender/data/balancingpaidworkunpaidworkandleisure.htm.

Chapter 2

1   Andrew Kohut, "From the Archives: In '60s, Americans Gave Thumbs-Up to Immigration Law That Changed the Nation," Pew Research Center, September 20, 2019, https://www.pewresearch.org/fact-tank/2019/09/20/in-1965-majority-of-americans-favored-immigration-and-nationality-act-2/.

2   Amanda Barroso, "Gen Z Eligible Voters Reflect the Growing Racial and Ethnic Diversity of U.S. Electorate," Pew Research Center, September 23, 2020, https://www.pewresearch.org/fact-tank/2020/09/23/gen-z-eligible-voters-reflect-the-growing-racial-and-ethnic-diversity-of-u-s-electorate/.

3   "Taste the Nation, from Your Couch," *NPR*'s Ask Me Another, July 17, 2020, https://www.npr.org/2020/07/17/892239135/padma-lakshmi-taste-the-nation-from-your-couch.

4   Author interview with Dean Jankelowitz, July 7, 2020.

5   Lisa Abend, "The Cult of the Celebrity Chef Goes Global," *Time,* June 21, 2010, http://content.time.com/time/magazine/article/0,9171,1995844,00.html.

6   Alan Jackson and Joann Cianciulli, *The Lemonade Cookbook* (New York: St. Marten's Press, 2013), viii.

7   Author interview with Lorena Garcia, July 14, 2020.

8   Jeff Gelski, "U.S. Annual Organic Food Sales Near $48 Billion," *Food Business News*, May 20, 2019, https://www.foodbusinessnews.net/articles/13805-us-organic-food-sales-near-48-billion.

9   Center for Nutrition Policy and Promotion, "Healthy Eating Index," USDA, January 31, 2019, https://www.fns.usda.gov/hei-scores-americans#.

10   "Plant-Based Proteins Are Harvesting Year-over-Year Growth in Foodservice Market and Broader Appeal," NPD, June 6, 2018, https://www.npd.com/wps/portal/npd/us/news/press-releases/2018/plant-based-proteins-are-harvesting-year-over-year-growth-in-foodservice-market-and-broader-appeal/.

11   Author interview with Jonathan Neman, December 3, 2020.

12   Danny Klein, "Sweetgreen Is Now Valued at $1.6 Billion," *QSR* magazine, September 2019, https://www.qsrmagazine.com/fast-casual/sweetgreen-now-valued-16-billion.

13   Clark Schultz, "Peloton, Apple and Lululemon Dominate in Evercore Survey of Young Adults/Teens," *Seeking Alpha*, October 29, 2020, https://www.fool.com/investing/2020/09/12/ceo-chipotle-will-rake-in-24-billion-in-digital-sa/.

14   Tom Kaiser and Nick Upton, "Episode 11 with Meredith Sandland and Christine Barone," *Food on Demand Podcast*, July 23, 2020, https://foodondemandnews.com/podcast/archive/.

15   Andrew Weil, MD, and Sam Fox, with Michael Stebner, *True Food: Seasonal, Sustainable, Simple, Pure* (New York: Little, Brown and Company, 2012).

16   Author interview with Rick and Elise Wetzel, July 6, 2020.

17   "Industry Perspective: Greg Creed—Yum!" KPMG, June 20, 2017, https://home.kpmg/xx/en/home/insights/2017/06/industry-leader-perspective-greg-creed-yum.html.

Chapter 3

1   In-N-Out history web page, In-N-Out.com, https://www.in-n-out.com/history.

2   "Jack-in-the-Box Drive Thru Sign," Smithsonian Institute, https://americanhistory.si.edu/collections/search/object/nmah_1417793.

3   "Our History," McDonalds.com, https://www.mcdonalds.com.mt/history/.

4   "12.4 Billion Drive-Thru Visits in 2011," *QSR* magazine, June 4, 2012, https://www.qsrmagazine.com/news/124-billion-drive-thru-visits-made-2011.

5   Sam Oches, "The 2018 QSR Drive-Thru Study," *QSR* magazine, October 2018, https://www.qsrmagazine.com/reports/2018-qsr-drive-thru-study.

6   "Starbucks Company Timeline," Starbucks.com, https://www.starbucks.com/about-us/company-information/starbucks-company-timeline.

7   Author interview with Brian Reece, October 6, 2020.

8   Author interview with Jane Gannaway, August 28, 2020.

9   Pat Lauscher and Jesse Poprocki, "Case Presentation: Taco Bell," University of Washington, Spring 2003, http://www.uwosh.edu/faculty_staff/wresch/case1a.htm.

10   "U.S. Real Estate," McDonalds.com, https://www.mcdonalds.com/us/en-us/about-us/franchising/real-estate.html.

11   Farley Elliott, "LA's Hardest Restaurant Reservation, n/naka, Now Available Via Bento Box," *Eater,* May 23, 2020, https://la.eater.com/2020/3/23/21191118/coronavirus-takeout-delivery-covid-19-n-naka-bento-box-news.

12   Everett M. Rogers, *Diffusion of Innovations,* 1st ed. (New York: Free Press of Glencoe, 1962).

13   "Yum! Brands and Grubhub Announce New U.S. Growth Partnership," Grubhub.com, February 8, 2018, https://investors.grubhub.com/investors/press-releases/press-release-details/2018/Yum-Brands-and-Grubhub-Announce-New-US-Growth-Partnership/default.aspx.

14   Rhian Hunt, "CEO: Chipotle Will Rake in $2.4 Billion in Digital Sales this Year," *Motley Fool,* September 12, 2020, https://www.fool.com/investing/2020/09/12/ceo-chipotle-will-rake-in-24-billion-in-digital-sa/.

15   Interview with Ali Velshi and Dr. Zeke Emanuel, "Bill Gates on Changing Behaviors to Fight COVID-19," MSNBC, April 24, 2020, https://www.msnbc.com/the-last-word/watch/bill-gates-on-changing-behaviors-to-fight-covid-19-82553413790.

16   Ashlee Kieler, "Groceries & Millennials: They're Buying Less, Shopping Online," *Consumerist,* October 31, 2016, https://consumerist.com/2016/10/27/groceries-millennials-theyre-buying-less-shopping-online/.

17   Jeffry Bartash, "Cost of Eating Out Is Rising a Lot Faster than Buying Groceries (and Cooking at Home)," *MarketWatch,* July 11, 2019, https://www.marketwatch.com/story/eating-out-is-getting-a-lot-more-expensive-than-buying-groceries-and-cooking-at-home-2019-07-11#.

18   Economic Research Service, "America's Eating Habits: Food away from Home, EIB-196" USDA, September 2018, https://www.ers.usda.gov/webdocs/publications/90228/eib-196_ch3.pdf?v=8116.5.

19   "Despite a Decline in Unit Count, U.S. Independent Restaurants Still Represent Over Half of Commercial Restaurant Units and Are Forecast to Spend $39 Billion in 2018," NPD, May 21, 2018, https://www.npd.com/wps/portal/npd/us/news/press-releases/2018/despite-a-decline-in-unit-count-us-independent-restaurants-still-represent-over-half-of-commercial-restaurant-units-and-are-forecast-to-spend--39-billion-in-2018/.

Chapter 4

1   Author interview with Kevin Abt, September 15, 2020.

2   Author interview with Michael Caito, August 18, 2020.

3   "Grubhub," Wikipedia.org, https://en.wikipedia.org/wiki/Grubhub.

4   Ibid.

5   Liz Welch, "How I Did It: Matt Maloney of Grubhub and Seamless," *Inc.*, November 2014, https://www.inc.com/magazine/201411/liz-welch/how-i-did-it-matt-maloney-of-grubhub-and-seamless.html#.

6   "What Is Grubhub?," Grubhub.com, https://about.grubhub.com/about-us/what-is-grubhub/default.aspx.

7   "DoorDash," Wikipedia.org, https://en.wikipedia.org/wiki/DoorDash.

8   "Uber," Wikipedia.org, https://en.wikipedia.org/wiki/Uber.

9   "Postmates," Wikipedia.org, https://en.wikipedia.org/wiki/Postmates.

10   Liyin Yao, "Which Company Is Winning the Restaurant Food Delivery War?" Second Measure, January 19, 2021, https://secondmeasure.com/datapoints/food-deliveryservices-grubhub-uber-eats-doordash-postmates/.

11   Ibid.

12   Kate Clark, "DoorDash, Now Valued at $12.6B, Shoots for the Moon," *TechCrunch*, May 23, 2019, https://techcrunch.com/2019/05/23/doordash-now-valued-at-12-6b-shoots-for-the-moon/.

13   Ida Mojadas, "Who's Killing the Taxi Industry," *SF Weekly*, June 13, 2019, https://www.sfweekly.com/news/whos-killing-the-taxi-industry/; "TNCs Today," https://www.sfcta.org/projects/tncs-today.

14   Todd Schneider, "Taxi & Ride-Hailing Apps in New York City," https://toddwschneider.com/dashboards/nyc-taxi-ridehailing-uber-lyft-data/#notes.

15   "Yellow Cab-Hailing App Arro Launches in New York City," CBS Local, September 2, 2015, https://newyork.cbslocal.com/2015/09/02/cab-hailing-app-arro-launches-nyc/.

16   "Orbitz," Wikipedia.org, https://en.wikipedia.org/wiki/Orbitz.

17   Author interview with Aaron Cheris, November 11, 2020.

18   Author interview with Fuad Hannon, September 25, 2020.

19   Author interview with Amir Nahai, November 5, 2020.

20   Tony Xu, "Form S-1 DoorDash Inc," November 13, 2020, https://sec.report/Document/0001193125-20-292381/.

21   "Nominal Food and Alcohol Expenditures, with Taxes and Tips, for All Purchasers," USDA Food Expenditure Series, June 2, 2020, https://www.ers.usda.gov/data-products/food-expenditure-series/; "U.S. Food Expenditures at Home and Abroad," American Farm Bureau Federation, November 13, 2019, https://www.fb.org/market-intel/u.s.-food-expenditures-at-home-and-abroad.

22   Ron Ruggles, "Off-Premise Orders Reach about 60% of Foodservice Occasions," *Nation's Restaurant News*, October 2, 2019, https://www.nrn.com/news/premise-orders-reach-about-60-foodservice-occasions.

23   Author interview with Rob Lynch, November 20, 2020.

24   Author interview with Yi Sung Yong, November 6, 2020.

25   Author interview with Zach Goldstein, July 16, 2020.

Chapter 5

1   "The 2020 Pizza Power Report: Taking Advantage of Digital Disruption," *PMQ Pizza Magazine*, December 2019, https://www.pmq.com/pizza-power-report-2020/.

2   Food Surveys Research Group, "Dietary Data Brief No. 11: Consumption of Pizza—What We Eat in America, NHANES, 2007–2010," US Department of Agriculture, February 2014, https://www.ars.usda.gov/ARSUserFiles/80400530/pdf/DBrief/11_consumption_of_pizza_0710.pdf.

3   Author interview with Mandy Shaw, November 11, 2020.

4   Author interview with Rob Lynch, November 20, 2020.

5   Author interview with Fred Morgan, October 23, 2020.

6   Author interview with Rick and Elise Wetzel, July 6, 2020.

7   "The Deep Dish: Food Trends in 2020," Doordash.com, https://blog.doordash.com/the-deep-dish-food-trends-in-2020-74656ce7621f.

8   Alexis C. Madrigal, "The 3 Big Advances in the Technology of the Pizza Box," *The Atlantic*, July 18, 2011, https://www.theatlantic.com/technology/archive/2011/07/the-3-big-advances-in-the-technology-of-the-pizza-box/242116/; Scott Wiener, "Scott's Pizza Chronicles: A Brief History of the Pizza Box," Serious Eats, August 9, 2018, https://slice.seriouseats.com/2011/07/a-brief-history-of-the-pizza-box.html; "Our Progress Key to Success," Dominosrecruit.co.uk, https://www.dominosrecruit.co.uk/history/.

9   Ibid.

10   Danny Klein, "Checking in on Domino's $130M Comeback Plan," *QSR* magazine August 2018, https://www.qsrmagazine.com/pizza/checking-pizza-huts-130m-comeback-plan.

11   Papa John's Press Release, "USA: Papa John's First Pizza Chain to Offer Nationwide Online Ordering," *Just Food*, January 10, 2002, https://www.just-food.com/news/papa-johns-first-pizza-chain-to-offer-nationwide-online-ordering_id74126.aspx.

12   Jonathan Maze, "How Domino's Became a Tech Company," *Nation's Restaurant News*, https://www.nrn.com/technology/how-domino-s-became-tech-company, March 29, 2016.

13   "History," Dominos.com, https://biz.dominos.com/web/public/about-dominos/history.

14   "The 2020 Pizza Power Report: Taking Advantage of Digital Disruption," *PMQ Pizza Magazine*, December 2019, https://www.pmq.com/pizza-power-report-2020/.

15   Jonathan Maze, "How Domino's Became a Tech Company," *Nation's Restaurant News*, https://www.nrn.com/technology/how-domino-s-became-tech-company, March 29, 2016.

16   "History," Dominos.com, https://biz.dominos.com/web/public/about-dominos/history.

17   Brian Heater, "Zume Will Provide Food Trucks for &Pizza," *TechCrunch*, September 19, 2019, https://techcrunch.com/2019/09/19/zume-will-provide-food-trucks-for-pizza/.

18   Author interview with Charlie Morrison, December 15, 2020.

Chapter 6

1   Ritesh Andre, "Dabbawala documentary," YouTube.com, January 8, 2020, https://www.youtube.com/watch?v=-9DuXJBGhGU.

2   Ritesh Andre, "Mumbai Dabbawala on Success through Synergy," TEDx Talks, January 8, 2019, https://www.youtube.com/watch?v=VYsR1KEOO7I&t=183s.

3   Author interview with Vivek Sunder, July 17, 2020 and September 2, 2020.

4   Prasanto K. Roy, "Mobile Data: Why India has the World's Cheapest," *BBC,* March 18, 2019, https://www.bbc.com/news/world-asia-india-47537201.

5   Gilles Guiheux, Ye Guo, Renyou Hou, Manon Laurent, Jun Li, and Anne-Valérie Ruinet, "Working in China in the Covid-19 Era," *Books and Ideas*, May 28, 2020, https://booksandideas.net/Working-in-China-in-the-Covid-19-Era.html.

6   Author interview with Abey Lin, July 22, 2020.

7   Email to author from Hans Chung, July 31, 2020; Billy Duberstein, "This Chinese Mobility Company is Up 150% This Year and Just Getting Started," *Motley Fool*, August 24, 2020, https://www.fool.com/investing/2020/08/24/this-chinese-stock-is-up-150-this-year-and-just-ge/.

8   Xing Wang, "Transcript of Q2 Earnings Calls," *Seeking Alpha*, August 21, 2020, https://seekingalpha.com/article/4370177-meituan-dianping-mpngf-ceo-xing-wang-on-q2-2020-results-earnings-call-transcript.

9   Jill Shen, "Meituan May Invest $500 million in EV startup Li Auto," *Technode,* June 29, 2020, https://technode.com/2020/06/29/meituan-may-invest-500-million-in-ev-startup-li-auto/.

10   David Lidsky, "The 2 Most Innovative Companies in the World Today Are Changing How Hundreds of Millions of Asian Consumers Buy Food, Book Hotels, and (a Lot) More," *Fast Company*, February 19, 2020, https://www.fastcompany.com/90298866/meituan-grab-most-innovative-companies-2019.

11   Ibid.

12   Restaurant Industry News, "Rise of the Indies: How Independent Restaurants are Keeping Ahead," *Restaurant Industry Magazine*, June 17, 2019, https://restaurantindustry.co.uk/2019/06/17/rise-of-the-indies-how-independent-restaurants-are-keeping-ahead-of-the-competition-with-flexible-funding/.

13   Zoe Wood, "Click and Collect Takes Off as Shoppers Buy Online and Pick Up in Person," *The Guardian*, June 8, 2011, https://www.theguardian.com/business/2011/jun/08/click-and-collect-takes-off.

14   "Who We Are," Ocado, https://ocadoretail.com/who-we-are/.

15   Office of National Statistics, "United Kingdom Population Mid Year Estimate," June 24, 2020, https://www.ons.gov.uk/peoplepopulationandcommunity/populationandmigration/populationestimates.

16   "United States 2019 Population Estimates," US Census Bureau, Vintage 2019 Population Estimates, https://www.census.gov/search-results.html?searchType=web&cssp=SERP&q=population.

17   S. Lock, "Most Popular Dining Brands in the United Kingdom (UK) as of October 2020," Statista, January 20, 2021, https://www.statista.com/statistics/950444/most-popular-restaurant-brands-in-the-united-kingdom-uk/.

18   Klaus Nyengaard, "Just-Eat is an INTERNATIONAL Company—End of Discussion!," blog post, February 10, 2012, https://klausnyengaard.com/just-eat-is-an-international-company-end-of-discussion/.

19   Klaus Nyengaard, "Just-Eat History: The First Business Plan," November 7, 2010, https://klausnyengaard.com/just-eat-history-the-first-business-plan/.

20   Mike Butcher, "The Europas Awards 2016 Honored the Best Tech Startups in Europe," *TechCrunch*, June 17, 2016, https://techcrunch.com/2016/06/17/the-europas-awards-2016-honored-the-best-tech-startups-in-europe/; "Records Break as Deloitte Announces the 2017 UK Technology Fast 50 Winners," *Deloitte,* November 16, 2017, https://www2.deloitte.com/uk/en/pages/press-releases/articles/records-break-as-deloitte-announces-the-2017-uk-technology-fast-50-winners.html.

21   Author interview with Former Deliveroo Executive, August 14, 2020.

22   "Deliveroo," Wikipedia.org, https://en.wikipedia.org/wiki/Deliveroo.

23   Jamie Powell, "Deliveroo and the Profitability Problem," *Financial Times,* November 11, 2019, https://ftalphaville.ft.com/2019/11/11/1573464859000/Deliveroo-and-the-profitability-problem/.

24   Nicholas Upton, "Market Share Data Gives COVID-Era Look at Third-Party Delivery," *Food on Demand*, May 14, 2020, https://foodondemandnews.com/05142020/market-share-data-gives-covid-era-look-at-third-party-delivery/.

25   "Ride. Swiggy Delivery Driver Monthly Salaries in India," Indeed, January 16, 2021, https://www.indeed.co.in/cmp/Ride.swiggy/salaries/Delivery-Driver#:~:text=Swiggy%20Delivery%20Driver%20monthly%20pay,47%25%20above%20the%20national%20average.

26   Jamie Powell, "Deliveroo and the Profitability Problem," *Financial Times*, November 11, 2019, https://ftalphaville.ft.com/2019/11/11/1573464859000/Deliveroo-and-the-profitability-problem/.

Chapter 7

1   "Hotel Owners vs. OTAS," Super Hospitality, https://www.super-hospitality.com/hotel-owners-vs-otas-relationship/.

2   "Can Food Delivery Apps Deliver Profits for Investors?" Morgan Stanley, February 21, 2020, https://www.morganstanley.com/ideas/food-delivery-app-profits.

3   Giuseppe Badalamenti, photo comment on Facebook, April 29, 2020, https://www.facebook.com/photo.php?fbid=2990762580989330&set=pb.100001668520076.-2207520000..&type=3.

4   Author interview with Murad Karimi, August 11, 2020.

5   Author interview with Jordan Boesch, August 4, 2020.

6   Nancy Luna, "Chipotle Mexican Grill to 'Experiment' with Raising Menu Prices on Third-Party Delivery Apps," *Nation's Restaurant News*, July 23, 2020, https://www.nrn.com/delivery-takeout-solutions/chipotle-mexican-grill-experiment-raising-menu-prices-third-party.

7   "Chipotle Announces Third Quarter 2020 Results Q3 Digital Sales Tripled Year-Over-Year And Accounted For Nearly Half Of Sales," Chipotle Investor Relations, October 21, 2020, https://ir.chipotle.com/2020-10-21-Chipotle-Announces-Third-Quarter-2020-Results-Q3-Digital-Sales-Tripled-Year-Over-Year-And-Accounted-For-Nearly-Half-Of-Sales, https://ir.chipotle.com/download/Delivery+Service+Revenue.pdf.

8   "Chipotle's Online Ordering Surge Bodes Well For Restaurants' Digital Efforts," Pyments.com, October 22, 2020, https://www.pymnts.com/earnings/2020/chipotles-online-ordering-surge-bodes-well-for-restaurants-digital-efforts/.

9   Author interview with Fred Morgan, October 23, 2020.

10   Author interview with Noah Glass, July 17, 2020.

11   Emma Rosenblum, "Line Cutter," *New York Magazine*, July 31, 2019, https://nymag.com/news/intelligencer/breaking/58181/.

12   Danny Klein, "The Digital Journey Evolves at Qdoba," *QSR* magazine, July 2020, https://www.qsrmagazine.com/fast-casual/digital-journey-evolves-qdoba.

Chapter 8

1   Rachel Abrams and Robert Gebeloff, "Thanks to Wall St., There May Be Too Many Restaurants," *The New York Times*, October 31, 2017, https://www.nytimes.com/2017/10/31/business/too-many-restaurants-wall-street.html.

2   Danny Klein, "Restaurant Prices Are Rising, and Traffic Is Declining," *QSR* magazine, November 2018, https://www.qsrmagazine.com/fast-casual/restaurant-prices-are-rising-and-traffic-declining.

3   Danny Klein, "Falling Guest Counts Is a Trend Restaurants Can't Escape," *FSR Magazine*, July 2019, https://www.fsrmagazine.com/fsr/finance/falling-guests-counts-trend-restaurants-cant-escape.

4   Source: Black Box Intelligence, used with permission.

5   Danny Klein, "There's Still Opportunity in Off-Premises for Restaurants," *QSR* magazine, July 2019, https://www.qsrmagazine.com/finance/there-s-still-opportunity-premises-restaurants.

6   Author interview with Michael Connor, November 17, 2020.

7   Tom Kaiser and Nick Upton, "Episode 11 with Meredith Sandland and Christine Barone," *Food on Demand* Podcast, July 23, 2020, https://foodondemandnews.com/podcast/archive/.

8   "H-E-B Meal Simple and Lakeway Police Department," YouTube video, https://www.youtube.com/watch?v=jAn0rNxui-4.

9   National Restaurant Association, "Consumers Are Expected to Continue Using Takeout and Delivery," *Hospitality Trends*, November 5, 2020, https://www.htrends.com/trends-detail-sid-113247.html.

10   Author interview with André Vener, July 22, 2020.

11   Author interview with Kevin Rice, September 3, 2020.

12   Author interview with Jonathan Neman, December 3, 2020.

13   Carley Milligan, "Galley Foods to Disappear Next Month as It Completes Merge with Sweetgreen," *Baltimore Business Journal*, January 28, 2020, https://www.bizjournals.com/baltimore/news/2020/01/28/galley-foods-to-disappear-next-month-as-it.html.

14   Author interview with Erle Dardick, August 27, 2020.

15   Tom Kaiser and Nick Upton, "Episode 11 with Meredith Sandland and Christine Barone," *Food on Demand* Podcast, July 23, 2020, https://foodondemandnews.com/podcast/archive/.

Chapter 9

1   Paul Sawyer, "GV leads $10 million investment in Kitchen United to Help Restaurants Expand through Data-Driven Kitchens," *Venture Beat,* October 8, 2018, https://venturebeat.com/2018/10/08/gv-leads-10-million-investment-in-kitchen-united-to-help-restaurants-expand-via-data-driven-kitchens/.

2   Matthew Lynley, "Travis Kalanick Is Already Back Running a Company with $150M Investment," *TechCrunch,* March 20, 2018, https://techcrunch.com/2018/03/20/travis-kalanick-is-already-back-to-running-a-company-with-a-150m-investment/; Rolfe Winkler and Rory Jones, "Meet Travis Kalanick's Secret Startup, Cloud Kitchens," *The Wall Street Journal,* November 7, 2019, https://www.wsj.com/articles/meet-travis-kalanicks-secret-startup-cloudkitchens-11573122602.

3   Andrew Chen, "Why We're Investing in Virtual Kitchen Co," November 14, 2019, https://a16z.com/2019/11/14/virtual-kitchen-co/.

4   Emon Reiser, "How This Softbank-Backed Startup Could Transform Parking Lots into Hubs for On-Demand Businesses," *South Florida Business Journal,* June 26, 2019, https://www.bizjournals.com/southflorida/news/2019/06/26/how-this-softank-backed-startup-could-transform.html.

5   Erika Adams, "High-Profile NYC Restaurants Are Moving into Soho's New 'Ghost Kitchen' for Delivery Only," *Eater,* August 26, 2019, https://ny.eater.com/2019/8/26/20833153/zuul-kitchens-opening-sweetgreen-junzi-sarges-soho-nyc; Garrett Snyder, "Rise of the Ghost Kitchens: How Virtual Restaurants Are Reshaping L.A.'s Dining Economy," *Food Hub,* October 7, 2020, https://www.food-hub.co/post/rise-of-the-ghost-kitchens-how-virtual-restaurants-are-reshaping-l-a-s-dining-economy.

6   Jennifer Marston, "Uber Eats Is Doing Ghost Kitchens. Here's How that Could Change Delivery," *The Spoon,* March 12, 2019, https://thespoon.tech/uber-eats-is-doing-ghost-kitchens-heres-how-that-could-change-food-delivery/.

7   Emily Tung, "DoorDash Kitchens Opens in the Peninsula," October 12, 2019, https://blog.doordash.com/doordash-kitchens-opens-in-the-peninsula-38fa32062c19.

8   Heather Haddon, "Latest Front in Food Delivery: Kitchens in Empty Malls," *The Wall Street Journal,* February 2, 2020, https://www.wsj.com/articles/latest-front-in-food-delivery-kitchens-in-empty-malls-11580644801.

9   Andrew Chen, "Why We're Investing in Virtual Kitchen Co," November 14, 2019, https://a16z.com/2019/11/14/virtual-kitchen-co/.

10   Author interview with Amir Nahai, November 5, 2020.

11   Author interview with David Kuo, August 17, 2020.

12   Author interview with Jane Gannaway, August 28, 2020.

13   Author interview with Ken Chong, August 7, 2020.

14   Author interview with Andro Radonich, November 5, 2020.

15   Plant Nation, "3 Largest and Fastest Growing Virtual Kitchen Company Launches Delivery-Only 100% Vegan Concept, Plant Nation," PR Newswire, May 22, 2020, https://www.prnewswire.com/news-releases/c3--largest-and-fastest-growing-virtual-kitchen-company-launches-delivery-only-100-vegan-concept-plant-nation-301064099.html.

16   Author interview with Christopher Petzel, November 13, 2020.

17   Author interview with Chris Baggott, November 17, 2020.

Chapter 10

1   Tina Bellon, "Factbox: What's at Stake in California's November Gig Worker Ballot Measure," *Reuters,* August 21, 2020, https://www.reuters.com/article/us-uber-california-factbox-idUSKBN25H2JH.

2   Author interview with Mostafa Maklad, July 24, 2020.

3   Dara Khosrowshahi, "I Am the C.E.O. of Uber. Gig Workers Deserve Better," *The New York Times,* August 10, 2020, https://www.nytimes.com/2020/08/10/opinion/uber-ceo-dara-khosrowshahi-gig-workers-deserve-better.html.

4   Scott Steinberg, "Budget-Minded Business Owners' Love Affair with Gig Workers Is Growing," CNBC.com, July 24, 2020, https://www.cnbc.com/2020/07/24/budget-minded-business-worlds-love-affair-with-gig-workers-is-growing.html.

5   Author interview with D'Shea Grant, September 25, 2020.

6   "New Study Shows What Consumers Crave in a Food Delivery Service," US Foods, May 19, 2019, https://www.usfoods.com/our-services/business-trends/2019-food-delivery-statistics.html.

7   Author interview with Jon Sewell, July 30, 2020.

8   Allison Lamberth, "The Fate of On-Demand Delivery," *Foodable Network*, December 6, 2019, https://www.foodabletv.com/blog/the-fate-of-on-demand-delivery.

9   Author interview with Aaron Hoffman, August 3, 2020.

10   Author interview with Roman Tsarovsky, July 28, 2020.

11   Diana Barr, "Panera Partners with Delivery Apps to Expand Its Own Delivery Service," *St. Louis Business Journal*, August 27, 2019, https://www.bizjournals.com/stlouis/news/2019/08/27/panera-partners-with-delivery-apps-to-expand-its.html.

12   Joanna Fantozzi, "After Holding Out on Third-Party Delivery, Panera Bread Dives in with DoorDash, Grubhub and Uber Eats Partnerships," *Nation's Restaurant News*, August 27, 2019, https://www.nrn.com/fast-casual/after-holding-out-third-party-delivery-panera-bread-dives-doordash-grubhub-and-uber-eats?NL=NRN-02_&Issue=NRN-02__20190827_NRN-02__606&sfvc4enews=42&cl=article_1_2&utm_rid=CPG06000002262948&utm_campaign=32867&utm_medium=email&elq2=8353769a930e466ca9c8ddbd8ec537dd.

13   Author interview with Marcus Higgins, August 5, 2020.

14   University of Oxford, "Happy Workers Are 13% More Productive," Phys.org, October 25, 2019, https://phys.org/news/2019-10-happy-workers-productive.html.

15   Author interview with Lloyd Wentzell, August 14, 2020.

Chapter 11

1   Author interview with Henry Roberts, July 9, 2020.

2   Author interview with Alex Canter, July 21, 2020.

3   Simplot Foods, https://simplotfoods.com/foodservice-brands/simplot-conquest/clear-coated-straight-cut-fries-skin-on/10071179030140.

4   Author interview with Andrew McClellan, October 13, 2020.

5   Author interview with Stephen Crowley, October 6, 2020.

6   Amit Kumar Garg, "Retail Lean Management—Desktop Research," Slideshare, https://www.slideshare.net/AmitGarg1/retail-lean-management.

7   Author interview with Scott Drummond, September 9, 2020.

8   Author interview with Brian Reece, October 6, 2020.

9   Author interview with Amir Nahai, November 5, 2020.

10   Author interview with Aaron Newton, August 10, 2020.

11   Author interview with Alex Beltrani, September 11, 2020.

Chapter 12

1   Simon Sinek, *Start with Why: How Great Leaders Inspire Everyone to Take Action* (Portfolio, 2009).

2   Author interview with Tressie Lieberman, September 18, 2020.

3   Ad Age Datacenter, "Marketing Fact Pack 2020," *Ad Age*, December 23, 2019, http://adage.com/d/resources/resources/whitepaper/marketing-fact-pack-2020.

4   Author interview with Amy Mason, August 21, 2020.

5   Eliza Barclay, "With Lawsuit over, Taco Bell's Mystery Meat Is a Mystery No Longer," *NPR*, April 19, 2011, https://www.npr.org/sections/health-shots/2011/04/22/135539926/with-lawsuit-over-taco-bells-mystery-meat-is-a-mystery-no-longer.

6   Patricia Cobe, "Give Me Mas," *Restaurant Business Online*, April 25, 2013, https://www.restaurantbusinessonline.com/marketing/give-me-mas.

7   Matthew J. Belvedere, "Yum Brands CEO: About Half US Population Eats Taco Bell Every Month," CNBC, October 12, 2016, https://www.cnbc.com/2016/10/12/yum-brands-ceo-about-half-us-population-eats-taco-bell-every-month.html.

8   "Taco Bell First QSR to Offer Vegetarian Certified Menu," Tacobell.com, October 1, 2015, https://www.tacobell.com/news/newsroomPage32.

9   Author interview with Jenn Parker, July 2, 2020.

Chapter 13

1   Author interview with Zach Goldstein, July 16, 2020.

2   Zach Goldstein, "The Four Horsemen of the Restaurant Apocolypse," *Medium*, September 12, 2019, https://medium.thanx.com/four-horsemen-restaurant-apocalypse-64947b3d9657.

3   "How Packaging Gives Apple's Buyers a Sensory Experience that Reinforces Brand," Personalics, February 3, 2016, https://www.personalics.com/2016/02/03/sensory-design-packaging/.

4   "Redefining a brand from Out-of-Reach to Accessible and Still Hip," Zaudhaus.com, https://www.zaudhaus.com/sugarfish.

5   Amelia Lucas, "DoorDash Eliminates and Reduces Some Commissions and Fees for Restaurants," CNBC, March 17, 2020, https://www.cnbc.com/2020/03/17/doordash-eliminates-and-reduces-some-commission-fees-for-restaurants.html; Kristen Korosec, "Uber Eats Waives Delivery Fees for Independent Restaurants during COVID-19 Pandemic," *TechCrunch*, March 16, 2020, https://techcrunch.com/2020/03/16/uber-eats-waives-delivery-fees-for-independent-restaurants-during-covid-19-pandemic/.

6   Author interview with Tressie Lieberman, September 18, 2020.

7   Author interview with Caroline Sizer, October 30, 2020.

8   Author interview with Kevin Rice, September 3, 2020.

9   Author interview with Stacie Colburn Hayes, October 29, 2020.

10   Author interview with Adam Brotman, July 28, 2020.

11   Author interview with Sebastien Pavy, November 11, 2020.

Chapter 14

1   Author interview with Alex Canter, July 21, 2020.

2   "Guide to Gen Z: Debunking the Myths of Our Youngest Generation," NPD, https://www.npd.com/wps/portal/npd/us/news/tips-trends-takeaways/guide-to-gen-z-debunking-the-myths-of-our-youngest-generation/.

3   "Launch a Virtual Restaurant," Ubereats.com, https://restaurants.ubereats.com/gb/en/innovations/virtual-restaurants/; Whitney Filloon, "Uber Eats' Path to Delivery Domination: Restaurant Inception," Eater, October 24, 2018, https://www.eater.com/2018/10/24/18018334/uber-eats-virtual-restaurants.

4   Author interview with Elyse Propis, October 29, 2020.

5   "Stories from Uber Eats Restaurants," Ubereats.com, https://restaurants.ubereats.com/us/en/restaurant-stories/.

6   Shannon Bond, "Uber Gobbles Up Postmates In $2.65 Billion Bet On Food Delivery," *NPR,* July 6, 2020, https://www.npr.org/sections/coronavirus-live-updates/2020/07/06/887961123/uber-gobbles-up-postmates-in-2-65-billion-bet-on-food-delivery.

7   Tom Kaiser, "Nextbite Offers Virtual Restaurants in a Box," *Food on Demand*, March 17, 2020, https://foodondemandnews.com/03172020/nextbite-offers-virtual-restaurants-in-a-box/#.

8   Author interview with Jenn Parker, July 2, 2020 and July 15, 2020.

9   Author interview with Geoff Alexander, July 14, 2020.

10   Author interview with André Vener, July 22, 2020.

11   Author interview with Jeff Appelbaum, July 17, 2020.

Chapter 15

1   Author interview with Andrew McClellan, October 13, 2020.

2   Author interview with Abey Lin, July 22, 2020.

3   Author interview with Lloyd Wentzell, August 14, 2020.

4   Author interview with David Kuo, August 17, 2020.

5   Author interview with Lorena Garcia, July 14, 2020.

6   "Sound and Food," YouTube, https://www.youtube.com/watch?v=w-oXtGfIEuc.

7   "Heritage Restaurant and Caviar Bar," ExploreTock.com, https://www.exploretock.com/heritagerestaurantandcaviarbar/.

8   Author interview with Noah Glass, July 17, 2020.

9   Author interview with Alex Canter, July 21, 2020.

10   Author interview with Adam Brotman, July 28, 2020.

11   Author interview with D'Shea Grant, September 25, 2020.

12   Sarah Fischer, "Coming to a TV Near You: Personalized Ads," *Axios*, January 25, 2019, https://www.axios.com/coming-to-a-tv-near-you-customized-ads-1548378037-e5553f3a-1ded-4cfd-9f5e-be89cd59cf69.html.

13   Perrin Braun, "Interview with Professor Jeffrey Blumberg, a Leader in Antioxidants Research, from Tufts University," *InsideTracker*, September 4, 2014, https://blog.insidetracker.com/interview-with-professor-jeffrey-blumberg-a-leader-in.

14   Author interview with Ken Chong, August 7, 2020.

15   Author interview with Nabeel Alamgir, July 30, 2020.

16   Author interview with Vivek Sunder, July 17/20 and September 2, 2020.

17   Author interview with Jonathan Neman, December 3, 2020.

18   Author interview with Scott Drummond, September 9, 2020.

19   Author interview with Lorena Garcia, July 14, 2020.

20   Sara Matheu, "US Foods Launches Ghost Kitchens Program to Help Operators Expand Off-Premise Dining and Create a New Revenue Stream," US Foods Press Release, August 19, 2020, https://ir.usfoods.com/investors/stock-information-news/press-release-details/2020/US-Foods-Launches-Ghost-Kitchens-Program-to-Help-Operators-Expand-Off-Premise-Dining-and-Create-a-New-Revenue-Stream/default.aspx.

21   "Cups and Lids," Freedonia, https://www.freedoniagroup.com/industry-study/cups-lids-3174.htm.

22   "Deliveroo Announces Reusable Packaging Partnership with Returnr in World-First Scheme—Deliveroo Foodscene," Deliveroo, July 18, 2019, https://au.deliveroo.news/news/sustainability.html.

23   Author interview with Henry Roberts, July 9, 2020.

24   Author interview with Tressie Lieberman, September 18, 2020.

25   Author interview with Charlie Morrison, December 15, 2020.

26   Author interview with Zach Goldstein, July 16, 2020.

27   Author interview with Jenn Parker, July 2, 2020 and July 15,2020.

28   Author interview with former Deliveroo executive, August 14, 2020.

29   Joelle Parenteau, "Why Restaurants are not F****d," *Medium,* May 18, 2020, https://medium.com/@joelleparenteau/why-restaurants-are-not-fucked-80383594c593.

30   Jordan Tyler, "PetSmart Partners with DoorDash to Offer Same-Day Delivery," Pet Food Processing, September 10, 2020, https://www.petfoodprocessing.net/articles/14104-petsmart-partners-with-doordash-to-offer-same-day-delivery.

31   Reprinted with permission from WD Partners, https://www.wdpartners.com/.

32   Andrew Lisa, "Jobs That Might Not Exist in 50 Years," *Newsweek,* December 5, 2020, https://www.newsweek.com/jobs-that-might-not-exist-50-years-1530811.

33   "The Drone Delivery Market, Forecast to 2024—Drone Deliveries Will Be the Fastest Growing Application Within the $43+ Billion Global Drone Market," Research and Markets, March 25, 2020, https://www.globenewswire.com/news-release/2020/03/25/2006020/0/en/The-Drone-Delivery-Market-Forecast-to-2024-Drone-Deliveries-Will-Be-the-Fastest-Growing-Application-Within-the-43-Billion-Global-Drone-Market.html.

34 Josh Fischer, "First Consumer Drone Delivery Service Takes Off in Virginia," Fleetowner. com, October 21, 2019, https://www.fleetowner.com/technology/article/21704392/ first-consumer-drone-delivery-service-takes-off-in-virginia.

35 "Amazon Prime Air Drones," https://www.amazon.com/Amazon-Prime-Air/ b?ie=UTF8&node=8037720011.

36 Sarah Wray, "More Delivery Robots Roll Out on UK Streets," *Cities Today,* November 26, 2020, https://cities-today.com/more-delivery-robots-roll-out-on-uk-streets/.

37 "Nuro Set to Be California's First Driverless Delivery Service," *BBC,* December 24, 2020, https://www.bbc.com/news/technology-55438969.

38 Arwa Mahdawi, "Would You Live in a House Without a Kitchen? You Might Have To," *The Guardian*, June 24, 2018, https://www.theguardian.com/society/2018/jun/24/ homes-without-kitchens-ubs-report.

GET YOUR EXCLUSIVE DIGITAL TOKENIZED NFT COPY OF

DELIVERING THE DIGITAL RESTAURANT

GO TO WWW.LEARN.DELIVERY/NFT